Successful Transformations?

STUDIES OF COMMUNISM IN TRANSITION

General Editor: Ronald J. Hill
*Professor of Comparative Government
and Fellow of Trinity College
Dublin, Ireland*

Studies of Communism in Transition is an important series which applies academic analysis and clarity of thought to the recent traumatic events in Eastern and Central Europe. As many of the preconceptions of the past half century are cast aside, newly independent and autonomous sovereign states are being forced to address long-term, organic problems which had been suppressed by, or appeased within, the Communist system of rule.

The series is edited under the sponsorship of Lorton House, an independent charitable association which exists to promote the academic study of communism and related concepts.

Successful Transformations?

The Creation of Market Economies in Eastern Germany and the Czech Republic

Martin Myant
University of Paisley, Scotland

Frank Fleischer, Kurt Hornschild
German Institute for Economic Research, Berlin

Růžena Vintrová, Karel Zeman, Zdeněk Souček
Czech Statistical Office, Czechoslovak Trade Bank and Management Focus International, Prague

STUDIES OF COMMUNISM IN TRANSITION

Edward Elgar
Cheltenham, UK ◆ Brookfield, US

Published by
Edward Elgar Publishing Limited
8 Lansdown Place
Cheltenham
Glos GL50 2HU
UK

Edward Elgar Publishing Company
Old Post Road
Brookfield
Vermont 05036
US

A catalogue record for this book
is available from the British Library

Library of Congress Cataloging-in-Publication Data
Successful transformations? : the creation of market economies in
    Eastern Germany and the Czech Republic / Martin Myant...[et al.].
    (Studies of communism in transition)
    Includes bibliographical references and index.
    1. Germany (East)—Economic conditions. 2. Czech Republic—
Economic conditions. 3. Germany (East)—Economic policy. 4. Czech
Republic—Economic policy. I. Myant, M. R. (Martin R.)
    II. Series.
HC290.782.S82 1997
338.9431—dc20   96–23168
                                                                  CIP

ISBN 1 85898 495 5

Printed and bound in Great Britain by
Hartnolls Limited, Bodmin, Cornwall

Contents

PART III CONCLUSION

Tables

Abbreviations

BfW	*Bundesministerium für Wirtschaft*, German Federal Ministry for the Economy
BVS	*Bundesanstalt für vereinigungsbedingte Sonderaufgaben*, Federal Office for Special Tasks Related to Unification, main successor to THA
CEFTA	Central European Free Trade Area
CMEA	Council for Mutual Economic Assistance, trading bloc including USSR and Eastern Europe prior to 1990
DIW	*Deutsches Institut für Wirtschaftsforschung*, German Institute for Economic Research, Berlin
EJL	*Entreprise Jean Lefèbvre*, French construction firm
ERDI	Exchange Rate Deviation Index
EU	European Union, since 1992
GDP	Gross Domestic Product
GDR	German Democratic Republic, East German state up to 1990
IfW	*Institut für Weltwirtschaft*, University of Kiel, Institute for World Economy
ISIC	International Standard Industrial Classification
IWH	*Institut für Wirtschaftsforschung, Halle*, Institute for Economic Research, Halle
Kč	*Koruna česká*, Czech Crown
Kčs	*Koruna československá*, Czechoslovak Crown
R&D	Research and Development

REER	Real Effective Exchange Rate
RMB	*Rationalisierungsmittelbau,* or *Rationalisierungs-mittel-Eigenbau,* explained on p.39
SITC	Standard International Trade Classification
SME	Small and Medium-sized Enterprise
SSŽ	*Stavby silnic a železnic,* Construction of Roads and Railways, Czech construction firm
THA	*Treuhandanstalt,* German agency administering former state enterprises up to December 1994
UNIDO	United Nations International Development Organization, Vienna

Acknowledgements

The research cooperation that made this book possible was funded by the European Commission's Phare ACE Programme 1994 which financed activities in Germany, the Czech Republic and the UK. It enabled the group to meet in Berlin in June 1995 under the auspices of the *Deutsches Institut für Wirtschaftsforschung,* the German Institute for Economic Research, and in Prague in November 1995 with further support from the *Friedrich Ebert* Foundation and from the Foundation for the Study of International Relations, Prague.

Assistance from the British Academy and help from the Institute of Economics of the Czech National Bank enabled Martin Myant to spend time in the Czech Republic in 1993 and 1995 and in Slovakia in 1994, which contributed to this research.

Introduction

With the collapse of communist power in central and eastern Europe in 1989, the great question for economic policy became the best means to ensure a 'successful' transformation of the various counties of the area into 'modern' market economies. A 'successful' transformation would be one that enabled the country to create a new economic system, to ensure rapid and sustainable economic growth so as to reduce, and ultimately to overcome the gap with the advanced countries of western Europe and, above all and most conclusively, one that led to acceptance as a developed market economy by the world's financial institutions, by governments and by intergovernmental organizations. Acceptance into the European Union could be seen as the crowning symbolic achievement.

The best-placed countries in the former eastern bloc appeared at the start to be the two countries with the highest per capita GDP, Czechoslovakia and East Germany, officially titled the German Democratic Republic or GDR. These terms will be used interchangeably in the following chapters, but following reunification, the broad area of the former GDR will be referred to as east Germany, signifying its new status as part of a larger state. This, of course, was an enormous advantage over other former members of the Soviet bloc. The new east Germany seemed to be able to pass many of the tests suggested above in one go, thanks to German reunification alone.

It immediately became part of the dynamic and prosperous German economy, with the prospect of substantial financial transfers to help ensure a speedy and smooth systemic transformation. There have been some signs of concern from part of the population at the completeness with which the whole heritage of the GDR seemed to be swept aside. Nevertheless, there was never any real question that the eastern part of the newly united Germany was to be assimilated into the existing Federal Republic of Germany, with a full acceptance

1

of its whole institutional and economic framework. No practical political alternative existed.

For Czechoslovakia, and particularly the Czech Republic, the process was never going to be so simple, but a number of factors clearly worked in the country's favour. Among these were the strong economic base, reasonable infrastructure and geographical location close to Germany. There was also a widespread expectation, based on the country's location and past history, that fate would put it back into the 'mainstream' of European development. This made it easier to gain acceptance for policies that could provoke more opposition elsewhere in east–central Europe. That was one of the differences between the Czech Republic and Slovakia which contributed to the breakup of the federation at the end of 1992 and the appearance of the Czech Republic as a separate state. Thus the political environment pointed to a great willingness in the Czech case, as in east Germany, to accept whatever was required to regain what was seen as a rightful place in a wider European community.

This book reflects the work of the authors within a research project on the restructuring of production and the changing nature of the enterprise in east–central Europe, supported by the European Commission's Phare ACE Programme 1994. The chapters are expanded, updated and substantially revised versions of papers presented at workshops in Berlin in June 1995 and in Prague in November 1995. They have been rewritten to fit together into a work that explores how far the transformations in these two cases should be considered 'successful', in the terms outlined above. Moreover, by providing a comparison between two cases that have a great deal in common alongside very substantial differences, the book points to possible wider conclusions on the nature of economic transformation in general. The focus is on answering the general questions of whether the changes that have taken place have created what can broadly be described as 'modern' market economies, and whether a basis has been laid for self-sustaining growth in the future.

Thus, for both cases, an assessment is made of the effects of past policies and of the structural changes that have taken place, with a substantial emphasis on the changes to, and within, enterprises. It would, however, have been illogical to provide precisely matching chapters for the two cases. Despite similarities in starting conditions and in ultimate objectives, the paths taken have, in a number of key respects, been radically different. Thus, the disappearance of East Germany as an independent state has meant that it cannot set its own macroeconomic policy framework. This area can therefore be passed over rather quickly in the case of east Germany, while in the Czech case it was a major sphere of policy concern, with a substantial influence on the course of economic restructuring.

Thus, Chapter 1, written by Kurt Hornschild, covers the broad policy framework for east Germany and summarizes its impact on the economy. Chapter 2, written by Frank Fleischer, gives the background to the organization of East German industry prior to reunification and then concentrates on the role of the *Treuhand-anstalt*, the agency put in charge of the state-owned companies of the former GDR, and its impact on the enterprise and sectoral structure. Chapter 3, also written by Frank Fleischer, develops on this, with case studies in large enterprises and a summary of the situation in small and medium-sized enterprises. The overwhelming conclusion is, at best, of a number of elements missing from a modern economic structure. Indeed, the very scale of financial transfers still required to maintain the east German economy suggests that it has yet to achieve a basis for self-sustaining growth.

Chapter 4, by Růžena Vintrová, outlines the macroeconomic policy framework in the Czech Republic, focusing on the theme of a possible conflict between pro-growth and anti-inflationary policies and pointing to a number of current policy dilemmas. Comparisons with east Germany are of little relevance for much of this, but Czech experience is set in the context of developments across east–central Europe. Chapter 5, by Martin Myant, summarizes the changes in the Czech economic structure, again pointing to possible similarities with and differences from other east–central European countries. Chapter 6, by Zdeněk Souček, outlines the changes within enterprises, based on a number of case studies. There is substantial overlap here with themes covered in the chapters on east Germany, but also important differences. Above all, the Czech enterprise was a far more active force in the transformation process, while its east German counterpart was typically left as a passive agent in the face of policies decided elsewhere. That, again, can ultimately be related to the absence of any independent east German political structure.

These policy differences have had a substantial impact on the resulting economic structures and on the course of the different transformation processes. Thus, far more could be carried through from the economic structure built up in the past in the Czech case, while east Germany has been left to a much greater extent to start from scratch. This east German way was dependent on the help of a rich partner and was therefore never a serious possibility for the Czech Republic. Nevertheless, there could be 'too much' continuity from the past in the Czech case, with frequent accusations that many established enterprises have felt little pressure to adapt to the new market environment.

The evidence here does not support this claim in its simplest form. Nevertheless, Chapter 7, by Karel Zeman, pursues a related theme demonstrating the extent to which the branch structure of Czech industry has not moved into line with that of other small developed economies. Continuity may, however, prove to be a great strength as part of a somewhat slower transformation process that appears to have typified the Czech Republic compared with east Germany. This, and other key points in the comparison and their possible policy implications, are taken up in the concluding Chapter 8, written by Martin Myant, which provides a critical comparison of the theoretical underpinnings of the two transformation strategies outlined in the earlier chapters.

PART I

The East German Transformation

1. East Germany's Way

At the time of reunification in 1990, the East German state enjoyed, by eastern European standards, a relatively high living standard and a substantial economic and industrial potential. In many respects, its economic structure was similar to that of West Germany. Both had industries with a strong export orientation, although East Germany exported to the CMEA countries while West Germany had its main markets in the western world. Reunification, however, effectively destroyed the basis on which the East German economy had functioned. It suddenly appeared to have the wrong sectoral structure and a labour force that was inappropriately qualified for the new situation. East German industry was losing not only its well-established markets abroad, but also its previously very safe domestic markets.

No prior preparations had been made for this new situation, either in East or in West Germany. Nevertheless, the political imperatives of the time meant that east Germany, referred to henceforth without the capital letter once it had become no more than a region within the reunited Germany, had to be integrated into western Europe as a part of Germany. Moreover, this had to be done rapidly, with no softening, intermediate stages. At the same time, the transformation process and accompanying structural changes had to be managed in such a way as not to threaten political stability.

In a relatively short space of time, those old structures that had failed in the past were swept aside. Above all, the big combines that dominated the old East German economy have been split up into smaller units and sold off to private investors. The infrastructure, which was very weak when set against west German standards and made east Germany unattractive for investors, has benefited from very substantial new investment.

7

In some respects, the results of this transformation can appear very impressive. With GDP growth rates of 8.5 per cent in 1994 and 6.5 per cent in 1995, east Germany is one of the most dynamic regions in the world. Moreover, it has achieved the intended integration into the European Union and become a solid component of the reunited Germany, with an economic structure dominated by private ownership.

Table 1.1 Key indicators of the east German economic level as a percentage of the west German level

	1991	1994
Gross domestic product	31	49
Personal consumption	50	67
Gross fixed investment	66	134
Disposable incomes	47	67
Unit wage costs	158	136

Source: DIW Wochenbericht, 1995, No. 27–8, p.467.

Nevertheless, the transformation has left a number of major unresolved issues. One of the clearest indicators of this is the need for financial transfers from west Germany. These have taken various different forms, but the total public transfers have increased from DM 133.5 billion in 1991 to DM 194.0 billion in 1995 (*DIW Wochenbericht*, 1995, No. 42–3, p. 734) totalling up to DM 848 billion over the whole period. This is equivalent to roughly DM 53,000 per capita and can be set against an east German GDP figure for 1994 of DM 258.3 billion. Moreover, this quite extraordinary level of subsidization has been accompanied by a dramatic fall in employment from more than 10 million before reunification to 6.3 million at the end of 1995, with 1.3 million registered unemployed. Thus, from a recorded level of employment in the GDR in 1987 of 477 per thousand inhabitants, east Germany had moved by 1995 to a level of 407 per thousand, against an equivalent west German figure of 435. Similarly, recorded unemployment had grown from zero to 15.3 per cent in 1994, falling back to 13.9 per cent in 1995, against a west German average figure in that year of 8.2 per cent.

Table 1.1 shows the broad comparisons of the levels of the east and west German economies, pointing in broad terms to aspects that could be seen as both 'positive' and 'negative'. Thus, there are clear signs of catching up from a previously very low level, with the high level of investment perhaps justifying hopes for future sustained growth. This needs to be supplemented with information on the performance of individual sectors, as shown in Table 1.2.

Table 1.2 Key indicators of sectors of the east German economy as percentages of west German levels

	Productivity		Wage costs		Employment
	1990	1994	1990	1994	1994
Agriculture	36	82			115
Mining and energy	31	73	75	87	117
Manufacturing	18	50	155	130	56
Construction	58	75	90	104	213
Trade	53	66	68	119	75
Transport	23	33	166	212	108
Private services	22	47	203	158	82
Public services	35	68	100	103	117
Total	34	55	107	131	94

Note: All figures are east German percentages of west German levels for the second half of the respective year. Productivity is measured as gross value added per employee in current prices. Wage costs are measured as income from employment per unit of output value. Employment is measured as a proportion of population.

Source: DIW Wochenbericht, 1995, No. 27–8, p.467.

Table 1.3 Productivity in east German mining and selected
branches of manufacturing as a percentage of west
German levels

	1991	1992	1993	1994
Mining	67.2	66.7	81.7	80.1
Chemicals	16.0	22.7	24.2	31.3
Machinery	22.9	31.1	37.7	41.4
Road vehicles	20.6	30.7	43.8	47.6
Consumer goods	16.2	37.1	49.3	59.0
Food, drink and tobacco	33.7	48.9	58.4	64.3

Note: Figures are for firms with 20 or more employees. Productivity is measured as gross production value per employee.

Source: As Table 1.2.

It is already possible to pinpoint some specific features of the east German transformation when set against countries of east–central Europe. In particular, the pace of the improvements in industrial productivity, but also of the decline in employment, look exceptional. As can be seen, the changes have been particularly dramatic in manufacturing, where the gap was previously at its greatest. This, as Table 1.2 shows, is a sector in which wage costs are still substantially above the western level, something that is quite unique compared with east–central Europe. There are even greater gaps in wage costs in transport and in services, but the products offered by those sectors are less mobile and there is therefore not the same impact of competition from the West. As a final comment at this point, there is one striking similarity with other economic transformations. That is, the improvement in agricultural productivity, accompanied by some decline in output.

Tables 1.3 and 1.4 further clarify the nature of the changes in industry. Table 1.3 again confirms the impression of a 'catching-up' process. This is the least pronounced in mining, where the difference was relatively small at the start. Even where changes have been dramatic, such as the machinery and road-vehicle sectors, the gap is still substantial. Moreover, Table 1.4 sets all of these productivity improvements in context. Thus the improvement in mining has been accompanied by a substantial decline in that branch's share in output,

Table 1.4 Sectoral structure of gross output from production industries in the east and west German economies

	East Germany		West Germany
	1990	1994	1994
Electricity and gas	12.4	13.2	6.4
Mining	9.6	3.0	1.7
Quarrying	2.5	5.1	2.3
Chemicals	4.0	2.7	10.8
Metalworking and railway equipment	2.9	5.4	1.5
Machinery	15.2	5.0	10.1
Road vehicles	2.7	3.0	9.6
Electrical engineering	8.5	5.1	11.2
Consumer goods	7.2	6.9	11.9
Food, drink and tobacco	8.3	9.2	9.1
Construction	18.1	34.5	7.3
Others	5.2	4.6	10.7

Note: All figures are percentages of the total from firms with 20 or more employees. The 1990 figures are from the last six months.

Source: as Table 1.2.

although it is still more important in eastern than western Germany. Chemicals, however, once a prominent part of the East German industrial structure, have been reduced to an extraordinarily low level. A similar fate has hit the once powerful machinery industry. By way of contrast, the construction sector has greatly increased on its already substantial share, and appears to be far more important in the East than in the West. Indeed, the slightly different figures in Table 1.5, from the end of the existence of the East German state, serve to show just how far the industrial structure has shifted from one that was in many respects rather similar to that of west Germany.

Table 1.5 Percentage shares of key sectors in total East German industry in 1989

	Companies	Employees	Turnover
Electricity and gas	1	4	8
Mining	1	6	4
Quarrying	3	3	2
Iron and steel	0	2	4
Chemicals	3	5	7
Metalworking and railway equipment	2	3	3
Machinery	14	15	11
Road vehicles	6	4	3
Electrical engineering	14	13	9
Consumer goods	27	21	13
Food, drink and tobacco	15	8	17
Others	14	16	19

Source: Statistisches Bundesamt, 1994.

This, then, is not a movement towards the west German industrial structure. Nor, as will become clear in later chapters, is it close to the structural changes in the Czech Republic. Indeed, Table 1.6 points to another east German specificity in the form of a rapid growth in investment levels. Generally across east–central Europe, these collapsed in the early phases of the transformation process. Moreover, public-sector investment fell particularly sharply as a result of policies of fiscal restraint. In east Germany, however, per capita investment levels have risen to a higher level than in the West and the difference is particularly large in public-sector investment, reflecting the strong orientation towards investment in the infrastructure.

Table 1.6 East German per capita gross investment as a percentage of west German levels, 1991–1994

	1991	1992	1993	1994
All	65	100	131	149
Private sector	61	92	126	142
Public sector	101	167	173	200

Source: BfW, 1995b, p.23.

Thus the most striking features of the east German transformation are the failure of the speedy integration into the wider German economy to open up possibilities for the export sectors of the past, alongside a revival of growth that has been partly public-sector led and that has centred around construction activities and, to a lesser extent, sectors that serve a very local market.

THE EAST GERMAN MODEL

In view particularly of the extent of the specificity of the east German transformation, it could appear at first sight that the differences from the Czech Republic are so great as to make a comparison almost pointless. As part of the Federal Republic of Germany, east Germany has been merged into an economically powerful partner and it was inevitable that this would lead to the rapid creation of an economic, social and political situation in some sort of harmony with that of the rest of the Federal Republic. This is a major difference in comparison with the eastern European reforming states which, by and large, are forced to bring about the transformation of their economic systems by their own efforts. East Germany can rely on west German help not only for major financial transfers, but also for providing a whole ready-made system of legal, economic and social institutions, including the necessary know-how.

Nevertheless, these differences in some respects make the comparison even more useful. The key point is that there were great similarities in the starting point and the goal, in many of the problems that have arisen in terms of economic policies and in the alternative solutions available on many specific issues. The differences are in the framework within which solutions could be sought. The initial similarity is obvious enough in the origins of all the economies of east–central Europe as integral parts of the socialist economic system, characterized by a planned or 'command' economy with enterprises incorporated into hierarchical structures, frequently with large combines as a key element. Although there was a division of labour in production both within and between the national economies of eastern Europe, the one thing that was lacking to any significant degree was the controlling element of competition. Thus, they all now share the common goals of transforming their national economies into systems operating on market principles, alongside integration into the world economy.

What could be described as the east German model for economic transformation had three immutable features. These were the adoption of the economic and social system of the Federal Republic, the reunification of the German currency, meaning that its external value was set by the overall situation of the Federal Republic, and the incorporation of the full legal system of the Federal Republic. Some economists in the early period argued for a gradual increase in the external value of the East German mark, based on a recognition of the limitations to the economic potential of the region. No matter how sensible such ideas might have been in economic terms, they were not politically feasible at the time. It would have been unthinkable to isolate east Germany, with its own currency and exchange rates, over any extended period.

Thus, the creation of the basic economic policy framework was ultimately determined by priorities set by the course of political developments. These, it could be said, set the context within which economic policy had to find the best available solutions. That often meant choosing what appeared to be the second- or third-best option, meaning that there was from the start no possibility of formulating a complete and coherent transformation strategy. Instead, the policy options available for east Germany could best be seen as analogous to regional policies in other large economic units which, by definition, have to operate within a broader, largely predetermined, framework.

Moreover, the Federal Republic of Germany was not prepared for unification and the collapse of eastern Europe. There was no contingency plan. There was, however, also no possibility of putting economic processes on hold until appropriate remedies for their future control had been developed. There had to be immediate action, beginning even before the economic objectives had been fully defined. Under these circumstances it is hardly surprising that it was not just the 'West German model' in general that was taken over. With it came whole catalogues of very specific measures that had been tried and tested in West Germany and had contributed to that country's economic success. They were, however, not necessarily appropriate for the specific problems of the East German economy.

INDUSTRY: THE PROBLEM AREA

Adjustment in industry was, and remains, particularly difficult. In contrast to other branches of the economy, the opening of the domestic market meant that industry was exposed to international competition virtually overnight. The introduction of the common currency in July 1990 is frequently blamed for the extensive collapse of east German industry. Clearly, the shock of revaluation had to have a very profound impact on the structure inherited from the past.

It is, however, now clear that, even had there been a phased revaluation of the currency, and had there been tariff barriers which could have been reduced gradually, the result would in the end not have been very different. In view of the productivity gap compared with west Germany, which was estimated at 70 per cent and even higher in the case of some export-oriented sectors, east German industry simply could not compete on price. Nor did it have the products that could be sold on western markets. The production processes developed within the planned economy could not match those in the West in terms of flexibility, quality or technological level.

Nor could the firms match the organizational techniques common in the West. There was a serious lack of management skills and business knowledge required for the new environment. These deficiencies are, of course, a common feature across all the east European reforming states, and raising the level of industrial competitiveness presents immense difficulties in all of them. The impact, however, has not been as dramatic as in the east German case, following that former state's speedy incorporation into the all-German economy.

A group from the DIW visited three of the largest consulting firms in the Federal Republic in the early stages of the transformation and discussed the comparative advantages of east German industry. They could find none. During these discussions, which also covered eastern Europe, it was concluded that western companies would enter into cooperation agreements only on the basis of equivalent technology and manufacturing philosophies. Even price concessions, which could, for example, be achieved by low wages, were considered insufficient to close the gap with the West. Thus, even from that early stage, experts were convinced that reaching western levels would be possible only through a considerable restructuring of industry, together with a renewal of fixed assets. This has clearly proved correct in the case of east Germany. There is every indication that it will prove at least as valid across the countries of eastern Europe which, therefore, still have to contend with considerable adjustment problems in view of the low level of investment in their industrial assets over the last few years.

A further factor made the initial conditions for east German industry particularly bad. Although it had appeared to be among the most efficient within the CMEA, its structure was remarkably similar to that of west Germany. Both countries' industries were highly export-oriented, and had broadly complementary markets. However, with the collapse of the CMEA, east German industry lost its traditional markets. It was not needed by western markets, where adequate capacity already existed. To avoid a major collapse it would have had to gain a sizeable share in new markets in a relatively short time. It would, however, have had to do this with products which west German industries were already selling successfully on the world market. The firms lacked many of the necessary prerequisites for this. Thanks, then, to the incorporation into the existing German economic structures, the east German production potential became effectively obsolete in one blow.

This fact alone need not have been fatal. The selection process in a market economy does not always favour the most efficient companies: market strength and financial power are frequently decisive factors in deciding the outcome of competition. In this, however, the western companies have equally clear advantages over those from east Germany and the reforming states. They had the experience of operating in a market economy, including well-established supply and customer relations, and they were usually way ahead where modern capital assets and financial power are important factors in deciding the outcome of competition.

The depth and specificity of these problems will become clearer in the context of the different possibilities opened to industry in the Czech Republic, as discussed especially in Chapter 6. The problems, however, were not satisfactorily reflected in the German government's policies towards industry, and for that matter other sectors, which centred essentially on the *Treuhandanstalt*, or THA. This institution was founded following a decree of the GDR People's Assembly on 1 March 1990, which was confirmed after German reunification. It was put in charge of the assets of state-owned enterprises and required to give priority to privatization, with less emphasis on rehabilitation, and to close companies where rehabilitation appeared impossible. As a supplementary objective it was to make every effort to safeguard employment in these enterprises. Nevertheless, the THA essentially stuck to very specific and limited goals. Only in the supplementary condition of 'maintaining employment' was there any sign of a mandate that could imply a more general role in helping towards the more familiar objectives of economic policy.

Indeed, for a long time the THA resisted pressures to take on issues of structural policy for which it did not consider itself qualified. This was despite an awareness from a very early stage that any action, or for that matter inaction, would also affect the development possibilities of whatever region or sector was concerned. To a great extent, this restricted role was defined from the start by the THA's subordination to the Ministry of Finance. Its freedom of action was also restricted by its dependence on the legal framework and philosophy of the old Federal Republic. This brought the principle of 'restitution of property rather than compensation', with the result that ownership in many cases was unclear for a longer period of time. The resulting uncertainty discouraged investment within enterprises and left the THA with no option but to wait until ownership issues were resolved, even where it might have had scope to consider active steps.

In the course of time, and when faced with changing problems, there were shifts in emphasis. At the start, it was assumed that privatization would yield more than DM 500 billion. These expectations had to be scaled down extremely rapidly and the THA finished its activities with a loss of DM 250 billion. It is clear from this that the potential of the east German economy was overestimated and the adjustment problems underestimated. A process of learning about the sheer scale of the problems stimulated the formulation of ideas for a more active rehabilitation of some industries and for the maintenance of some industrial sites. Examples include shipbuilding, as well as the chemical, iron and steel industries, and are taken up in more detail in Chapter 3.

At the end of 1994, the THA had completed the major part of its work, with the lion's share of the property it originally administered transferred to private hands. However, the transformation process was far from complete. The THA's successor organization, the *Bundesanstalt für vereinigungsbedingte Sonderaufgaben*, the Federal Office for Special Tasks Related to Unification or BVS, was entrusted with controlling the contracts negotiated by the *Treuhandanstalt* and privatizing the remaining enterprises. According to the BVS, substantial public funds will be needed to keep enterprises afloat, meaning that in the coming years the financial obligations of the THA's successor, totalling approximately DM 100 billion, must be met (*Tagesspiegel*, 8 May 1995, p.13). Thus, despite total public transfers to east Germany of DM 848 billion of public money between 1991 and 1995, plus the THA's loss of DM 250 billion, east Germany is still far from being an independently viable region within Germany. It still suffers from a range of specific problems across industry, construction and the hotel and catering sectors. This is a shocking discovery. It should, however, not be seen purely as a judgement on the work of the *Treuhandanstalt*, as the ultimate root cause lies in the weakness of east Germany's competitive capacity.

Thus, as explained in Chapter 3, the THA's initial hope of speedy privatization could never be a solution for the former large-scale enterprises, particularly when complex and integrated production processes made impossible simple subdivision into smaller units that would be attractive to outside investors. This, however, created a major dilemma when set against the THA's initial strategy. A sudden and complete collapse of these firms was unthinkable, if only for reasons of political stability, but maintaining production was extremely expensive. Nevertheless, that second option was frequently chosen. This could have been a logical approach from a regional or east German perspective had active steps been taken to develop a more secure future for these sectors. There were, however, few cases of this. Partial exceptions were shipbuilding and the iron and steel industries, but any rehabilitation plans have aroused controversy as they concern industries which even in west Germany find it difficult to survive without subsidies. Moreover the volume of subsidies necessary — DM 1 million per job maintained — is very considerable.

A further dilemma surrounds the case of the chemical sites in the region of Halle and Bitterfeld, which is discussed in Chapter 3. BVS thinking in 1995 envisaged the use of more than DM 10 billion of public funds in the 'chemical triangle' alone, while critics have argued that these funds should have been used for technologically advanced projects rather than investing in old industries. That option, however, has been taken only in a few exceptional cases, such as that of the firm Jenoptik which was supported from very early on, and of the semi-conductor enterprise, Halbleiterwerk, in Dresden. It is still not yet clear if these technology-intensive projects will prove successful.

Indeed, ideas for a structural policy oriented more towards the sectors of the future may be in line with economic theory, but they are not in line with political realities. The time factor poses an insoluble problem. The task in east Germany and the reforming states is not one of building up a new industrial structure alone. It involves the dual task of destroying an existing industrial structure while simultaneously creating a new one. The trouble is that the fastest and most certain part of this process has proved to be the destructive one. As long as new growth in new sectors cannot match the pace of decline in traditional sectors, the obvious danger is of intolerable social costs.

Moreover, support to new growth is constrained by the requirements of the European Union's support and subsidization policies, which limit Germany's freedom of manoeuvre.

Nevertheless, the complexity of the issues involved in the privatization of the east German economy did lead to some degree of adaptation in the THA's strategy in ways that had major implications for the newly emerging east German economic structure. For a considerable period, it gave priority to offering east German companies to west German firms operating in the same sector. In many cases, however, privatization processes were drawn out over a long time period. German investors frequently only revealed a serious interest when foreign buyers appeared. There were also bogus offers in order to deter rivals. No doubt this is understandable from a company's point of view, but such behaviour was detrimental both to companies and to regions. There were some successes where good conditions and substantial grants proved especially attractive to companies which were looking for new production sites, intending to expand or change their production range, or which had obsolete production facilities themselves and were forced to undertake major investment to remain competitive.

In many cases, however, interest was minimal. Those firms which used to be research-intensive and export-oriented had particular difficulty in finding buyers. Even when research facilities were separated from parent companies, western investors had virtually no interest in taking them over, generally preferring to start from scratch. This almost always appeared more promising than trying to maintain and develop from operations of companies that had failed to prove themselves in the past. Indeed, takeovers were often motivated by the desire to establish 'extended work-benches', covering for short-term capacity gaps in a west German operation. The only other major area of attraction was in those activities where proximity to the market was important. Thus banking, insurance, trade and construction, and the quarrying, printing, food and semi-luxury goods industries made rapid progress.

Generally, however, west German industry already had its production sites close to the consumer markets and also had comparatively modern assets. There was little reason for large-scale industry to take over east German production facilities. The results can be seen clearly in Table 1.4, with the declining representation of sectors typically dominated by large-scale export-oriented enterprises alongside the survival or even growth of construction and consumer-oriented sectors. With this has come the disappearance of the large enterprises that had dominated the east German economy in the past, and the appearance of a structure dominated by small and medium-sized enterprises.

EAST GERMANY'S PROSPECTS

A joint report by three major German research institutes, the German Institute for Economic Research (DIW), the Institute for World Economy of the University of Kiel (IfW) and the Halle Institute for Economic Research (IWH), was compiled for the Federal Minister for Economic Affairs of the Federal Republic of Germany and reported in its Economic Bulletin in September 1995. This makes it clear that the process of catching up is under way, but that considerable gaps still remain, particularly in industry. The report illustrated the structural deficiencies within the east German economy around several points. These relate to the sectoral pattern of production and employment, the scale of companies, the integration into a cross-regional division of labour and the geographical distribution of production sites. Some of the key data are provided in Tables 1.2, 1.3 and 1.4.

As previously demonstrated, the share of manufacturing industry in east Germany's gross output is only half as high as in west Germany, while the share of the construction industry is three times as high. Indeed, the construction industry in the East has clearly overtaken manufacturing industry in terms of gross output. This difference from the West could be seen as a reflection both of the depth of the economy's collapse and of the effects of renewal with clear signs of a fresh start in some activities. The construction industry, protected from cross-regional competition by high transport costs, profits from reconstruction without having suffered from the dramatic decline that affected other sectors. On the other hand, manufacturing was hit more severely by the shock of transformation than any other sector and has yet to recover completely. Enterprises in that sector have been concentrating on material- and labour-intensive production for which longer-term prospects are generally considered to be relatively poor.

East German enterprises are also deficient as far as company size is concerned, and this complicates their integration into the all-German division of labour. One group of enterprises, and this applies particularly to privatized, former THA-administered companies, are often no longer large enough. Another group, and this applies especially to newly-formed companies, are still too small. There is a striking difference even in the mining and manufacturing industries in east Germany where larger companies are poorly represented compared with west Germany.

The share of foreign trade in the overall turnover of east German industry has hardly changed since 1991, as local production has been geared to an ever greater extent towards the domestic market. The overall figure of 12 per cent in 1994 was less than half the figure of 27 per cent recorded for west German industry. It can be added that all business sectors showed lower export rates than their opposite numbers in the West, with particularly dramatic differences for road vehicles — 7 per cent of east German output exported against 44 per cent for west Germany — and electrical engineering — with figures of 10 per cent and 32 per cent, respectively.

These figures conceal the fact that there are major shifts in the regional structure of foreign trade although, according to foreign trade statistics, a large part of these exports is still going to eastern Europe. There has, however, been a substantial change, with exports from east Germany to central and eastern European countries declining in importance. Instead, supply relations have been established with partners in western countries, though not on a large enough scale to compensate for the loss of markets in the East. This reorientation applies especially to businesses owned by west German companies and able to use their existing sales networks.

The continual decline of exports by east German firms to central and eastern Europe gives cause for concern. It cannot be attributed to the difficult economic situation in the reforming states alone, not least in view of the business successes of many west German companies in these countries. This points yet again to the general competitive weakness of east German companies. They have difficulty regaining a foothold even, and perhaps particularly, in the reemerging markets in the East. Indeed, the once powerful investment goods sector has suffered an especially severe decline. All in all, the east German economy accounts for less than one-tenth of overall German exports of goods and services. By way of contrast, east Germany's share of the population is 19 per cent. Needless to say, its share is also low on the west German market, even though it apparently finds it easier to gain a market share there than abroad.

The low level of integration of east German companies in the cross-regional division of labour is closely linked to another structural problem. This is the disappearance of company headquarters in the new federal states. Generally speaking, western investors focused primarily on those activities most closely linked to production itself. East German subsidiaries have largely been relieved of other functions, such as research and development, marketing, organization of sales and the development of long-term business concepts.

Even the benefits of this degree of integration into the all-German economy are not evenly spread across east Germany. It is no more of a homogeneous regional unit than is west Germany or, for that matter, many other countries. There are major disparities which have their roots far in the past. The North was always dominated by agriculture and small-scale business production, while industry was concentrated into the centre and the South. Little changed even in the forty years under socialism, despite some partially successful attempts at industrialization on the coast and on the river Oder. For the future, however, the development prospects of individual regions in east Germany are ultimately determined by whether or not they have favourable transport links to neighbouring economic centres. It is no accident that investment projects have up to now been concentrated along the main traffic arteries. This points to an enormously important role for investment in the infrastructure as possibly the most effective method of promoting long-term investment.

Despite all these difficulties, east German industry has undergone a structural change without parallel in the five years since the currency, economic and social union. Indeed, the recent GDP figures point to a major production boom. The hourly productivity rate had already doubled by the end of 1992, and by the end of 1994 it was three times as high as at the beginning of 1991. This, however, still left productivity levels in east German industry far below those of west Germany. It was only in the second half of 1994 that 50 per cent of the west German level was attained. Despite substantial pay increases, unit wage costs are declining. This, however, is not yet a universal phenomenon. As Table 1.2 indicates, unit wage costs in the second half of 1994 in manufacturing were still on average 31 per cent higher than in west Germany.

In order to obtain a more detailed picture of the state of east German industry than the available statistics allow, the DIW carried out a poll of industrial companies in the period from March to June 1995. Usable questionnaires were returned by 2,800 firms covering 180,000 workplaces. The results point to the continuation of considerable obstacles to east German industrial development. The movements of wages and salaries, and the lack of capital, feature prominently as continuing problems. There has been a noticeable rise in complaints from enterprises about the failure of purchasers to make payments, and this is associated with the critical liquidity situation, a problem mentioned with increasing frequency. There was less concern than in the past over difficulties with the conversion of production, with finding new markets and from the burden of old debts.

A large number of enterprises have drawn their own conclusion from wage trends. They are becoming increasingly reluctant to follow the west German practice of fixing minimum wage levels through collective bargaining. Small businesses, especially, have broken away from collective bargains covering whole sectors. This causes problems not only for trade unions but also for the employers' associations, as there is now little willingness to join an employers' organization committed to collective bargaining.

According to the results of the questionnaire, east German industry expected an increase in turnover for 1995 of about one-fifth, compared with the previous year. This would point to faster growth than between 1993 and 1994. Major hopes are focused on foreign markets where sales are predicted to increase by about a half. There should also be significantly higher sales than in 1994 into western Germany. It is noteworthy that those companies, whose main competitors are based in the old *Länder* or abroad and who are therefore exposed to particularly strong competition, have the greatest expectations of increased turnover. Generally, therefore, the enterprises were extremely optimistic, not just as far as turnover is concerned but also with regard to profits. Many companies, which were still incurring losses in 1994, believed that in 1995 they would balance the books or even make a profit.

Nevertheless, the long-term future development of east German industry depends essentially on the scale and speed of investment activity. A significant growth in investment has been achieved since 1991, a large part of it facilitated by the privatization of companies entrusted to the THA. As a rule the THA negotiated job agreements and investment levels with purchasers and in return made concessions on the purchase prices. The results of the questionnaire indicate that these firms invested DM 29,000 per employee in 1994. That is DM 8,000 more than the DM 21,000 invested in those companies which had to make do without such 'startup subsidies'. Moreover, in approximately two-thirds of the companies privatized with investment guarantees, the firms themselves claim to have invested beyond the level agreed in the purchase contract, while only about one-tenth of purchasers failed to undertake the agreed level of investment.

On average, those companies which had already come to a decision planned to reduce their level of investment in 1995 by just one-tenth as compared with 1994. This results primarily from a fall in investment from those companies still owned by the BVS, the successor to the THA. On the other hand, privately managed companies, both independent ones and those controlled by larger groups, planned to invest about the same amount in 1995 as they did in 1994. Only a few firms planned to increase their capacity. For the time being the expansion phase appears to be complete, particularly in large companies. The results of the questionnaire indicated overall that no further increase of investment could be expected from within the present stock of companies during 1995. Nor, however, was any reduction anticipated. It is not possible to confirm, from the first results for 1995, how far this has been the case.

This apparent stability of investment must be set against the extent of the decline in the labour force. Industrial employment by 1995 was only about 600,000 compared with 3 million before reunification. It could be assumed that further job reductions were possible even with increasing industrial production, as productivity levels were still about half those of west Germany. It is, however, unclear how the weaknesses stemming from the absence of larger enterprises will be overcome. The situation is still particularly unfavourable in such formerly research-intensive and export-oriented sectors as chemicals and mechanical engineering. In these sectors, large companies are often important customers for other firms and the focus of industrial research activity. This rather suggests that east Germany will continue to be a structurally weak region within Germany for a considerable time to come. That will certainly apply to industry, if not to other sectors.

WERE THE POLICIES WRONG?

In the light of this assessment of the weaknesses in east German industry, and even while accepting that there has been a strengthening of some positive trends, it does seem reasonable to ask whether economic policy, and maybe also economic theory, should not be judged to have failed. The same questions can be posed again about the possible inappropriateness of introducing the Deutschmark at the actual exchange rate chosen. From a purely economic point of view, an independent east German currency with flexible exchange rates would certainly have been a possible option for a transition period. Pressure would thus have been reduced during the adjustment period, leaving time and room for manoeuvre.

Another frequently cited source of unsatisfactory performance, and a background factor in the need for large financial transfers to east Germany, was the rapid rise in wages and salaries. The obvious criticism is that costs were thereby pushed upwards too rapidly in a period when production and productivity were falling. There was a mismatch between the movements in these two economic quantities. This argument is right as far as it goes. However, it overlooks the fact that remuneration has different functions, which meant that some degree of mismatch was inevitable.

It is useful in this context to differentiate between three areas in which wage levels influence developments. These are the impact of wages on costs, the impact on demand and what can be termed the 'integration function'. Different levels of wages and salaries were needed so that incentives could begin to work. Given the low startup level, this differentiation alone had to lead to increases in remuneration. In addition to this, wages and salaries were adjusted to the 'new price level' which was introduced with unification, together with integration into the social system of the Federal Republic. Although higher wages and salaries meant company costs were rising rapidly, there was also a stimulus to purchasing power. This led to an improvement in sales conditions for some east German producers. It affected in particular housing, the construction industry, energy, trade, banks, insurance companies, the service sector and many craft workshops, all of which have been areas of rapid progress in east Germany. However, the high level of wages and salaries, which initially went far beyond the net product, meant that the company sector as a whole initially incurred losses. Thus, a large part of the transfers went into consumption rather than investment.

Increases in pay levels were also necessary for political reasons. This is their 'integration function'. Too large a gap could even have rendered impossible the necessary cooperation between east German and west German experts in east Germany. There would also have been a greater incentive for employees to look for jobs in west Germany. Excessive pressure from migration would have risked creating political and social unrest. Thus, again, one strong line of 'defence' for the policy decisions taken is that a strictly 'economic' logic was inapplicable. Political expediency meant that longer-term isolation of east Germany through flexible exchange rates was not feasible. The whole adjustment process followed a path of political necessity while the economy had to find the best possible solutions under these circumstances.

Moreover, despite these high wage levels making some forms of economic activity unprofitable, other important steps have been taken to increase investment which, as Table 1.6 shows, was comfortably above the west German per capita level. Important steps have been taken in setting up the administration and extending the infrastructure, which have greatly improved east Germany's attractiveness as an industrial location. This will continue, not least because it is seen as politically highly desirable. If investment in east Germany can be kept at a high level and financed through redirecting resources from consumption, then the united Germany will emerge greatly strengthened. A special Solidarity Supplement Tax, paid by households with higher incomes in 1991 and 1992 and reintroduced in 1994, was an indication of the possibilities of restricting consumption in favour of investment in east Germany, although it accounted for only 0.2 per cent of total tax revenues in 1994.

Nevertheless, there is no doubt that mistakes were made, even if some might be judged 'unavoidable mistakes' in view of the starting conditions and the problems which had to be surmounted. The most serious errors, apart from the restitution of property before reimbursement, could be grouped around three general headings. The first was the generally short-term view on the instruments of the economic policy. Most of the promotion programmes were established for a relatively short time and then prolonged and changed. This did not provide the stability required for making confident investment calculations. The industrial support programmes would have been more effective if they had been in force for a longer period of time and then reduced step by step.

The second error was the lack of courage to speak out in favour of a more active, regional, structural policy, while the third was an excessively narrow definition of the mandate for the THA, the policies of which were determined primarily by business management criteria rather than by national economic ones.

In assessing the results and the economic policy measures taken, one must also be aware that development policy in east Germany is designed to achieve the maximum benefit for the national economy as a whole. In other words, it is concerned with benefits for west as well as east Germany. That immediately differentiates the objectives of policy making in this case from the objectives that could be pursued in the countries of eastern Europe. This point is often overlooked, but it had a major influence on the approach to industrial development and related policy measures, helping to explain why hardly any attention was paid to questions of a specific industrial policy framework. Thus there were no attempts to foresee or plan the future industrial structure. There was no conception, for example, of the possibility of developing industries of the future, such as those concerned with protecting the environment.

The point, of course, is that such a conception for the industrial direction of east Germany would immediately have affected west Germany and vice versa. Since the necessary influx of know-how and capital had to come mainly from the West, and since the state had to leave the structural orientation to market forces, a situation was bound to arise in which, at least in the short term, purely east German interests moved backstage. The political aim was not to come to an optimum for east Germany but for the whole Republic. If the present modern production capacity in east Germany competes with the production in the West, the result will be a zero benefit for the whole German economy, assuming that there is no difference to the growth in demand.

Nor was east Germany intended to become a Trojan horse. This is what could have happened had foreign investors been attracted to set up modern production facilities through generous subsidies, and then started competing with west German industry. In this context, one should mention the high level of investment support with the possibility that up to 35 per cent of the costs of assets can be underwritten through a combination of investment subsidies and tax allowances. This is a major incentive, particularly for companies either looking for new locations in Europe or having to renew outdated facilities.

In practice, however, it was not particularly important to the relatively modern west German industry. Companies there were discouraged primarily by the long-term weakness of the global economic situation, together with uncertainty about the future of east Germany and the difficulties in understanding the complex tax and subsidy systems. There has, therefore, been relatively minor interest in the concessions on offer, although this could, of course, change in the future.

Thus, incorporation into the all-German economic structure, and the logic of the policy priorities that followed from that, have meant that, for the foreseeable future, there can be no solution to the problems faced by the export-oriented, research-intensive industrial core of the old East German economy. The chemical industry and electrical and mechanical engineering were, and are, bound to face massive difficulties. Comprehensive transfers and promotion measures were necessary both to cushion the shock effects resulting from the introduction of the currency union and to initiate a fresh start or restructuring. There has, however, been no strategy on new regional, technological or structural goals. Instead, state involvement has so far centred on maintaining old industries. There are reasonable grounds for fearing that deeper state interference in shaping structures may actually end up creating structures that will need to be subsidized for a long time to come. It is, for example, more than doubtful whether the subsidies given to the shipbuilding and steel industries will lead to permanent jobs in the quantity expected. By the end of 1997, the subsidies paid will have exceeded DM 13 billion in the chemical industry and DM 2 million in the steel industry, leading to the calculation of the cost of a workplace at more than DM 1 million.

WHAT POLICY SOLUTION?

It is clear that all the weaknesses of the east German economy cannot be blamed on insufficient state help and nor can, or indeed should, they all be reduced through immediate state action. The deep structural deficiencies in east German industry can only be eliminated very gradually over a long time period. It also has to be accepted that the politically desirable integration into the western economic system had a range of less fortunate economic consequences which limit the freedom of manoeuvre in economic policy making. Nevertheless, government policies can play an extremely important role in helping to reduce the east German economy's structural weaknesses.

It is possible here to distinguish between two broad approaches to state support. The first is promotion of a region's 'endogenous' potential. In regional policy this has frequently been considered as the key to success. It points to using subsidies to reduce weaknesses in existing companies, such as low capital resources, market access, a lack of R&D capacity and a low level of innovativeness. Programmes for strengthening the potential for new firm formation should be included here. In general, if east Germany is to regain importance as an economic location, then know-how as well as capital have to flow into the region. This requires continued strong commitment by foreign investors. This, however, will only happen if east Germany can offer comparative advantages over other regions. Since such advantages are not inherent, they will still have to be created through subsidies for a long time to come.

Consequently, a second major support approach must include measures to make the overall location characteristics more attractive for investors. These have to be long term if they are to be effective. Major investors must be won to plump for east Germany as a location for research-intensive and export-oriented production, and they will only do this if all the relevant characteristics of the region are judged desirable.

The complexity of this task follows from the extent of the east German structural weaknesses. Thus a fully-formed, modern industrial structure requires a full range of companies differentiated by size and linked together in reasonably stable networks. East Germany is deficient here, with its domination by small and medium-sized enterprises. Not only does it need bigger firms, it also needs their integration into an effective network linked to the publicly-funded research infrastructure. Indeed, without large enterprises, which generally have the ability to make use of the research results of public institutions, the potential for smaller firms is also very restricted. They are often dependent on larger firms as their major customers.

This has important implications for policy making towards east Germany. Unification and integration into both the German and the global economy caused a considerable structural crisis in east Germany. For more than 40 years, the economy had been based on criteria which are no longer valid today and will not be in the future. The products and production processes developed in the past are inappropriate to future requirements as they cannot meet the demands of the market economy. Companies also developed particular sizes and fields of specialization, which for the most part are no longer required today.

A process of 'creative destruction', the central point in Schumpeter's model of economic development, is essential. Initially, however, this means an extensive depreciation of both fixed assets and human resources. Particular jobs and skills will become obsolete as part of this renewal. Neither economic theory nor practice provides adequate solutions for overcoming such problems. Theories relying on the comparative-static approach point to the assumption that it will be possible to create a new equilibrium through a relevant salary, price, monetary and financial policy. However, the problem lies in mastering the process of adjustment.

Democracies are stable only if they are based on human satisfaction. However, a substantial fall in national income cannot be avoided during the economic transformation on account of this depreciation process. The situation therefore cannot be compared directly with the post-war reconstruction after 1945. In that case, destruction had already taken place and the only open question was how to go about reconstruction. It could also be assumed that prosperity would increase every year. In this sense east Germany has considerable advantages over the eastern European reforming states, since the fall in national income can be at least partially compensated by integration into the Federal Republic and help from west Germany. Also, capital and know-how are made available for the process of renewal.

To summarize east German experience, then, a general collapse of industry could not be prevented, despite large transfers. New products had to be developed, production processes and assets had to be renewed, new supplier and customer relations had to be established. The renewal process was and remains strongly dependent on an influx of western capital and of know-how in the broadest sense. It is, however, clearly not a process in which speedy success can be taken for granted.

Set against this background, the problems for the Czech Republic and the other reforming states of eastern Europe appear to have a great deal in common with east Germany's. They do have the ability to isolate their domestic markets, by holding their currency at a low rate and by other measures to restrict imports. They can also maintain a high level of price competitiveness, thanks to low wage levels.

Nevertheless, these advantages do not solve the problem of long-term competitiveness that has hit the east German economy more immediately and with greater force. In all cases the former export-oriented enterprises, often the more technologically advanced part of the planned economies, have found it particularly hard to survive. These firms, too, depend largely on the flow of capital and know-how from the West in order to make products which are competitive in both price and quality on the international market. But they will also need western partners to gain access to the market, either as suppliers or within a cooperative framework. In economic policy terms this means that attractive conditions have to be created for western investors. Low wages and salaries alone are not enough. Political stability and a monetary policy geared towards stability are prerequisites for creating confidence in the national economy, but even with those, foreign investors will commit themselves only if the basic legal conditions and tax incentives, as well as the infrastructure, are favourable.

There is clearly scope here for considering what instruments of industrial policy could be used to help the restructuring process. There are, however, dangers in simplistic analogies. Thus the experiences of Japan, South Korea and other east Asian countries are often cited as cases in which active industrial policies were important. They, however, started from different positions both when compared with east Germany and when compared with the countries of eastern

Europe. Thus, for example, rapid industrial growth started from a position in which their industries were not yet developed.

By way of contrast, the Czech Republic, like east Germany, faces the different problem of restructuring on the basis of a well-established industrial structure. Moreover, Japan in particular had a larger internal market, which can be seen as an important precondition for the success of the kinds of industrial policy that it adopted. Above all, the countries of east Asia were not nearly as closely integrated into their environment as the states of east–central Europe soon will be. They may not lose their separate economic identity, and they may not gain the benefits of a richer partner with the suddenness and to the same extent as east Germany. They will, however, be more closely integrated into, and therefore increasingly dependent on assistance from, the European Union. The forms and extent of this assistance will be key factors in determining the fate of their transformations. There is a strong case for arguing that, as in east Germany, this outside help should be concentrated primarily on building up the infrastructure while also opening up access to the west European market. That, however, may not be adequate on its own to ensure economic success.

2. The Role of the *Treuhandanstalt*

The transformation of the enterprises inherited from the GDR into private companies has been a long and complex process, strongly influenced by the structure that existed before reunification. This background is essential to an understanding of why, in most cases, the establishment of fully competitive private companies has proved to be so difficult. The basic position of enterprises within the GDR's planned economy, with its attendant economic policies, will therefore be discussed in some detail here, in so far as they are relevant to the companies' situations. Changes in the political, legal and economic framework of the companies resulting from the introduction of the Deutschmark are described next, followed by a concluding discussion of the problems of the privatization of *Treuhand*-administered companies. It is impossible to cover all points in detail, but the general discussion indicates clear problems with the chosen strategy for the transformation of the east German economy. Chapter 3 amplifies the point with detailed descriptions both of the privatization of larger industrial concerns, taking the chemical industry as an example, and of the emergence of small and medium-sized enterprises.

AN OVERVIEW OF THE PROBLEM

Despite its high level of development relative to other CMEA countries, the internal problems of the old economic order were perhaps more severe in the GDR than anywhere else. A number of negative influences came together, including the economic policies of the GDR leadership, the problems within the system of centralized planning, the economy's organizational structure and its technological and market orientations. Together these had so restrictive an impact on the competitiveness of combines and companies that the international solvency of the GDR was coming under serious threat before the end of the 1980s. Despite the outward appearance of stability, forces were at work that made the transformation into a market economy ultimately inevitable.

Currency reunification and the introduction of the Deutschmark in east Germany brought about a radical change in the economic system. Central control and planning bodies lost their powers while the ownership of state-owned, nationalized companies passed mainly into the control of the *Treuhandanstalt*, the THA. The most important exceptions were the core state institutions such as the *Deutsche Post*, the postal service, *Deutsche Reichsbahn*, the railways, the administration of roads and waterways and those companies or institutions directly controlled by central, regional or local authorities. The THA's task, as defined in the Law on the Privatization and Reorganization of State-owned Property passed on 17 June 1990, was the promotion of 'the structural adjustment of the economy to market requirements, in particular by influencing the development of companies which could be rehabilitated into competitive enterprises, and by their privatization'. It was to work for 'the emergence of companies able to survive in the market' and for 'a more efficient economic structure', both to be achieved 'by the sensible dismantling of company structures'. In practice this meant that the THA acted as a limited interim owner. It tried above all to sell the companies it administered to investors, only assuming the wider functions of a shareholder when this could not be avoided.

These companies remained legally independent. The THA was not conceived as a head office and, although it did retain decision-making powers over their finances, it was not liable for their losses in cases of bankruptcy. Its role, then, was purely to help in their transformation into fully independent private companies capable of operating successfully in a market economy. This implied radical changes to their internal structures, to their market orientations and to the division of labour between them. Companies often had to break new ground, becoming involved in a complex division of labour at both the German and the international levels.

Previously, of course, the country had been isolated by the autarkic policies of the GDR's leadership, and by the almost exclusive ties with the CMEA countries. It had, however, held a very specific foreign trade advantage in comparison with its partners in central and eastern Europe, as the European Community considered the GDR to be a part of the Federal German economic area. East German goods could therefore be sold into the European Community duty-free. This, however, was of increasingly limited benefit as the CMEA functioned in such a way as to give very limited scope for the development of a complex division of labour, based on the complementary production of goods of a high technical level. Instead, specialization remained at the most rudimentary level, with the Soviet Union providing primary products and energy which the eastern European partners bought in exchange for manufactured goods.

This failure to create a modern and sophisticated division of labour within the CMEA was reflected in the declining relative efficiency of East German industry, and hence in a deteriorating export performance. Moreover, the limited nature of the GDR's participation in the international division of labour was reflected in limitations on the internal division of labour. The link was partly direct as, unable to afford the materials and parts they needed from western markets, enterprises increasingly had to produce their own inputs. It was also partly caused by policy choices, with the GDR probably suffering more than other CMEA countries, with the possible exception of the Soviet Union, from deformations resulting from the generalized establishment and subsequent development of combines. This was to make the opening of the economy to the West, followed by privatization, particularly traumatic.

The argument here is that the nature of the structural change from 1990 onwards, and its distinctiveness compared with the countries of east–central Europe, cannot be explained purely as a result of direct competition from western rivals. It is, of course, difficult to establish the relative importance of the different factors. It would, however, be an oversimplification to attribute everything only to the 'currency shock' and to the way in which formerly state-owned companies were privatized. These factors operated against the background of a structure inherited from the past which already suffered from severe weaknesses and distortions.

The main aim during the transformation of companies was the reestablishment of overall competitiveness under the new conditions of a market economy. Clearly, the declared political aim of the east German economic transformation — self-sustaining economic development — is dependent on a sufficiently large proportion of industrial enterprises achieving competitive status. The goal could be said to have been achieved when the regional 'national product' is greater than regional consumption, and when the region will only need financial transfers on a scale consistent with financial equalization already familiar from the former federal states.

This, of course, might involve a substantially different sectoral structure from that inherited at the time of reunification. The former GDR had developed a 'complete' branch structure as was inevitable for a separate national economy, particularly under the semi-autarkic conditions imposed by the system of central planning. This cannot serve as a yardstick for the future development of the regional structure. Nor is it inevitable that industry should enjoy a similar status to that in other regions of Germany. Nevertheless, the new structure will not be created from a completely blank sheet. Rather, it will emerge as a combination of previously existing elements that can achieve competitiveness at least in the medium term, of old elements that continue to survive and of completely new developments. All of these will have to be integrated into the overall economic structure of Germany.

BEFORE REUNIFICATION

The broad sectoral breakdown of the GDR's industrial structure in 1989 was shown in Table 1.5. Table 2.1 indicates the breakdown by size of industrial unit. Again, as was typical in centrally-planned economies, there was a strong bias towards larger organizational forms, with 88 per cent of employees in units employing 500 or more, which also accounted for nearly 89 per cent of total output. The picture in the old East Germany, with 76.7 per cent of employment in enterprises with more than 1,000 employees and an average employment per enterprise of 944, points to a substantially higher level of concentration than in Poland where, in 1989, 65.3 per cent worked in enterprises with more than 1,000 employees and the average employment level was 669. In Czechoslovakia, however, there were even fewer smaller enterprises and the average employment per industrial enterprise was 2,064 in 1989. The dramatic changes there are discussed in Chapter 5. Unfortunately, it is impossible to provide precisely comparable figures for east Germany in later years.

Table 2.1 Size distribution of East German industrial enterprises in 1987

Number of employees	Percentage of total		
	Enterprises	Employment	Output
Up to 100	18.7	1.1	1.2
101–500	40.3	11.0	10.1
501–1,000	16.3	12.2	10.9
1,001–2,500	15.5	25.9	24.3
2,501–10,000	8.6	39.8	41.5
More than 10,000	0.6	10.0	11.9

Source: Statistisches Jahrbuch der DDR, 1989, p.139.

Even this does not tell the full story. The industrial structure of the GDR was characterized by the organization of production into 'combines', built around large firms. Even the bulk of small firms, which had been allowed to exist through the 1950s and 1960s, were nationalized in 1972, and have been fully integrated into the combine structures. This has involved either direct incorporation or reorganization of their production programmes, leaving them totally dependent on the larger enterprises. The only important exceptions are approximately 300 very small, private industrial businesses, which managed to survive in the GDR right up to 1989, and the producer craft cooperatives, some of which were sizeable firms.

The term 'combine' was originally used for an organizational form incorporating vertically-integrated production phases, starting with the raw material and ending with the finished product. However, reforms in the 1970s centred on the comprehensive policy of organizing the economy into larger economic units, and as a result state-owned companies were generally attached to a combine, even when this did not bring together vertically-integrated production phases. Thus the 'combine' concept came to be used to group companies by very heterogeneous criteria. It could, for example, be applied to a holding company for firms producing a particular kind of commodity. Thus there were metallurgy combines, which had existed since the 1950s, handling everything from ore mining to the production of metals and semi-finished products. There were also combines for 'shipbuilding', 'railway-vehicle construction', 'agricultural-machinery manufacture', 'microelectronics' and so on. This structure created internal production monopolies and, because of the state monopoly on foreign trade, customers were at their mercy.

Both the functional structure and the scale of these enterprises frequently proved an obstacle to rational management. A 'parent company' was conceived as the production control centre and was meant to coordinate the structures of the combine. This made sense where the parent company was a final producer. However, in other cases the GDR leadership still insisted on adhering to its formal principle, and a holding company was set up even when the division of labour pointed to no obvious candidate as a parent firm. This could have surprising results. Thus, in a number of combines, specialized departments were formed out of industrial research institutes and production units for the improvement of the production processes, creating the so-called *Rationalisierungsmittel-Eigenbau*, or RMB, units. In some cases these were given the status of parent companies. In other cases specific production units could be honoured in this way.

Thus, company profiles were no longer designed around the objective of satisfying demand. Instead, they were fashioned to fit in with the preconceived and rigid notion of a combine structure which had been elevated to the level of a universal principle. By 1989 there were 221 combines, 126 of them answerable directly to the relevant ministries responsible for the various sectors of industry. The remaining 95 were controlled in the first instance by their district councils and ultimately by a coordinating ministry, responsible specifically for district-controlled industries.

The structuring of combines was in theory to be based on a branch principle. However, time proved the impossibility of maintaining doctrinal purity. To give one example, from the very beginning, roughly 60 per cent of production in mechanical engineering was undertaken outside the mechanical engineering combines. The reason was that plant assembly and installation and the bulk of technical services simply could not be separated from the principal activities of the user enterprises. The unreliability of deliveries from other enterprises — a familiar feature of the shortage economy and of the increasing difficulties in foreign trade — meant that each combine became increasingly autarkic, supplying as much of its own needs as it could. This applied to components of more complex finished products and increasingly also to investment goods. This, of course, was the background to the emergence and increasing importance of the RMB departments and plants, the growth of which appears as something of an East German speciality, symptomatic of the limitations to the wider division of labour in the economy as a whole. They developed, constructed and produced equipment both for the improvement of production processes and for replacement of old equipment across whole combines.

As a result, 'specialization and the division of labour were largely restricted within the framework of combines rather than spreading across sectors' (IWH, 1991). It became increasingly difficult to create new divisions of labour between companies belonging to different combines, or to engage in flexible exchange when that would have been advantageous. Instead, combines were forced to take on jobs that were foreign to them. Thus they created their own building divisions as well as the RMB units. Investment goods producers undertook consumer goods production, and combines typically had their own transport divisions. This had a range of serious consequences, among which was the separation of production from research. It was also inevitable that much of the capacity in these subsidiary activities was underutilized.

The combines thus became 'self-supporting organisms' rather than competitive enterprises. Indeed, in 1986, at the time when investment was at its very lowest level, 18 per cent of investment in plant was accounted for by the construction efforts of the combines themselves. This inevitably restricted the scope for improvements in productivity, despite some extraordinarily determined individual efforts, partly because enterprises could not take advantage of the benefits of a more complex division of labour across the economy and partly because they were weighed down by the need to undertake a wide range of peripheral activities. They even had to carry much of the burden of social services, including kindergartens, health centres, sanatoria and holiday homes.

There were, of course, exceptions to this generally negative verdict. Some firms blessed with skilled and competent personnel were able to create successful engineering businesses out of their RMB units. Some of these were to prove better equipped to jump into the market environment than many production enterprises. This, however, does not affect the overall picture. The industrial division of labour was seriously hampered by the development of autarkic combine structures. Towards the end of the 1980s, the employment level in RMB units was roughly equivalent to total employment in machine-tool combines themselves. However, outside the mechanical and electrical engineering sectors, these units generally lacked the qualified staff that would have been required to use their capacity rationally.

This 'comprehensive' combine creation, including the later degeneration of the combines into quasi-autarkic economic units, did not exist to anything like as great an extent in the other CMEA countries. Czechoslovakia, for example, broadly completed nationalization of the economy earlier than the GDR and a slightly different organizational structure took shape. Admittedly combines — the *Výrobní hospodářské jednotky*, or economic production units — were created, but not around such all-embracing principles and without the later striking interventions in the internal division of labour. Even the management structures were often designed in a more flexible way. There were 'managements for specific fields' with relatively independent businesses while, in some other areas, combines incorporated firms with some degree of independence. This may be one of the reasons why a proportion of the firms in these countries can still fall back on the traditional networks of division of labour and continue to find markets for their products. There is, of course, also the protection from the undervalued currency, which to some extent dilutes the impact of the confrontation between inherited structures and the force of international competition. Even in these countries, however, the firms face the problem of creating a more rational division of labour.

The combine system fitted in with, and became an integral part of, a rigid and autarkic system of central planning, with all its negative features and inflexibilities. It may have been an advantage for a specific, basic pattern of the division of labour, but the limitations of the firms' areas of competence were a serious drawback where market conditions pointed to the need for a flexible organization of production. The firms had no freedom of decision making on the nature or volume of their outputs, or over the sales structure. Those wishing to reform the economic system had been trying since the mid-1960s to do away with this rigid regimentation. The leadership, however, had always been cautious because of its reluctance to relinquish any of its own power and because of a fear that the stability of internal supply relations could be jeopardized.

The negative consequences of its centralized powers are well known. The central planners measured a company's performance mainly in production volume in marks, which led to many well-known distortions. One example was that inexpensive goods needed by the market were given a low priority. When it came to fixing plans, companies fought for low plan quotas, in order to be able to exceed them, but not by too much, because good performance was punished in the next planning cycle with even higher quotas. Only the state felt direct economic pressure for higher performance. It transferred this strain 'downwards' in the form of ideological pressure and tried to motivate workers through periodic political campaigns.

This system had a deadening effect on motivation within enterprises. Initiatives 'from below' were often ineffective. Changes by companies in their production range threw the central planning balances into disarray. Even though there were rewards, for example for inventions and feasible innovations, the shortage of investment funds increasingly prevented the implementation of anything new. This paralysed all initiative and was reflected among other aspects in the declining technical quality of 'new' products. It can also be demonstrated by figures on the number of patent applications from the GDR in West Germany which fell by 67 per cent in the machinery industry, by 69 per cent in electrical engineering and by 86 per cent in the chemical industry between 1970 and 1985.

The rigidities of centralized planning were associated with a substantially different financial system from that of a market economy. Above all, the state budget was far more closely linked to the financial affairs of enterprises. Even companies and combines that were meant to be operating under the so-called economic accounting system did not have true financial autonomy. They financed production and investment nominally out of their own revenues and from loans from the state banks. In effect, however, this depended entirely on conditions laid down by the state. Thus, irrespective of the concrete income and expenditure situations in companies, the state demanded a transfer of profits, set as a percentage of the planned profit, of taxes on fixed assets and, from the 1980s, on employment. The state, however, covered possible company losses by subsidies. It was therefore possible for the central authorities, by setting plan targets and by deciding on subsidy levels, to determine in total the financial position of enterprises. In 1988, transfers of profits and a variety of taxes on companies accounted for approximately 70 per cent of state revenue. Income taxes were far less important.

Companies had to produce under the terms of the central 'accounting system' and were allotted appropriate quotas of energy and materials. The 'MAK' accounts, meaning accounts for material, equipment and consumer goods, regulated the allocation and consumption of virtually all important goods in conformity with the plan. Financial conditions, as described above, were set in line with the terms of the MAK accounting. The setting of prices could, however, contain a strong element of irrationality and could be influenced by the producers.

Many prices were not fixed by the market but were meant to reflect production costs. These producers were frequently domestic market monopolies and, over a period of time, the purchasers lost any ability they may once have had to replace domestic products with imports. Thus the producers themselves were under no pressure to reduce costs, and cost-plus pricing amounted to a promise of an easy life. Prices charged by producers were in turn either increased by taxes set at differing rates for individual products, or they were lowered by price support so that 'basic goods' could be offered to the population at stable prices. Thus, it could be said that the state control of prices gave some protection to consumers, thereby deadening the direct impact of the monopoly practices of producers. This, however, had to be paid for with special taxes on industrial goods, partly aimed at 'absorbing excess purchasing power', but also a convenient way for the state to raise finance which could cover the subsidies on rents, public transport and various basic consumer goods.

In such a system, company profits bore only the vaguest relationship to business efficiency: in the same way, losses did not always mean inefficiency on the part of the individual company. This naturally complicated enormously both state planning decisions and company management decisions, hampering the elimination of inefficient production and the emergence of a more successful system.

That financial system from the past has left traces even today. Within the rules handed down to enterprises, the ratios between self-financing and the use of credits were specified in advance. Within this, investment was financed primarily by credits. This is the original source of the 'old debts' inherited by enterprises from the days of the GDR. Investment decisions, however, were taken at ministerial rather than company level, as part of a dialogue with the managing director of the combine in question. Thus, companies were not free to use as they wished any profits they could make. They were, therefore, unable to determine the direction of major changes. Their only degrees of freedom were in the exploitation of ways to lower costs that did not require major investment and in dictating prices to domestic customers, who were often unable to choose different suppliers.

There are a whole range of reasons why, by and large, companies should not be 'blamed' for the generally excessive cost level of production in the GDR, even though firms may often not have exploited all the possibilities open to them. Weaknesses included the limited participation in both the national and international divisions of labour, the restrictions on investment — limiting the possibilities for utilizing the results of research and development — and the constraints imposed by the policy of full employment. The centralized allocation of energy and other materials also restricted firms' ability to reduce unit costs by increasing output levels. The fundamental point, then, was that company managements had severely limited powers.

The fairly comprehensive integration of even small companies — in so far as they were still in private hands in 1972 following nationalization — into the structure of combined enterprises, meant that the last chances were lost for flexible production capable of satisfying demand. In particular, this had a negative effect on the production of components of more complex goods and on the satisfaction of consumer demand. There was a considerable volume of excess purchasing power among the population in the form of savings, which could not be spent because of the inadequacy of the goods on offer. At the beginning of 1990, this backlog of excess purchasing power was estimated at approximately DM 30 billion and the State Office for Prices had the task of 'absorbing excess purchasing power' by raising the prices of industrial consumer goods.

This, however, could not prevent a degeneration of the system of central planning that was visible both in the behaviour of enterprises and in the behaviour of the centre. At the enterprise level, managements ordered special production 'outside the plan' and sought help through mutual favour networks in an effort to maximize production and to overcome the most pressing supply bottlenecks. The last few years, especially, saw a lively barter trade by companies, which could of course only be joined by those who had something to offer in return. This special 'black market' could never replace a functioning international, or far less a national, division of labour. Producers of consumer goods, in particular, were left high and dry. However, company managements had somehow to learn to help themselves by improvising where there were problems and by circumventing the obstacles created by state regulation.

At the same time, the centre was reacting to the growing economic problems by taking more power for itself. Centralization, however, could never be a solution for an advanced and complex economic system and the centralized allocation of an ever broader range of goods became ever less effective. Even in the case of standardized parts used throughout the economy, it became increasingly difficult to keep production in line with the plan. Thus, the companies' influence on planning declined, while the 'leadership of the party and state' increasingly closed its eyes to economic realities. They decided on plan targets without seriously assessing whether they could be achieved and without even noticing the growing imbalances. Moreover, in the 1980s everything that could be sold off was requisitioned for export to the West in order to prevent state insolvency. The companies could not rely even on the delivery of materials that had been allocated to them on paper in the plan. Rolled steel and fuel, for example, were exported in large quantities, creating shortages on the domestic market.

Indeed, the key factor in the growing problems of the GDR economy throughout the 1980s was its declining foreign trade performance, which was both a consequence of its systemic weaknesses and increasingly a contributory cause. The point was that the leadership responded by resorting ever more to solutions that exaggerated the degree of autarky both of combines and of the economy as a whole. The extent of the difficulties can be illustrated by raw figures. From 1971 to 1980 the total trade deficit was roughly VM 21 billion, with the valuta, or foreign-trade, mark equivalent to 2 East German marks in 1970. From the start of the 1980s, the government cut back on imports and was able for a time to restore a trade surplus, although at substantial cost to the domestic economy.

Thus, the reduction in western imports often made it impossible to buy even spare parts for imported plant. Despite immense efforts, it was not possible to substitute domestic products or imports from the East. Capital equipment producers came under especially heavy pressure, facing the dilemma of whether to export, or whether to cover for the disappearing imports by trying to develop and produce substitutes. This solution, however, often presented still more problems.

The drawbacks of import substitution were perhaps most dramatically illustrated by the case of the replacement of mineral oil by brown coal as an energy source. The effect was almost fatal. The background in this case was a change in policy from the Soviet Union. The GDR had been using products derived from Soviet oil to sell in the West for hard currency. The Soviet partners naturally resented this 'Roubling around'. They wanted to use the export of oil and its derivatives to help ease their own hard currency problems. Deliveries to the GDR were reduced and the Soviet side also sought, in return for continuing deliveries, 'investment participation' in the form of foreign currency or goods with a foreign exchange value. As a result, the GDR had to reduce drastically its crude oil consumption, without having the technological preconditions for efficient alternatives and also without being able to reduce its exports of petroleum products to the West. This led to fuel shortages internally and, as an additional consequence, to catastrophe on the roads because there was not enough bitumen for repairs.

It was possible to increase brown coal output but, because of bottlenecks in the investment sector, unprocessed brown coal was transported and burned. The freight transport system, which was already antiquated, was grossly overburdened, while environmental pollution increased and the efficiency of the energy sector declined drastically. Thus, the attempt by the investment and R&D sectors to find substitutes for imports exacerbated rather than solved the problem.

Thus, the GDR economy increasingly lost the ability both to guarantee the standard of living of the population and to cover the most urgent investment needs. The state accepted credits from the West in order to maintain consumption levels and at least to cover the most serious gaps in production but, because of the decreasing efficiency of production and external trade, these debts could not be serviced in the normal way. The state's difficulty in meeting payments meant that almost anything available had to be exported but, as a rule, no 'normal' profits could be made by the GDR exporters who had to force their way on to the market with dumping prices. The purchasers of the exported goods naturally took advantage of the GDR's weakness. It is, therefore, hardly surprising that companies after privatization were typically unable to regain their export markets in the West. Under the new economic conditions, they had to demand prices that covered costs and those were prices that customers were not prepared to pay.

Table 2.2 Ratio of earnings from exports to the West, in East
German foreign-trade marks, to domestic production
costs, in East German marks

Year	Ratio
1970	0.536
1980	0.454
1985	0.275
1988	0.246

Source: IWH, 1991.

As the level of national debt increased, the export targets for enterprises became ever harder and more unrealistic. The plan in 1986 to 1990 was to reach a balance of trade surplus of VM 23.1 billion, but in 1989 the government accepted that it would end the period with a deficit of VM 6 billion. Subsequent assessments of what was achieved have been rather negative. Thus, trade with non-socialist states has been characterized as having 'mainly a stop-gap function' in the acquisition of foreign currency (IWH, 1991) and a strong bias towards a highly raw material-intensive product range, reflecting the country's technological backwardness and the effects of the western embargo on advanced technology. Especially from the middle of the 1970s, the terms of trade for this structure of export goods rapidly worsened. The point can be illustrated with the figures from Table 2.2, showing the ratio between earnings from exports and their domestic production costs. The figures show both a steady worsening in performance and indicate the impossibility of the task facing the planning authorities towards the end of the 1980s. Thus, the planned export of VM 16.1 billion to the West in 1988 would have required a product of DEM 65.4 billion, equivalent to 40 per cent of the country's national income. In 1970, a product of DEM 30 billion would have been sufficient for the same level of exports (IWH, 1991).

Thus, to repeat a point that has already been made, this declining foreign trade performance was met by a strengthening of combine autarky. This allowed for the continuation of obsolete processes with equipment generally eliminated only when totally incapable of operating. As the basic safety and technological–organizational preconditions for quality production became an acute problem, so breakdowns increased and firms' repair units grew until their size bore no rational relationship to the level of production. In 1988, 12 per cent of all employees were involved in repair work, double the proportion in West Germany (Schäfer and Wahse, 1990). Thus, the need for replacement investment was met in an inefficient way which itself gave little scope for the introduction of technological advances. In 1989, 85 per cent of depreciation costs were marked down to maintenance while, in sectors such as metalworking and heavy machine construction, the amount spent on maintenance actually exceeded the total annual sum set aside for depreciation (Wetzker, 1990).

Despite this, the 'leadership of the party and the state' chose strategic options that only exacerbated the problems. Thus, they pursued ambitious investment and technological development projects for the development and production of microelectronics components and for the automation of production in the mechanical engineering industry. There were even new, modern business plants, built with equipment imported from the West. R&D efforts and the limited investment funds were concentrated on these prestige projects. This was the GDR leadership's attempt to bypass the western technology embargo, but the price was high. One consequence was that there were no resources for the investment necessary to increase the technical level of production in the majority of combines, which gained very little from the special projects. Thus, this strategy did nothing to overcome the wider problems of a very unfavourable industrial structure with excessive use of raw materials and energy and 'capital stocks' which were 'worn out and technically obsolete. Company production employed excessive material and labour. Both productivity and profitability were correspondingly low' (Wetzker, 1990).

With the disappointing results of these misguided investment projects, it proved impossible to coordinate planning and production in such a way that the ambitious production and export targets could be met. The structure of production could not be improved, partly because the increasing difficulties with exports made it impossible to finance imports of enough new equipment and technology. Moreover, the past failure to become involved in a complex division of labour left many East German firms committed to supplying the domestic market. There was no possibility of transferring these resources to facilitate new projects with export potential, while production for the limited domestic market inevitably meant production on a relatively small scale. Calculations show that 65 per cent of the range of goods available on world markets were produced in the GDR, but only 50 per cent in the USA and a mere 17 per cent in the old Federal Republic.

The picture, then, was of an economy struggling merely to survive. Thanks to enormous pressure on the domestic economy, a foreign trade surplus of VM 1 billion was achieved in the period 1986–1988, but the debt service level had reached VM 13 billion. Gross debt had grown from VM 2 billion in 1970 to VM 49 billion in 1989, equivalent to four times the level of exports in that year. Indeed, a final, unpublished report from the State Planning Committee to the ruling party's Politburo on 30 October 1989, reported that export earnings in 1989 could cover only 35 per cent of the country's outgoings on debt service plus imports. The expected economic collapse of the GDR, inevitable given those economic conditions, was prevented only because the political system collapsed first, opening the way for the subsequent economic transformation.

THE *TREUHANDANSTALT* TAKES OVER

The metamorphosis of the former GDR economy — leaving aside issues relating to the preparation for monetary union — did not begin with the privatization of the economy. The starting point was rather the collapse of combine structures and the transformation of companies into independent businesses. For many enterprise managements it was a time of hope. With the economic and monetary union with West Germany on the horizon, they looked forward to greater freedom and independence. The ties which had linked companies to the planning system and the combine structure fell away, giving opportunities for, and indeed compelling, a complete redefinition of company modes of operation and integration into new delivery and supply networks. The workforces of many companies removed politically discredited managers and 'elected' new managements in the wake of the 'peaceful revolution', while the Modrow government, in some of its last acts before reunification in 1990, legalized the establishment of new private companies and allowed for the return to former owners of the companies nationalized in 1972. In all, approximately 3,000 companies left combine structures which, in turn, began more generally to disintegrate.

All state-owned enterprises were taken over by the newly-established *Treuhandanstalt*, the THA, which guaranteed the interim financing of production immediately after the currency unification and the introduction of the Deutschmark in July 1990. The majority of these companies were undoubtedly not competitive and their weaknesses were quickly exposed. It had initially been assumed that up to 70 per cent of the firms would make losses from monetary union and that 30 per cent of the firms, with more than 1.1 million employees, would be in acute danger of going bankrupt. In reality more than 90 per cent of the concerns were threatened with insolvency.

The THA was immediately faced with the task of preventing a financial catastrophe. It used loans to maintain liquidity and loan guarantees to ensure that production did not collapse completely, thereby at least keeping open the possibility of restructuring and rehabilitation. It transformed the former state-owned combines and enterprises into TH-incorporated firms, henceforth referred to as TH-companies, and helped them to draw up an opening balance sheet in Deutschmarks while developing business strategies. Those companies considered capable of being rehabilitated were provided with capital resources equivalent to the average amount of capital of comparable west German companies (THA, 1994). The THA took over outstanding company debts, which had been devalued at the rate of 2 East German marks to 1 West German mark at the time of monetary union, and redistributed the obligations by a special formula which took the average loan debts of west German companies as the baseline.

The THA called on high-level representatives of west German political and economic life to become members of the boards of large TH-companies, in the hope that this would assist those companies in their search for new markets and for integration into new corporate networks. Thus, representatives of the direct competitors of the TH-companies gained access to the TH-company managements. By constituting company boards in this way, the THA intended to transfer know-how and support to companies inexperienced in the market economy. Clearly, at the same time, this gave the competitors in the same business a certain 'control position' from the outset. The possible consequences could be seen in several cases, such as that of SKET AG, the former Magdeburg heavy machine construction combine. Some members of its board may have been less than helpful in the search for export orders (Hornich et al., 1993).

Nevertheless, despite such reservations, the THA's activities as an interim owner, many of which were directed towards weathering the shock of monetary unification, should be seen as a substantial achievement. It has tended to go relatively unnoticed amid discussions of the problems of privatization itself, although it represents a unique feature in comparison with the transformation processes in the other formerly socialist countries. It coincided, however, with other equally specific east German developments which created exceptionally severe problems for companies. Thus, they were hit by the immediate influx of west German companies, seizing the opportunity to extend the business upswing at a time when other western industrial countries were already at the start of a recession. This did enhance the state's ability to finance the costs of unification, but it made it much more difficult for east German companies to defend 'their' domestic market.

THE PRIVATIZATION PHASE

The Berlin-based *Treuhandanstalt* and its branches in the new federal states were the key actors in the privatization of the state-owned industries. It ensured that the former GDR's combines were split up and the production programmes of large enterprises were cut back to their main business areas. All service sectors were separated and privatized independently. The emerging small and medium-sized businesses could be sold more easily. The THA was also responsible for returning formerly nationalized concerns to their previous owners and this, too, contributed to the dissolution of major enterprises and to the emergence of medium-sized or small firms.

At the same time, some entrepreneurs with particular business ideas set up new companies with selected staff and with equipment and premises either bought or given from former large-scale enterprises. In some cases, as a result of company liquidations, parts of the old company property were used to set up smaller, new companies. In the scientific field as well, when the Academy of Sciences was dissolved, industrial enterprises emerged using the existing capacity for the production of scientific instruments. Finally, in many cases, craft production units were hived off and became small industrial firms.

These reorganization processes had a major influence on the structure and scale of companies, on the division of labour and on the competitiveness of part of east Germany's manufacturing industry. The net effect was that, seriously reduced in both staff and capacity, a large proportion of the former state-owned companies, or parts of former combines, set themselves up as private, small or medium-sized companies. Thus, as a rule, single large enterprises and combines were converted into large numbers of medium-sized firms.

Relatively few businesses were privatized as large companies. GDR statistics showed approximately 3,400 firms with more than 20 employees in 1988, employing in total about 3 million. By the end of 1990, there were 5,900 manufacturing companies with more than 20 employees. The number of companies continued to grow during privatization, with the number of registrations consistently exceeding the number of liquidations. At the same time, the average number of employees per company fell dramatically. The growth in the number of companies dropped sharply at the end of the privatization period in 1994, by which time all formerly state-owned enterprises, with relatively few exceptions, had been privatized or wound up. By the end of 1994 some 12,500 industrial firms had emerged, employing about 600,000.

Unfortunately, there are no up-to-date statistics classifying firms by size. The most recent figures are from September 1993, when privatization was still in full swing. Sixty two per cent of industrial employees worked at that time in companies with fewer than 500 employees. Only 8 per cent were employed in larger companies with a workforce between 300 and 500. A further 38 per cent of employees worked in companies employing 500 or more. The average level of employment per company was about 112. That number had fallen by the end of 1994, at which time only about 20 per cent of privatized or reprivatized companies were owned by east German entrepreneurs (BfW, 1995a, p.6). Table 2.3 shows the breakdown by sector, again indicating the dominance of smaller firms as gainst the dominance of larger units before reunification.

Table 2.3 East German companies by business sector at the end of 1994

	Number of companies in thousands	Number of employees in thousands	Average number of employees per company
Artisans	148	1,200	8
Trade	142	470	3
Services	102.5	735	7
Medium-sized industry	12.5	600	48
Free professions	75	195	3
Total	480	3,200	7

Source: BfW, 1995a.

Privatization changed more than just company size. It also brought a reshaping of many aspects of relations concerning the division of labour in east German industry. New company owners brought distribution and supply networks with them, while trading and distribution organizations were often sold separately from their related production units, significantly reducing the competitiveness of the latter. The appearance of outside suppliers broke down the autarky of the combines with their grossly exaggerated degree of vertical integration. The stable supply links within former combines were either destroyed or put under serious threat.

The net effect was that the majority of east German companies lost a large share of their domestic market even before privatization had started and the full force of competition had been felt. These, of course, were markets which they had often served rather poorly as monopolists. Under the impact of these rapid changes in organizational structure, the east German enterprises made a late start in responding to the new market conditions and many were 'missing from the market' in the crucial years of 1990 and 1991.

The collapse of the previously existing system for the division of labour and sales, alongside the advanced wear and tear on plant and equipment meant, according to figures from the Federal Statistical Office, that by 1991 roughly 55 per cent of fixed assets in manufacturing inherited from the GDR and more than three-quarters of plant and equipment were no longer useable. This was referred to at the time as the 'peaceful bombardment' of the east German economy. It can be added that 20 per cent of equipment had already been written off before reunification, although it was still in use. To this extent, then, part of the reduction in capital stock could be seen as a welcome clearing-out operation. Nevertheless, even that part of inherited fixed assets which could still be used provided an insufficient basis for a new start. It had to be integrated into new operational structures, and investment was essential to prevent still further deterioration. However, the actual decision to undertake investment renewing these fixed assets — or rather for creating a modern capital stock in east German industry — depended on the strategies of the new owners once privatization had been achieved.

The TH-companies awaiting privatization were still solvent despite dramatically shrinking sales. They, however, suffered from very limited powers and a lack of managerial expertise relevant to a market economy. Moreover, they had an essentially weak market position, not least because they could give no guarantees to customers in view of the uncertainty of their future. The privatization philosophy of the THA meant that these businesses could initially invest only in an 'investor-neutral' way. In other words, decisions on basic changes in production profiles and technology were to be left to the future owners. Thus, for a long time these companies were not allowed to invest in technological changes, even though reorientation in the market frequently demanded just this. This was a particularly severe handicap when set in the context of the collapse of exports to the East, the shrinking domestic sales and the rapidly rising wage levels. Weighed down by these multiple burdens, enterprises often found that, even when technical equipment appeared to be usable after 1990, production could still be unprofitable.

The dwindling employment prospects in TH-companies after 1990 created a very heavy 'social pressure' on the population to become self-employed. Many new companies were formed by partial takeover of part of an existing firm. In many cases, however, the operations were highly risky. This was particularly true of a large proportion of those units that were hived off from larger firms, such as R&D units, general service sections and subsidiary production departments, which had been sold as the main enterprise restricted itself to its core activities. It also affected new companies that could be formed out of the special firms set up by the government to create temporary jobs in areas of underemployment.

In a number of cases, newly-separated companies were formed with the hope of retaining the parent concern as the main customers. However, the parent companies were frequently split up and privatized in separate parts, or wound up altogether, leaving the newly-established small companies high and dry. In TH-companies facing liquidation, workers at independently operating units within such firms tried to save their jobs through management buyouts and by joining in purchasing schemes for their businesses. In quite a few cases, such small firms lost the markets for their traditional production programme as part of increasing regional deindustrialization and had to switch to new production, or give up altogether. There were, of course, some successes, particularly where parent companies and the *Treuhandanstalt* gave comprehensive support. For months, working within the parent company, individuals or units were able to plan their moves towards independent status and were given leases, equipment and licences at very favourable rates.

PRIVATIZATION STRATEGIES

The transformation of a state-owned enterprise into a private company does not end with the act of sale to a new owner. This is particularly true of the privatization of a large-scale enterprise in which the business strategy of the new owner is crucial to the company's survival prospects in a market economy. This was recognized in the THA's general privatization philosophy. Its slogan, as proclaimed in its publications, was 'privatize quickly, rehabilitate decisively and close carefully'. In practice, however, the greatest emphasis was put on privatization, which was presented as 'the best form of rehabilitation'. The report of the THA board on the completion of its activities in December 1994 (THA, 1994) still maintained that 'the experience of recent years still clearly demonstrates that the best way of achieving urgently needed rehabilitation in most companies is by gaining a new, experienced, business-oriented owner, able to bring management skills, technology, markets and new products'.

It was, therefore, important where and how the potential buyers were sought for TH-companies and which of the interested parties was chosen. In particular, it was important for competitiveness, both for the privatized companies and for east Germany's overall status as an industrial location, that the buyers intended to introduce technologically advanced production programmes. The potential for this was greatest in the case of western companies extending their capacity by buying east German firms. There was less to be gained from the movement to the East of less sophisticated forms of production, or product lines which were being phased out.

This latter phenomenon came to be known as the 'extended work-bench'. East German firms filled what could be only a short-term gap in a west German firm's production plans. In some cases this could have been an interim solution, which might become a first stage in a longer rehabilitation process. Employment could be maintained for a period at least. Nevertheless, capacity extension without advanced products hardly ever provides a satisfactory long-term solution and therefore cannot create future job security. As was later shown, these 'extended work-benches' were very dependent on the economic position of their parent companies. A fall in sales by the parent company frequently led first to reductions in output from the subsidiary firms.

Many TH-companies — and often also groups of companies that had been linked together in the past — preferred privatization as a single unit, which they saw as offering the best chance of rehabilitation and future job security. Declining sales, however, as a result of competition at the start of the recession, and because of the disappearance of exports to the East, frequently compelled companies to give up any such hopes. They had to accept the splitting-up of the activities and the resulting disruption of established relationships. The central service units and the 'rump companies', which were left after separation and sale, could often only be wound up. Even the new owners of privatized parts frequently started a further phase of integration involving the closure of sections of the companies, themselves often only parts of former enterprises, that they had bought. It was, therefore, often very difficult for the THA to find buyers who would guarantee investment and jobs. The extent to which this could be achieved often depended on accepting a significant reduction in the sale price of the assets. This, then, was one of the factors depressing the price at which companies were sold.

Moreover, although the THA selected buyers from an assessment of their business strategies, its thinking depended in practice on the ideas developed by its personnel. As a rule its experts had, and had to have, experience in the corresponding sectors of the economy in West Germany. Some of them had been released by their own companies for a limited period of time. They attempted to push through their own conceptions, within the framework of the privatization philosophy of the THA, and received the maximum political backing. Controls from outside were therefore minimal.

This had two immediate consequences. The first was that preference went to buyers whose ideas fitted with rather specific established preconceptions, while those with 'non-conformist' business strategies were more likely to be rejected. The second, and even more important, consequence was that there was some room for manoeuvre in shaping regional industrial structures, although this was employed in very diverse ways. Political interests, and even the interests of competitors, sometimes played a major role. On the political side, east German provincial governments were represented on the THA Supervisory Board and had some scope to influence privatization policy, but they were very late in recognizing the need to try to preserve and build from the basis inherited from the past or to formulate any form of regional structural policies. Attempts by the federal and state parliaments to exert greater control also started very late, coming only after criticisms of the THA's strategy and of a number of questionable sales decisions. Even then, they failed to make the THA's privatization practice any more transparent.

Nevertheless, and despite an insistence that it was taking decisions on purely commercial criteria and without any reference to a conception of structural policy, the THA was able to take decisions with far-reaching structural implications. East German potassium mining is a case in point. In 1993, the THA forced closures, although there were purchasers genuinely interested in the companies and despite employee resistance, including sit-ins and hunger strikes, lasting into 1994. The outcome, and one with far-reaching structural implications, was greater concentration of decision-making power in this sector into the hands of a big western chemical company. Another case, covered in more detail in Chapter 3, was the sale of part of the chemical industry to the US company Dow Chemicals, which also has major structural implications.

Despite this relative freedom of manoeuvre for THA managers, the decisions on the privatization of the largest enterprises were typically extremely difficult. There were three main reasons for this. The first was that the employment situation of whole regions often hung in the balance. The second was that there was often no market available for the firms' productive capacity. The third was that these decisions could be expected to affect the corresponding west German production sites. In a number of cases the THA supported, against the interests of west German competitors, the continuation of iron and steel production, of shipbuilding and of part of the chemical industry, in order to safeguard jobs in areas of potentially high unemployment.

The problem was that sale to private owners alone could not promise a secure future for these and other industries as there was not a great deal of desire, beyond some quite specific activities, to acquire east German companies. The main reasons for this are to be found, first, in the objective interests of potential outside investors, second, in the actual operation of the THA's privatization strategy and, third, in the lack of capital among potential east German investors.

Thus the first, and most important, limitation derives from the objective interests of the investors, the would-be purchasers of east German companies. As a general rule, production sites with sufficient capacity to meet demand already existed in western Europe. The only arguments favouring east Germany as an investment site would be capacity extension, some sort of cost advantage or the quest for new markets. Where goods which were difficult or especially expensive to transport were concerned, proximity to markets was a persuasive argument for taking an interest in THA companies. This applied to production of materials and parts for the construction industry, to production of glass bottles and other containers, to service and trade companies and to the production and installation of power-station equipment. There were also some quite specific and limited opportunities for buying existing east German companies as a means to broaden a west German firm's product range. These rather limited advantages were, for the great bulk of western firms, more than outweighed by a number of very solid reasons against such acquisitions.

Thus, potential investors would have had to contend with uncertainties over the development of political, institutional and macroeconomic conditions. It was clear that the institutional framework would eventually correspond to that of the former Federal Republic. This was an advantage compared with the situation in other transforming countries. Nevertheless, some time was needed to ensure the full adoption and then stabilization of the west German political, legal and economic framework. Moreover, economic changes, including the destruction of the old industries did not, as a rule, allow investors to make clear assessments of potential investment sites. Regional deindustrialization worried producers and suppliers of services, for whom industry is the customer. There was also a further source of uncertainty in the well-known difficulties in resolving disputes over ownership rights for some property.

Moreover, even east German demand did not necessarily require east German production capacity, as it could often be covered by capacity reserves within the west German economy. Thus, reunification often pointed to the case for capacity expansion in the West, or to higher imports. Reindustrialization in east Germany even carried the threat of a new source of competition. Moreover, although it might have been expected that labour-intensive forms of production would move from the high-wage areas to the East, resistance both from firms and from trade unions made any movement of capacity a difficult undertaking. In fact, the wage differential compared with west Germany could not play a decisive role in location decisions, partly because it was considered a transitory phenomenon within the unification process and partly because the really important differentials in wage levels were with eastern Europe. Indeed, there was a noticeable decline in interest from western firms in acquiring additional capacity in east Germany with the start of the recession in 1991. Under these circumstances, the reticence displayed in west Germany or abroad was understandable.

There would hardly have been any industry left in east Germany had it not been for special policies aimed at protecting particular regions and for the public financing of privatization. Even with that, however, it has so far proved impossible to stimulate a substantial enough level of industrial inward investment. Indeed, it is questionable whether, in view of the objective reluctance of investors to transfer production to east Germany, investment promotion could ever have achieved a satisfactory result. There were, of course, further objectives, as capital promotion was not aimed just at attracting industrial investment. It also supported privatization in general and facilitated investment by east German-owned companies themselves. As, however, the existing industrial basis was still very weak, and the existence of many firms could not yet be considered secure, the state will have to give financial support to industry for a long time to come.

When set against this assessment of the interests of potential investors, the weaknesses in the THA's privatization strategy as it developed in practice become clearer. This is the second of the main reasons for the disappointing results of attempts to attract buyers for TH-companies. The THA was set on finding outside investors with real expansion aims, and very often preferred any western offers over attempts at indigenous regeneration. It tried to find purchasers with substantial capital resources, hoping they would bring technological and marketing know-how, and above all easier access, to the market. For the reasons given above, in many cases this could not be successful. The views of the TH-companies themselves were often given little weight, although they, too, were often keen to find some form of partnership with western firms. The THA, however, sought to persuade west German competitors to step in in the belief that they could provide management know-how. In the case at least of the larger enterprises, the THA made very substantial efforts, informing potentially interested parties, organizing sales meetings and calling for public tenders at international level for those companies which proved harder to sell.

The emphasis on rapid privatization alone also had a further unfortunate consequence. Would-be purchasers could afford to 'play for time' in order to scout out their east German rivals, often without eventually taking them over. During this period, thanks to the THA's insistence on 'investor-neutral' investment, no major rehabilitation projects could be undertaken. Moreover, every TH-company opened its doors for any businessman who feigned an interest. Thus TH-companies not only had a late start. They also had massive competitive disadvantages, which reverberated after privatization. All of this was reflected in reduced levels of profitability, meaning a reduction in purchase prices and hence of privatization revenues, to the detriment of the THA's overall balance.

The THA moved away from its policy of 'investor-neutral investment' only in the final stages of privatization, agreeing to finance rehabilitation investment so that companies *could be* privatized. This, of course, meant that company takeovers became increasingly profitable for the purchasers at the expense of an effective subsidy paid by the state. Even then, however, the implication of the THA strategy was still to favour outside investors. The potential east German investors were hampered, quite simply, by their lack of capital.

This was the third factor restricting the overall level of interest in buying TH-companies. The better-placed, larger and more competitive enterprises passed most easily into west German or foreign ownership although, of course, that often involved their subdivision. The specially desirable parts were sold to buyers who could offer the best conditions and the firmest guarantees, and that meant west German or foreign investors. The THA often still had to offer considerable price concessions for the less-attractive companies, including deferral of debt repayments, covering for past losses, taking over credit obligations, covering the costs for repairing ecological damage and helping with the costs of new investment. The THA resorted to east German would-be purchasers only when, after every effort had been made, there was no one else interested. Thus, although a comparatively large number of small and medium-sized enterprises did pass into east German hands, these tended to be the ones with the worst chances of successful rehabilitation. About 20 per cent of the TH-companies passed into the hands of east German owners, most of them as management buyouts.

In September 1993, the THA took an initiative aimed at lowering company purchase prices so that east German would-be buyers could afford them. This involved the separation of ownership of land and premises from the ownership of companies. This, however, still left the new companies at a serious disadvantage. The point was that ownership of real estate serves as a rule as collateral for bank loans. Companies that do not own their premises, therefore, suffer from a low credit rating and have only a limited ability to finance current output expansion or new investment through credits. Moreover, any benefits to the firms in a lower purchase price could be partially cancelled out by the owners of premises demanding higher rents. This vicious circle might have been broken by local authorities offering a sufficient quantity of affordable properties, set aside for business purposes with options to buy, and by promoting location changes for smaller domestic businesses. This, however, the east German local authorities lacked the financial resources to do. Nevertheless, and despite the weakness of their starting conditions, these management buyouts have been no less successful than other privatized firms. By the end of 1995, one-third could be said to have overcome their startup problems, while two-thirds were still battling to achieve a reasonable degree of stability.

THE RESULTS OF PRIVATIZATION

From the outset, considerable state commitment was absolutely essential for the transformation of those businesses that had grown up within a planned economy into private companies that could cope with the new economic conditions. Even after the relatively rapid privatization of the majority of companies, the state still cannot withdraw from the economy, as long, that is, as the aim continues to be the creation of the foundations for self-sustaining growth. The 'price' of privatization by selling companies to powerful investors, was that the state frequently had to participate in various forms of rehabilitation. In the case of some large enterprises, and in spite of all the THA's efforts to the contrary, the state remains a shareholder, at least for the time being. The main examples are in chemicals, steel and heavy engineering.

Without state commitment, there would have been no private commitment, although even that is still below the level necessary for rapid economic rehabilitation. The original economic strategy of using state investment in the infrastructure to create conditions for encouraging investment in other sectors, gave an impetus to the construction industry and related businesses. It has not so far proved adequate to the task of encouraging a more general industrial development. A real investment boom could only have been achieved on the basis of somewhat different methods of privatization.

The basic decision, later revised, to favour restitution was a mistake. This led to the return of companies and premises to former owners, or their sale to investors to finance compensation for those former owners. Only an unambiguous priority for investment, right from the beginning and whether linked with former owners or other investors, could have mobilized large-scale private investment.

It was also unfortunate that the privatization policy of the THA, contrary to what was laid down in its mandate, concentrated excessively on the rapid sale of companies, often involving their subdivision into smaller units. A differentiated rehabilitation and privatization policy depending on the actual competitive situation and the state of the companies, sometimes even involving rehabilitation before privatization, would probably have kept more enterprises viable. It could, therefore, ultimately have led to a smaller burden on public funds. The best way for the THA to have encouraged the rehabilitation of east German companies would have been to demonstrate clearly that east Germans could do it, if necessary, themselves.

Forcing the pace of privatization and proclaiming a final date for it only facilitated the power game played by those who were interested in buying. An alternative would have been to employ professionals with experience in rehabilitation who could help indigenous businesses overcome their know-how deficiencies. This could in the end have saved state funds, as such costs should be set against the state investment grants and other subsidies, often agreed in the sales of unrehabilitated companies, as well as the low prices at which companies were eventually sold. Moreover, encouraging and helping firms to try to rehabilitate themselves would have encouraged the management of the TH-companies themselves to develop their own ideas and strategies. There certainly was potential here, as has been demonstrated by the example of 63 TH-companies which remain in public ownership but with management contracted out to four business management companies, each of which runs firms in a variety of sectors. Had such a practice been used more widely, then both managements and workforces would have been able to contribute to their companies' rehabilitation rather than being passively exposed to privatization.

Different decisions, both of principle and on sales, as well as more flexible privatization and rehabilitation methods, would probably have yielded better results. This judgement is hardly new. By 1992, at the latest, it was clear that the way in which the THA was fulfilling its mandate was bound to lead to far-reaching deindustrialization. As early as autumn 1992, the federal government proclaimed that the 'security and maintenance of the industrial core' in east Germany would be one of the THA's future tasks, and this led to a change in strategy, formalized in June 1993. There was some controversy around fears that this would mean the rehabilitation of traditional industries without any perspective, to the detriment of investment in 'industries of the future'. Whether these fears are justified depends on the nature of the rehabilitation. Moreover, even the industries of the future need a regional industrial environment. Indeed, a further aspect of policy that can be sharply criticized is the lack of emphasis on the maintenance, or introduction, of R&D-intensive production, and indeed of R&D capacity itself.

A substantial transfer of financial resources over an extended period will be necessary if east Germany's economic power and living conditions are to reach the west German level. Unfortunately, the privatization strategy itself has in some respects made this more, rather than less, necessary. Industry has now been reduced to so small a level that it probably cannot provide the basis for self-sustaining growth. Moreover, privatization has proved to be very expensive. When the THA as such completed its work at the end of 1994, handing over its legal responsibilities to the BVS and other bodies that were meant to ensure the completion of its tasks, the overall privatization deficit was put at between DM 260 and 270 billion. This was, and still is, financed through the capital market with roughly half accounted for by loans. The repayment of liabilities was taken over by the state budget in 1995 in the form of a separate fund. The THA took over DM 101 billion of company debts from the GDR era, more than 80 per cent of the total level, paid DM 44 billion for cleaning up ecological damage, and spent DM 154 billion on the financial rehabilitation of companies. They expect returns from sales to total DM 73 billion.

In its final report, the THA set its deficit against the DM 206 billion of investment promised by companies, plus agreements to maintain or create 1.5 million jobs. The extent of expenditure for structural change in east Germany was justified with reference to the considerably greater volume of public spending on structural change in west German regions over the last 40 years. In east Germany, however, the structural changes associated with privatization were supposed to be completed within four and a half years, although they certainly cannot be considered complete as yet.

Thus, in conclusion, the pressure of events has led to a gradual evolution away from a 'pure' privatization strategy. At the start, the THA repeatedly declared that it had no intention of using privatization as a means to carry out structural policy and that its sales decisions were based mainly on the merits of individual commercial cases. There was some relaxation of this in cases where agreements with Brussels demanded more active steps. Examples were the iron and steel industry and shipbuilding.

More recently the THA, or its successor organization the BVS, has been participating in the rehabilitation of medium-sized industrial enterprises, most notably by the contracting-out of management in the companies it still owns. Thus, it is engaged in a hesitant state industrial policy directed towards the emergence of private industrial structures, with the intention of leaving future developments mainly to the market. Moreover, in many cases, supplementary negotiations of purchase contracts have become necessary in order, for example, to put company purchasers on an equal footing with the owners of reprivatized businesses, or to give greater weight in the price to the firms' earning capacity. The BVS also helps companies with healthy business strategies when they have run into difficulties through no fault of their own. These are clear, if belated, signs of a recognition that a whole range of support measures are necessary in order to safeguard the fragile industrial base.

3. East Germany's New Firms

As the previous chapter has shown, privatization led to the breakup of the large enterprises inherited from the GDR. The key question is whether the smaller firms that generally emerged out of this process have provided, or can be expected in the future to provide, a satisfactory basis for self-sustaining growth in the east German economy. To help shed further light on that, the discussion in this chapter covers three broad, interrelated themes. The first is the break-up of large firms, with case studies from the chemical industry alongside some references to other sectors. The second is the small and medium-sized industrial enterprises, or SMEs, which emerged either out of privatization or out of new firm formation from scratch. In this context, the term SME is used to refer to firms employing fewer than 500, not belonging to a larger corporate group, and with activities clearly centring on manufacturing or extractive industries. The third is an assessment of the structural weaknesses of the east German economy with particular reference to problems of R&D.

THE FATE OF BIG FIRMS

There were substantial differences in the fates of the major enterprises in east Germany, both during and after privatization. Some businesses in the electrical and power-plant construction fields, for example, were taken over by the western market leaders relatively early and seem to have done relatively well. In many cases, however, the breakup of complex organizational structures associated with the restructuring and privatization of the major industrial concerns, especially where successive production stages were tightly interwoven, risked making their competitive positions even worse. These were cases in which the negative effects of the currency shock were further exacerbated by the process of privatization. Examples included the major chemical concerns in Saxony-Anhalt and Saxony, the shipyards in Mecklenburg-Western Pomerania, heavy machine and plant combines in Saxony-Anhalt, Saxony and Brandenburg, metallurgical combines and railway-vehicle production plants in Brandenburg.

As a rule, these major industrial enterprises were not only the biggest employers in their regions, but they frequently represented *the* industrial activity in their regions. In some cases they were involved in sectors in which there is overcapacity in the EU as a whole, and which are therefore subject to production quotas. In other cases these industries may, with EU approval, receive state subsidies abroad, shipyards and metallurgical industries being examples. As far as the shipyards, plant-construction combines and many other large enterprises are concerned, most production had previously been exported to the East. Despite intensive efforts to maintain these exports after 1990, nothing could be done beyond slightly slowing the pace of decline.

The chances of privatizing such companies were very small, and decisions were taken at the highest government levels in 1992 and 1993 to maintain the industrial sites, reversing the original decision by the THA that they should be dissolved. There were also individual cases in which the enterprises themselves proved successful in fighting off THA decisions that they should be closed down. Examples include a company producing lubricants, a motorcycle plant, a refrigerator company and some chemical production lines in Bitterfeld.

To a certain extent each case tells its own story. However, many of the problems can be illustrated from case histories, and a particularly important example is the chemical industry that was based around major works in Leuna, Schkopau, Bitterfeld-Wolfen and Böhlen. These included giant combines, such as Buna in Schkopau with 27,100 employees in 1989, Chemiekombinat Bitterfeld, employing about 28,500 and Filmfabrik-Fotochemisches Kombinat Bitterfeld-Wolfen with about 20,900 employees, although in no case were all those employees based at the parent plant. The chemical industry as a whole accounted for 35 per cent of all industrial output in Saxony-Anhalt in 1991 and more than 60 per cent in the core of the region.

There were extremely close links between the different combines' production processes. Thus, for example, a key starting material was crude oil and gas from the Soviet Union, which came into Leuna. This produced petrol, for sale direct to consumers, but also further inputs, including methane for Bitterfeld and materials for the production of ethylene at Böhlen, which in turn provided inputs for Buna and, to a lesser extent, also for Leuna. These complex interconnections were to prove important in the development of restructuring and privatization strategies.

The information that follows is based on investigations by the DIW in the so-called 'chemical triangle' in the Halle area (DIW, 1993), supplemented by information produced by the THA in the period 1991–1995. It is only possible here to give a very broad, generalized overview of the privatization aims and the steps taken. This makes it impossible to describe all the twists and turns in privatization intentions and activities, of which there were many. Nevertheless, the general picture is clear and more detailed case histories can be found elsewhere (Hornich et al., 1993).

The enterprises produced petroleum products and chemical raw materials, as well as chemical consumer goods such as dyes, plastics and plastic goods, photographic chemicals and films. Much of the output was aimed at the East German market and, in line with the autarkic tendencies of the old economic system, there was an attempt to produce the most complete range of chemical finished products. The claim in the GDR was, 'es gibt nichts auf dieser Welt, was nicht kommt aus Bitterfeld', or there is nothing in this world that does not come from Bitterfeld. Such autarky, of course, carried a cost, and large production volumes were achievable only when domestic demand could be supplemented with exports to the East. Exports to the West played a less important role, except for the case of petroleum products referred to in Chapter 2. In general, however, production levels were too small at the time of reunification, leaving the east German producers at a cost disadvantage. Both the production range and the technology of the chemical companies were seen as outdated and the rehabilitation of the majority of these enterprises, it was estimated, would prove very expensive.

Before 1989, much of the chemical industry had been built up around the production and utilization of calcium carbide as a starting point for basic organic chemicals in the manufacture of plastics and fibres. The process used brown coal as a basic input, which had to be transported in bulk by rail. The result was both energy-intensive and environmentally unfriendly. This is why an almost immediate switch was made to petrochemicals as the source of starting materials and the calcium carbide plants were closed down and dismantled.

The extent of integration of production processes was also reduced, with a greater dependence on purchasing intermediate inputs from outside as, in view of the small scale of east German production, these were believed to be cheaper. Power stations using brown coal were either modernized or closed down and replaced by modern plant, thereby sharply reducing the expensive transport of unprocessed brown coal and the waste products from its combustion. This has already had a major effect on productivity in that sector and has led to a considerable reduction in the level of environmental pollution. It did, however, place a heavy burden on the declining chemical industry with the need to invest in change and reconstruction.

Areas of business activity were reassessed and classified in all enterprises. Those core businesses which remained prominent were separated from subsidiary businesses and from those activities which were to be discontinued. Where possible, any unit that could be given a clear classification as to its field of activity was split off from the core business. This fitted with managements' view that it was unrealistic for the firms to hope to compete in the area of basic chemicals. They saw the future in high quality and more specialized products and therefore saw no need to continue with the large and complex organizational structures inherited from the past.

Nevertheless, given the high degree of technological interdependence between stages of the production processes, the combine in Leuna and the Buna combine in Schkopau initially aimed to achieve privatization as two complete enterprises. It quickly became clear, after some attempts by the THA and parallel steps from the companies, that this course of privatization was unrealistic. No one was interested in purchasing the concerns intact and nor, to this date, has it been possible to bring together consortia out of potentially interested parties. Thus, in the case of the Leuna enterprise, a form of privatization was prepared involving 'packaging' into parts. Central activities and services would be grouped together into a single enterprise, which would then sell its services to the firms established out of the parts of the combine. The advantages of purchasing centralized services, considered together with the closeness of technological integration would, it was assumed, become so obvious that the operators of the individual firms would later become shareholders of a central, coordinating service firm. A real estate company would provide the company with land, which would first be cleared and then sold or leased to chemical companies which would reprocess the products manufactured in Leuna. The central Leuna-Research was hived off as an independent concern since no one could be found who was interested in taking it over. Small, decentralized research groups have been privatized with defined areas of business activity.

The management of the Buna concern did not see any way to separate its business areas and, despite the difficulties, it continued to aim for privatization as a single company. It was also able to reach agreement with the THA, under which it could invest and transform its technological level. Bitterfeld, however, suffered a more dramatic fate. Only a very few promising product lines could be identified out of this giant concern's 'supermarket' of consumer goods, developed mainly for the GDR market. It is unclear whether any consideration was given to the possible introduction of potentially more profitable product lines. Instead, since 1992 the strategy has been to develop a 'chemical park', meaning an area where the infrastructure for chemical production is available and on which only chemical production, or production or services directly connected with the chemical industry, can be undertaken.

This means that most of the non-viable business areas will be dissolved and a 'chemical park' company founded producing chemical base products and also offering central services for incoming chemical firms which, it is hoped, will be attracted. These services are to include energy and water supplies, the disposal of waste water and waste products, the transport infrastructure, telecommunications, supply of chemical raw materials, technical gases and process materials, repair and plant construction services, business services, site protection and a fire service. The assumption was that the companies set up on the chemical park would emerge from a variety of sources. Among them would be western chemical firms seeking the advantages of a chemical processing site where chlorine factories are allowed. There were also hopes that newly-established east German businesses would use the site alongside the remaining privatized individual companies of the former chemical combine. Most of the plants and their parts were sold in 1992 and 1993, although the existing equipment has generally been used for totally different production processes. The R&D departments, however, became superfluous with the closure of most of the production of the former combine, and their staff either went into a Bitterfeld rescue company or suffered redundancy.

More recently the chemical company Bitterfeld–Wolfen, the successor to the Bitterfeld chemical combine, attempted privatization as a single unit. Most of the combine's subsidiaries outside Bitterfeld had by then broken away, leaving the company with control over five business areas plus the central administration of the former combine. Sales, however, fell away in the years after 1990 even more rapidly than the company could close its unprofitable sites. As a result, no firm could be found willing to take over the remaining company.

There was, however, no possibility of achieving a regeneration of the area by bringing in completely different industrial activities. Politicians and managers, and also the THA, were all against allowing the use of the Bitterfeld–Wolfen chemical park for other business activities. The local authorities were already offering sites for other industries in these areas. Nevertheless, some investors have come. The first, specialist chemical firms include a quartz glass plant and Bayer–Bitterfeld, with a medical, paint and adhesive plant. The Bayer concern was, in 1995, the largest so far of the 170 new arrivals. Initially, investors were interested primarily in participating in the modernization of the chemical park's central services, such as waste-water disposal, industrial power stations and technical gases. In conclusion, then, the success of the strategy is by no means assured. This becomes particularly clear from a discussion of how these broad ideas on restructuring the industry had to be modified when confronted with hard realities in the context of specific privatization strategies evolved within the THA.

PRIVATIZING BIG FIRMS

The THA, using the advice of prestigious management consultants, developed, and tried to implement, a broad strategy for the revival of the chemical industry. It tried to ensure conditions on site for the competitive supply of raw materials for chemical production. It also sought to respect the technological linkages in chemical production processes. It, therefore, did not aim to destroy, but rather to expand and where possible to privatize as single companies, units that were closely interrelated. It also tried to privatize as single units firms that had similar product ranges. It aimed to keep together starting materials — such as mineral oil derivatives, methanol and ethanol — and related technological units involved in producing intermediate products, such as the olefin group. Single firms were also to be created for related finished products, such as similar organic chemicals, plastics, dyes, cleaning liquids and glues.

The complexity of the interconnections between these firms, as already referred to, was compounded by the location into different companies of stages in processes linked to petrochemicals, such as crackers, and the relevant further reprocessing stages, such as olefin production. They were also on different sites, in Halle and Leipzig, although partially interconnected by pipelines.

There was even competition between TH-companies over which locations could expect replacement investment, itself a precondition for maintaining sufficient capacity for future requirements. The problem was that investment on a single site could replace in total the capacity of the existing plant on various sites. This complicated problem area gave rise to complicated privatization solutions. In the case of chemicals, every privatization complex was to be sold as a whole, meaning that the distribution organisations had to be sold as well. This was somewhat different from some other sectors in which distribution organizations were often sold off separately, a practice that could cause some disruption as foreign trade firms for different sectors had been partially integrated into the combines during the 1980s. In these cases, then, privatized companies, which formerly shared common distribution organizations and foreign trade companies, have been forced to create new, similar structures in competition with those separately-privatized firms.

The first step was the privatization of the most important raw material supplier, the Leuna mineral oil company. The THA transferred the management of the old Leuna refinery to a German–French consortium to which Leuna's remaining petrochemical processing branches were also sold. Conditions included a commitment to construct a new, modern refinery in Leuna and to guarantee the production of petrochemical base products on the site. Following this, the Buna company also joined in the Leuna investment in order to reduce the risks for the French partner. This business was a particularly attractive one for the investors, as the petrol station company,

Minol, was part of the package. Moreover, the THA agreed to take over the losses of the old Leuna refinery, the operations of which are to be terminated only when the new refinery comes on stream. The Leuna refinery has been taken out of the Leuna chemical association, but will remain under the THA until it is closed down. The supply of chemical gases was also separated off and privatized.

Following this logical, first move in the privatization process, the next steps became increasingly complicated as privatization of processing branches, such as the olefin complex, were linked to basic decisions about investment. Thus, privatization decisions were tied in with attempts to ensure investment for the processing branches on their current sites, as opposed to the alternative of bringing in materials by pipeline. However, the purchasers of individual operations of TH-companies had a vested interest in avoiding over-dependence on one supplier of intermediate products. This was difficult to reconcile with the logical requirement for new sites for production capacity to be close enough either to minimize, or effectively to eliminate in total, the costs of transport between them.

These problems associated with the attempt to privatize stages separately could explain why the next steps towards privatization, particularly of the olefin complex, were put off until the end of 1994 and were still not finalized during 1995. This delay over privatization, and hence also over investment, hampered the ability of these branches to achieve a satisfactory position on the competitive chemical market. It thereby contributed to the closure of further product lines and to a further decline in employment. Even before privatization, most of the individual business branches had been reduced to medium-sized firms, generally with fewer than 500 employees.

The THA found the idea of developing more specialized and higher-quality chemicals very attractive and this played a major role in its thinking on the privatization of the large chemical enterprises. The THA thought it would attract major chemical concerns from west Germany or abroad as investors for Leuna and Buna. Subsidies would tempt them to the new sites, partly for normal replacement investment that would otherwise have been undertaken elsewhere. Foreign investors could well be interested in the German chemical market, especially for goods related to the construction industry, or simply to gain a site within the EU. Basic materials for a sophisticated chemical industry would be produced in the former TH-companies at competitive enough rates to stimulate reprocessing firms to move into the area. This had happened in the past — immediately after the Second World War and even earlier on some sites — in the case of major west German chemical companies, such as Bayer in Leverkusen and BASF in Ludwigshafen.

This idea went one step beyond the enterprise management's chemical park concept and conflicted with their hope of creating their own capacity for producing specialized chemicals. Their reasoning was that the costs in basic chemicals were too high and they therefore could not hope to establish a competitive position. There was, of course, no guarantee of success with more specialized chemical products, but the chances of finding market niches did appear to be greater there.

In practice, the THA's hopes were not always realized. There was already intense competition in Germany for sites for industrial replacement investment. Those with a potential interest in the sites in the East adopted the familiar waiting position, showing a greater interest only in 1994. Thus, the decision to sell the Buna concern and the whole olefin production complex — including parts of the Leuna company, the Buna company as a whole and the chemical company in Böhlen near Leipzig — to the US multinational Dow Chemicals was taken by the THA's successor, at precisely the time when the THA itself was being wound up. Ownership was not transferred until June 1995.

Dow aimed to create a new operational base with a sophisticated and sizeable capacity in central Europe. This, they hoped, could be used as a springboard for gaining better access into eastern European markets. It has, however, become clear that the product lines that were previously produced by the TH-companies have been either partially integrated into buyers' company profiles or closed down altogether. There is, therefore, no doubt that the firms, already hit by the preceding fall in turnover, will shrink even further with full privatization. According to its President Bill Stavropoulos, Dow intends to close down capacity for DM 100 million annual turnover, but will establish new plants with a potential of DM 600 million annual turnover. Altogether, DM 4 billion are to be invested in these three sites, more than DM 3 billion of which will be contributed by the state, with Dow contributing new technology, management skills, and the benefits of its global connections (*Wirtschaftswoche*, 1995,

No. 23, p.64). It is, however, still unclear exactly what form the investment will take.

A somewhat different example is afforded by the Wolfen film plant, which emerged out of the core business of the former photochemical combine that had manufactured ORWO films. It fought a long battle to be privatized as a film plant with its own specific profile. On two occasions a distinguished consultancy firm, and one that was frequently used by the THA, confirmed that this TH-company could be rehabilitated. However, the film plant's management and the THA were unable to agree on the precise rehabilitation measures to secure the enterprise's future, and the THA therefore refused to release funds. All the film plant's main rivals, in both Western Europe and the USA, showed intense interest in participating in the film plant, but then withdrew.

The THA's strategy, contrary to the aim of the management, was to privatize some sections of the technological processes while closing down the rest of the firm. Indeed, it frequently made clear that closure was the ultimate intention. Meanwhile, the company management was struggling to keep a position in the market by introducing new products and trying to switch to new technologies. This, however, was severely hampered, and a significant reduction in costs effectively ruled out, by the THA's refusal of credits for a new film-coating system. The THA even sold the ORWO trademark of Wolfen Films, which legally belonged to the Wolfen film plant, in a combined deal for the sale of the Berlin X-ray film plant to a well-known American corporation from the photographic sector. Legal objections finally forced a reversal of the trademark sale.

At the beginning of 1995, the BVS took a formal decision to close down the film plant, but the liquidator continued to negotiate with interested parties over the sale of a part of the film production plant. Then the R&D section dissolved itself and finally, in August 1995, the BVS published its decision not to produce any more film in Wolfen because of the high losses. It nevertheless accepted the offer of an investor wishing to have films that were produced elsewhere by outside firms, packed with the ORWO trademark. The very fact that such a deal was possible rather indicates that there could well have been a place for ORWO in the growing, competitive film market.

The immediate consequence of the BVS decision has been a reduction of the 700 staff employed at the Wolfen plant to 200. Some of these were to be employed in packing film, while some the BVS was intending to transfer to other jobs in Wolfen. This compares with an employment level of 15,000 in the film plant in 1989 and makes Wolfen one of the places recording the greatest job losses in east Germany. The fall, however, has been held in check in Bitterfeld where, despite a drop from 18,000 to 700 jobs between 1989 and 1993 in the chemical combine, jobs have been maintained around the preparation for the 'chemical park'. More generally, the Wolfen case demonstrates very clearly the conflicts of interest which inevitably arise in the course of privatization. It is, however, very difficult, if not impossible, for those on the outside to make an objective assessment of the different parties' arguments.

Thus, the full reorganization and privatization of the major enterprises has yet to be completed and the problems have been handed over, together with the so-called contract supervision, to the THA's successor organization the BVS, the Federal Office for Special Tasks Related to Unification. In some cases, sales decisions have already been taken in principle, although the precise details have still to be negotiated. The contractual partner of the THA or BVS can still refuse to sign the final contract of sale, as has happened in some cases in the past. In the majority of sales negotiations, the decisive issue seems to be the extent of the BVS's preparedness to participate in startup losses and rehabilitation investment.

The obvious question is whether, given the accumulating cost of cash assistance and the expectation of state investment and equity participation, it would not have been more advantageous for the TH-companies to be rehabilitated early on, with the help of western managers with experience in rehabilitation of enterprises elsewhere. The firms could then have been listed on the stock exchange as viable companies. In east Germany, extraordinary though it may seem, no attention was paid to the experiences of rehabilitation and privatization of state enterprises in West Germany, such as the car manufacturer Volkswagen or the chemical concern VEBA, in the mid-1960s. In these cases, the state's proprietary function was retained for many years until privatization was viable.

The example of the large chemical enterprises shows particularly clearly the problems that arise from splitting up the old structures. It is a problem that has to be confronted in all the transforming countries. It would be unrealistic to expect to find buyers for all large companies who can lead them into international competitiveness. The problem is that precisely those sectors with major production capacity are the ones that have lost their markets, following the collapse of exports to the East and especially to the former Soviet Union. Competitors on the world market are naturally unenthusiastic about giving up market shares, and that applies with particular force to the metallurgy and chemical industries.

Rehabilitation of existing enterprises, therefore, usually depends on devising offers on a completely different basis, which once again typically implies radical technological changes. There is usually no other way to gain market access. Moreover, the size of the enterprises and amount of capital required points to the need for purchasers' consortia, meaning that a number of firms have to see an advantage in their joint involvement. Under these circumstances, conflicts of interest are unavoidable. The THA, however, has attempted actively to stimulate the creation of such consortia, while the potential purchasers have responded by attempting to minimize their risks and by demanding passive state participation and high investment subsidies.

When these conditions have been accepted, the advantage of privatization by sale to outside investors could be realized, with new private capital flowing directly into the enterprises. That, however, is incompatible with rapid state withdrawal at the point when ownership is transferred. As the discussion of Czech enterprises in Chapter 6 indicates, this is not a uniquely east German problem. In those parts of eastern Europe where privatization has been achieved by vouchers and other forms of widespread share distribution, the newly privatized companies have been left struggling to find the resources for necessary investment. There is no obvious solution without state participation.

As a general rule, the case is overwhelming for dismantling the inherited structure of large enterprises, both to promote the modern division of labour and to facilitate privatization. There may be a few exceptions to this, where that structure already incorporates an efficient division of labour. Nevertheless, east German experience does show that something should be carried forward from the preceding structure. Above all, it makes sense not to maintain links between closely-related parts of a production process. The creation of central service enterprises has been shown to increase the value of the site of such formerly very large concerns.

Conditions are slightly different across other sectors, but

privatization is also under way, though not yet completed, in most of the east German large enterprises outside the chemical industry. Some firms in the so-called management companies are close to completing rehabilitation, and await privatization decisions. The management is among the potential buyers in parts of the mechanical engineering industry. A buyer was also found in 1995 for a major company in railway-vehicle construction, which had previously appeared as a major problem case.

The major shipyards were also privatized, and a Belgian company was found willing to buy the last steel and rolling mill on the river Oder, long held by the THA. The EU agreed to special rehabilitation subsidies for these once large enterprises, in exchange for agreements not to expand capacity and to impose some partial plant closures. The levels of employment were thereby reduced to about the 500-person mark in these enterprises, too. Needless to say, state participation in subsidizing investment is substantial in all these difficult privatization cases.

In a few cases, large enterprises have emerged out of several medium-sized companies through privatization. Some west German enterprises, previously classified as middle sized, have grown by buying subsidiary companies in east Germany. In general, this involves conglomerates of west and east German companies from different branches often combining construction with manufacture. Examples include a group bringing together shipyards, machinery manufacture and plant construction, while other cases have seen breweries and glass factories come together, and the merger of recycling firms with paper manufacturers and producers of packaging materials with trading subsidiaries. In these cases, new networks have been taking shape, fulfilling one of the expectations which optimists had looked forward to from privatization as whole.

Nevertheless, the point remains valid that large enterprises are now the exception in the structure of east German industry. This points to the absence of an important precondition for the reindustrialization of the region, for the consolidation of small and medium-sized industrial and service companies and for the continuation and development of industrial research.

THE FORMATION OF SMEs

A strong emphasis has been placed on the role of the independent small and medium-sized enterprises, or SMEs, in economic development both in theory and in German economic policy. In West Germany's past they made a substantial contribution to the flexibility of the division of labour and to the innovative renewal of the industrial structure. They thereby contributed substantially to the stabilization of employment. In west Germany, more than 90 per cent of companies, classified according to the criterion of the number of employees, are SMEs. An increasing, although statistically unquantifiable, number of these belong in fact to major companies. For east Germany it was hoped that the transformation into a market economy would lead after privatization to a substantial reorganization of the formerly state-owned enterprises into a new industrial structure, based upon SMEs, in which state intervention would be kept to a minimum. The extent to which this hope could be realized naturally depended on the actual course of developments in the east German economy.

The formation of independent SMEs was at first dependent above all on the terms laid down for privatization and reprivatization. Following the conclusion of the privatization phase, it is dependent on the setting up of new companies or on the relocation of existing ones from outside. When the transformation began in east Germany, there was a shortage of both entrepreneurs and managers with market economy experience. Private individuals were very rarely able to accumulate sufficient capital in the former GDR, but support from the state in giving access to capital sources — rising from DM 0.2 billion in 1991 to DM 1.2 billion in 1995 — has enabled east German entrepreneurs to participate to a substantial extent in both the privatization and the formation of new companies.

Other help from early on has included the creation of Centres for Technology and New Businesses in which new businesses have been offered cheap accommodation with a good infrastructure, as well as free advice for the startup phase. It was, of course, taken for granted that east Germany's economic revival would be helped by a commitment on the part of the previous owners to whom nationalized concerns had been returned, and by investment from west German medium-sized companies. New SMEs were never expected to be the sole source of economic recovery.

In numerical terms, at least, it does appear that a very substantial transformation has taken place. About 3,000 industrial concerns have been created through management buyouts, the method of privatization for more than 20 per cent of all companies. More than 6,300 firms were returned, the great majority to former east German owners. About 2,400 of these were industrial companies (*DIW Wochenbericht*, 1994, No. 20, p.322). In the first quarter of 1995 the total number of medium-sized firms, although not covered in official statistics, was estimated by the Federal Ministry for the Economy at about 12,500 (BfW, 1995b), including a very high proportion of firms with fewer than 20 employees. The 12,500 industrial businesses have about 600,000 employees, meaning an average of 48 employees per firm. In the newly-created firms, employment is about five per company and the risk of failure is high. When account is taken of other sectors as well as industry, it can be assumed that east Germany has roughly 500,000 businesses with some 3.5 million workplaces, meaning on average seven people per firm.

There are, however, substantial differences in how these new, small firms have developed. Two paths can be identified, depending on whether the firms were effectively given, or had to fight for, a position in the market. Generally speaking, privatization could lead to the creation of east German SMEs as a supplement to the traditional west German structure, or as genuinely new businesses struggling in areas of intense competition. East German newcomers were poorly equipped to face this on account of their limited access to capital resources.

As a general rule, those enterprises taken over by west German, or other larger outside firms, were integrated into the acquirer's division of labour and marketing strategy. This has given them a reasonable guarantee of future integration into the new all-German economic structure. The outcome, however, has not always been ideal. A number of companies were acquired purely as a means for overcoming immediate capacity problems, the so-called 'extended work-bench', with the accompanying risk of an increased dependence on the overall economic situation. In some other cases, individual companies were bought up by competitors, either to eliminate competition or simply to make a profit from selling off their assets.

The situation was substantially more difficult for SMEs with no ready-made route into the west German economic structure. This could apply to firms taken over by west German individuals without an industrial background, rather than functioning and successful firms, and to firms either obtained or newly set up by east Germans. In the main they had, and still have, to fight for access to the market. As a general rule, their delivery and supply relations appear to be much less secure than in the case of subsidiaries of west German companies.

The general prospects for medium-sized firms deteriorated with the decline of large-scale industry in east Germany. Their traditional activities had been geared towards supplying either inputs or services to major enterprises, covering public procurement at all levels, but especially in the regions, and satisfying consumer demand at the local level. Exports had not been a major area of activity for the medium-size businesses, except indirectly in so far as they had been suppliers for major industrial export companies.

As the traditional customers disappeared, so a period of intense competition began. In almost every case, west German enterprises had sufficient capacity to cover east German demand. The only exceptions were a few innovative products. Overall, the pattern now is that the subsidiary sales organizations of the west German large and medium-sized industries have been, or will be, expanded into east Germany. The few newcomers to the region with production companies generally brought their traditional suppliers with them.

There is, moreover, a tendency for local markets to decline in importance. Everywhere, medium-sized firms are competing with long-distance deliveries from other companies. Under such conditions, even filling market niches and meeting regional needs is possible only with products that are consistently competitive, although there may still be some gaps in the market not covered by the major companies and some scope for exploiting the advantages of specific locations, such as proximity to Berlin.

The modern retail business is dominated by wholesale chains, which can organize their purchases across regions. To gain entry to this market, the newcomer must offer product and price advantages, demonstrate the capacity to deliver regularly and be able to survive the pressures of competition. In addition, the newcomer in Germany must pay special 'taxes', such as auditing costs, stock control costs and 'shelf money'. The task was anyway going to be exceedingly difficult as, even in the public service supply organizations, in the railways and the postal service, supply positions were already occupied. Thus, any newcomers had to push out traditional suppliers. Moreover, they also had to face the threat of competition from east–central European companies which, thanks to exchange rates and wage levels, could often offer lower prices.

These amount to pretty daunting conditions for newly-formed or rehabilitated firms, and explain why very many east German enterprises cannot yet find a secure place in the market. There were and are major trade barriers created by west German competitors, such as the presentation of a 'negative image', cartel agreements, price dumping, head hunting of staff and connections between administration and industry. An example of this was the attempt by an east German enterprise to bring the first CFC-free refrigerator on to the market. Competitors left no stone unturned in their attempts to prevent this. When it was finally clear that they had failed, they simply included similar refrigerators in their own production and sales programmes.

In the past, not even east Germany's public procurement practices have made sufficient use of the possibilities of giving orders to companies from the region, even though east German companies are given some degree of preferential treatment. They were to be awarded a public procurement contract, even if their bids were 10 per cent more expensive than those from competitors. Thus, the THA and major enterprises have tried through their own voluntary purchasing initiative to push east German goods in an attempt to establish the firms in the market. The initiative is making a little headway, with east Germans increasingly buying east German products, and this is stimulating a recovery on the east German consumer goods market.

A realistic, medium-term assessment of the chances for developing a competitive medium-sized industry in east Germany must take account of the immense changes in the structure and potential technological level of industry. The key change is the breakup of the major industrial enterprises and the creation of a more flexible structure around smaller firms. In some cases firms are following the cost-cutting strategies associated with such current buzz words as lean production, profit centres, outsourcing and industrial restructuring. Increasingly, major industrial concerns are employing small, flexible structures, while keeping links that point to a recognition of the continuing advantages of cooperation within groups of companies.

Nevertheless, a number of changes are serving to reassert the advantages of larger firms. Among these are the increasing internationalization of production and research, the growing pace of change in basic technologies and the automation of production, distribution and communications. In an effort to exploit discoveries of prestigious scientific centres abroad, there is a tendency for major enterprises to establish R&D facilities close by, either alone or in 'strategic alliances' with competitors. A prominent German example is the electronics firm, Siemens.

Thus, the R&D facilities of large firms are moving outside Germany, a practice that is obviously beyond the capability of smaller firms. Moreover, smaller firms face even greater difficulties in exploiting the results of technological progress, which often requires substantial levels of investment. Final producers, for example in the automobile industry, increasingly pass their cost pressures, resulting from the competitive international market, on to their suppliers, forcing the latter into compromises, mergers and rationalization moves. Entering such networks during a period of radical change demands massive technological advances from potential newcomers. Given the weak capital position and R&D base of east German firms this is, to say the least, a difficult undertaking.

This shows up very clearly both the limitations and the potential role of medium-sized companies in a modern division of labour. Current economic changes point to the need for an ever greater concentration on R&D potential and to the need to be able to finance the investment required to reach the new levels of technological development. It is an open question whether the medium-sized firms or the enterprises still linked into larger structures are the better placed to take advantage of the possibilities arising out of innovation and the changed division of labour in the future. The former may, therefore, be unable to assert themselves, either on the east German market or elsewhere. The question requires research. It is, however, pretty clear that any economic policy directed exclusively towards medium-sized companies will fail to help these firms win a satisfactory position within the new overall German industrial structure, or even within an east German regional structure. The problem, however, is that large enterprises have now become rather scarce in east Germany. East German policy therefore inevitably tends to be a policy directed towards medium-sized companies.

There is no reason to doubt that firms have been making every effort to remain competitive, despite their poor starting conditions. Industry, however, has been very seriously reduced in aggregate terms within the east German economy, as discussed in Chapter 1. Thus, it contributed 19 per cent of east German GDP in 1994 compared with a west German figure of 28 per cent. Moreover, sectors that are in long-term decline account for almost three-quarters of the east German net product. Thus, the branch structure of industry is weak and the structure of the enterprises, as it has emerged, is fundamentally flawed, with the very weak representation of research-intensive, export-oriented sectors of chemicals, mechanical engineering, rail-vehicle construction and electrical engineering. Together these account for only 27 per cent of gross industrial value added, compared with 47 per cent in west Germany. Indeed, the revival of growth in the east German economy since 1994 has been predominantly due to firms oriented to the local market only, while in 1994 total east German output from all sectors still accounted for only 60 per cent of total east German consumption (*DIW Wochenbericht*, 1995, No. 27–28, p.465).

There are sectoral variations in the progress made towards full competitiveness by east German firms which reflect the wider nature of the transformation and point to different conditions and possibilities for the emerging SMEs. The greatest progress has been made in the food industry. Production serving construction has obvious advantages in view of the extent to which east German recovery to date has depended on a revival in construction itself. Quarrying, alongside steel and light metal construction firms, has taken particular advantage of this. The position of the investment goods industry, affected in part by the development of the economic situation and the enormous structural changes, is the most difficult.

Even within sectors, the fate of individual firms varies widely. Some companies have fought their way into new markets or found niches from which they can compete successfully with western rivals. Many firms, however, have a long way to go and have not even achieved a level of profitability that can ensure survival and stability. The continued existence of companies not yet integrated into the all-German economic system is only possible thanks to state assistance. In 1994, more than 300 east German firms went bankrupt every week. Even in 1995, despite an improvement in the overall economic situation, there was no letup in the wave of bankruptcies, as credits were coming up for repayment.

The depth of the difficulties that this represents can be illustrated by a comparison with the effects of privatization itself, during which some 20 per cent of functioning companies created out of the former combines were closed down. This is measured as a share of the so-called gross company stock within the THA's overall portfolio as at 31 December 1994, covering all the 13,815 firms, irrespective of sector, which emerged from the dismantling of the structure of the former nationalized economy. The only cases excluded from the figures are the so-called 'remainder' or 'shell' companies, which were left behind when the 'active' companies broke away from their old structures. Thus, the figure of 20 per cent of companies dissolved does not include the closure of newly-established companies while privatization was still under way.

The majority of companies succeeded in retaining a core of qualified personnel despite the relatively uncertain future and comparatively poor levels of pay. During the recession, employment levels in many firms fell to a minimum. Despite the limited investment capacity the technical gap was clearly reduced, thanks to state support for investment, which was reflected in improvements undertaken during the normal replacement of equipment. By the end of 1994, 40 per cent of the equipment stock employed had already been replaced, allowing on average a 35 per cent growth in productivity per year since the beginning of 1991. Despite this, as has been argued, the new companies are still weak in innovative products, as they do not have the R&D facilities. They also suffer from continuing difficulties in finding markets outside their regions, from shortcomings in managerial ability and from poor pay conditions for employees.

A LASTING STRUCTURAL WEAKNESS?

Substantial structural alterations in favour of more research-intensive production could be considered a precondition for viable, sustained growth in the east German economy. In a country with high salaries, such as the Federal Republic, only technologically sophisticated products, or products requiring complex, system-integrated processes, have any long-term market future. This points to the seriousness of the implications of the decline of the structural share in east Germany of precisely those research-intensive branches that should provide the basis for self-sustaining growth. It is true that the rate of unemployment in the east German regional economy had stabilized by 1995, but there was still no expansion in the number of secure employment positions.

Despite extensive capital and site promotion, it has not yet proved possible to encourage the migration of the right sort of companies to the extent that would create a noticeable growth in employment. Small west German firms have moved their businesses to east Germany, but not in significant numbers while, for reasons already explained, it is not a particularly enticing investment site for large firms. In 1989 and 1990 there were some major investment projects in the motor industry as a result of political encouragement. Mercedes-Benz, Opel and Volkswagen — the so-called 'flagships' of German industry — built new assembly plants in east Germany, but most of the inputs still came from outside the region. Volkswagen had some previous links with the East German motor industry, having supported investment in motor and gearbox production. It became the owner of these new plants as the investment was completed. Some other western companies set up some joint ventures with enterprises in the closing weeks of the GDR's existence, but most were on a small scale and relatively unsuccessful. Significant new commitments have been rare, with Siemens's construction of a computer-chip plant in Dresden being an outstanding exception.

Thus, the general conditions for the structural renewal of industrial production based on the potential of industry located in east Germany are not particularly favourable. Research facilities, especially in major industries, were broken up or decimated during privatization (*DIW Wochenbericht*, 1995, No. 6). With the disappearance of company head-quarters from east Germany, centralized R&D facilities were generally put in jeopardy. The major enterprises' R&D units lost touch with production during privatization and were separated from the production units, if they survived at all, and privatized as 'Research Ltd'. They had to find a market niche for their research services independent of their mother companies. Many will fail in this, not least because German industry has been reducing its research expenditure for some time. They will find it very difficult to keep up with the related problem areas of developing production and markets from the outside.

The THA did not think it was part of its mandate to maintain R&D capacity, and treated this just like any other partial production process which could be hived off in the interests of dismantling the old structures. In order to preserve research sites, the THA would have had to set the continuation of R&D departments as a clear criterion when assessing purchasers' offers.

More generally, however, the fall in R&D was not the result of specific decisions relating to R&D alone. It was rather an inevitable consequence of the kind of structural transformation that has taken place in east Germany. It follows, above all, from the changes in the structure of firms both by size and by sector of activity.

Thus, in west Germany, which is frequently taken as a benchmark for evaluating east Germany, private-sector research is concentrated in large firms and in a small number of branches. As many as 80 per cent of industrial R&D staff are employed in firms with 1,000 and more employees, which also account for 84 per cent of private-sector industrial research expenditure. These large firms are clearly the best placed both to finance costly research projects over an extended period and to market the results on an international scale. Small and medium-sized enterprises frequently enjoy advantages in customized research by taking existing technology and varying, developing and deploying it flexibly to provide solutions for specific, usually small-scale, demand segments.

It is sometimes concluded from this that SMEs are more innovative than large companies, but such comparisons are rather unhelpful. For an economy to be strong in technological terms it requires a highly differentiated sectoral structure and a good mixture of large, medium-sized and small firms, all conducting research. To this extent, west German structures meet a number of important criteria for ensuring technology transfer from basic research to applications.

Public bodies play an important role, especially in fundamental research, but applied research oriented directly to innovations and experimental development, what is normally termed industrial R&D, is primarily the responsibility of private firms. Thus, even of the total DM 80.7 billion spent on R&D in 1992, the private sector accounted for two-thirds, suggesting that research in the main is steered by market forces. In financial terms, the next most important bodies were universities and specialist research institutes, either government owned or run as private non-profit-making bodies, which accounted for 16 per cent and 15 per cent, respectively, of the overall research budget.

With a total volume of DM 1.3 billion in 1992, east Germany accounted for about 2.4 per cent of the R&D expenditure undertaken by German manufacturing industry as a whole, although its industrial output was equivalent to slightly more than 5 per cent of the west German level. Moreover, clear differences emerge between the two regions if the analysis differentiates between firms of different size categories. In east Germany, a quarter of private-sector R&D expenditure in 1992 was generated by firms with fewer than 100 employees, while firms with 1,000 or more employees actually accounted for just less than one-quarter of the total.

This comparison needs to be set in context around three points. The first is that, to judge from the number of staff employed in R&D, east German industry still has a research base. Although the number of research staff employed by firms fell from 85,700 in 1989 to an estimated 16,000 at the end of 1993, this does represent a smaller decline than that for output, suggesting some decoupling of output from research.

The second point is that east Germany has adopted the west German public-sector system for encouraging and facilitating technology transfer, including offices for that purpose in universities and colleges, ten specific institutions supported by the Federal Ministry for the Economy providing a network of contact points offering advice on new technologies, product strategies, management, market data and research cooperations. There are also nine institutions supported by the Federal Ministry of Research and Technology in the new federal states, six of which are computer-integrated manufacturing (CIM) technology transfer centres and a number of further bodies and agencies giving support for technology transfer and innovation.

Thus, federal bodies moved quickly after reunification, setting up and funding the operation of various agencies from 1992 onwards. Apart from the benefits of advice, more than 2,000 firms received direct financial help in that year for activities that included supporting R&D personnel, undertaking research preparatory to market entry and conducting research under contract to other bodies. It is therefore clear that government bodies have taken serious steps aimed at strengthening R&D in east Germany.

The third point, however, is that these efforts have still left industrial research in a very precarious position. The key issue is partly the structure of industry in the region, with the weak representation of research-intensive, export-oriented sectors. Even within those sectors, however, the east German share in total research spending is frequently lower than would be justified by the share in total German output, as shown in Table 3.1. The weakness, of course, is the absence of large east German firms.

Table 3.1 R&D expenditure in east and west Germany in manufacturing industry

	Research spending in DM billion		East Germany as percentage of German total	
	West, 1991	East, 1992	Research spending, 1992	Industrial output, 1994
Chemicals	10,660	171	1.6	2.5
Machinery	5,180	369	6.6	4.6
Road vehicles	10,335	28	0.3	2.8
Electrical engineering	13,630	336	2.4	3.9
Precision mechanics and optics	812	48	5.6	2.1
Total	52,455	1,304	2.4	5

Source: Gemeinnützige Gesellschaft für Wissenschaftsstatistik, 1993.

As a rule, western investors have installed production capacity without making provision for any R&D facilities. Arguments about the benefits of placing research close to the customer and near to the market do not seem to apply to east German industry, for which internationally recognized standard figures for the proportion of turnover spent on R&D also seem irrelevant. In many cases, the R&D staff of existing TH-companies have taken other jobs within the firms. Top performers often voluntarily moved to rivals because of the uncertainty over their futures. However, some firms, which have recognized the value of keeping their own R&D capacity, have succeeded in maintaining a nucleus of their original capacity and in retaining the best staff. They have been helped in part by state support for R&D, which is estimated to have accounted in 1995 for 50 per cent of the total expenditure in enterprises. Since there are now virtually no major enterprises based in east Germany, in-house R&D capacity there is usually employed by SMEs.

This means that a number of significant preconditions for an effective technology-transfer system are not yet in place. In addition to a broad technology spectrum, such a system requires corporate structures encompassing large, medium-sized and small firms all pursuing R&D, to which know-how can be transferred from academic research institutions and in which it can be developed. Without that, the current level of employment in R&D can be expected to fall in the years to come.

Moreover, east German companies are unanimous that it is very difficult to penetrate markets, even with innovative products. The problem lies in the high degree of stability of established delivery and supply networks. Some of the major firms' successor companies, such as Jenoptik, a part of the Zeiss concern which emerged from the Karl Zeiss combine in Jena, have tried to find a foothold with innovative products and to make use of innovative services on a regional scale. This company, however, faced major difficulties in entering the market, and has subsequently turned to distribution partnerships with international concerns.

A whole new range of 'technology-oriented firms' were set up with state support at just the time when R&D capacity within enterprises was being dissolved. Their founders have tried to find a market for innovative products or processes. The promoters hope that this will lead to the creation of points around which a basic renewal of the industrial structure can crystallize. As a rule, insufficient time has passed for innovations to establish themselves on the market. The companies therefore cannot yet be considered secure. Indeed, they are as yet neither growing nor investing to any significant extent.

In addition to these, there are a number of smaller SMEs which are already successfully marketing innovative products but which, because of their restricted financial margins, cannot grow rapidly. Thus, there are also first attempts at developing a high-tech area, for example in the fields of microelectronic and optical-electronic components, in instrument construction, in medical and environmental technology and in some branches of the chemical industry. Their contribution to the overall east German economic structure is still very small and dependent on state support as, even where outside capital participation could be sought to overcome the lack of resources within companies, owners are frequently frightened of the possible loss of independence. They often lack the experience or expertise that might enable them to attract dormant partner holdings or to look for partners in areas where conflicts of interest are likely to be small. Since the owners are often both researchers and entrepreneurs simultaneously, they simply do not have the time to carry out both functions well and in parallel. As elsewhere in the world, researchers are often bad entrepreneurs.

Movement of production facilities from West to East on any significant scale, however necessary that may be, is likely to be difficult to achieve in the foreseeable future. It would depend on marketing the location to make it genuinely competitive with locations in western Germany. Support for economic activities would have to be adapted more carefully to the structural deficiencies of the region's industry. Above all, support should be targeted towards particular activities that could fit with a conception for the region's long-term development.

Apart from possible short-term cash assistance to bridge startup difficulties, this points to a medium-term strategy involving financial participation in firms with promising innovations, while also increasing the innovative capacity of those companies which could play a long-term role in creating an economic structure with long-term potential. This could involve the creation of new 'technology-oriented' enterprises. It is also undoubtedly points to the need to give carefully-targeted support to ensure stability and to allow for the future development of key companies that have the potential to play a major role in the development of a modern industrial structure, even if they have not so far proved themselves to be particularly innovative. It is, however, clear that an active policy of state intervention is essential if the structural weaknesses of the east German economy are to be overcome.

PART II

The Economic Transformation in the Czech Republic

4. Stability Before Growth?

Economic policy in the early stages of the Czech transformation within the Czechoslovak federation centred on macroeconomic issues. Stabilization measures, similar to the standard IMF package for less-developed countries suffering from internal and external disequilibrium, were combined with the freeing of prices and external trade. This was the core of the package introduced in January 1991, following similar measures adopted in Poland in January 1990. Liberalization measures were to create an environment in which the market could start to function. Inflation was to be held in check by restrictions on the money supply and on domestic demand, while the external balance was protected by sharp devaluation. The immediate effect of this, coinciding with the collapse of trade within the CMEA, was a dramatic fall in output alongside a sharp rise in inflation. Official statistics point to a drop in GDP of 14.2 per cent and an inflation rate of 56.6 per cent. Later years have seen a resumption of growth, starting in 1994, and a stabilization of inflation levels at less than 10 per cent.

Despite the passage of time, and the broadening of economic policy measures into other areas, most obviously including privatization, much of the emphasis still centres on holding inflationary pressures in check rather than on encouraging restructuring and growth. The assumption continues to be that macroeconomic stabilization plus privatization are the best, and sometimes it seems the only, steps needed to ensure satisfactory economic restructuring. The following analysis of the impact of the macroeconomic framework points to a less certain conclusion.

Despite reasonably favourable starting conditions, the economic level of the Czech Republic fell further behind comparable western European countries at the start of the transformation, and rapid growth over the coming years will be required to secure the conditions for full integration into the European Union. It can be argued that the anti-inflationary bias in macroeconomic policy has hampered recovery in the level of investment and left policy makers with a series of dilemmas that probably cannot be resolved with macroeconomic measures alone. If growth is to be ensured, the trade balance restored to the equilibrium it lost during 1994 and inflation reduced to well below 10 per cent, then the government will need to consider active measures to encourage restructuring at the micro-level. Ultimately, stabilization and growth with restructuring cannot be seen as alternative policy objectives, as the failure to achieve the latter will threaten the achievement and maintenance of the former.

THE STARTING CONDITIONS

The Czech lands started their transformation with several advantages over their neighbours in east–central Europe. They had a long tradition of industrial development stretching back into the Austro-Hungarian monarchy before the First World War and through into the independent Czechoslovakia between the wars. Indeed, they were industrially the most developed part of the Austro-Hungarian monarchy, with two-thirds of the industrial output of the whole empire. In the late 1930s, Czechoslovakia had a higher per capita GDP than neighbouring Austria and ranked fifteenth in the world. The economically more-developed Czech lands occupied tenth place, not far behind Belgium and Holland, with an annual per capita GDP of about $200 in the prices of the time.

Czech industry produced a wide range of goods. Several leading engineering enterprises, including the arms producer Škoda of Plzeň, the Prague heavy engineering combine ČKD, and the Moravian arms manufacturer Zbrojovka Brno, established world-wide reputations and were respected for a number of significant innovations. Light industry, the leading sector in the initial phases of the industrial revolution, was also a well-developed export sector, with capacity substantially greater than the domestic market. Among the best known are the shoe manufacturer Baťa, set up in the Moravian town of Zlín in 1894, and the well-established glass, china and textile industries.

After the Second World War, the Czech economy fell behind the developed economies of the world both in quantitative and especially in qualitative terms. Meaningful economic incentives ceased to function in the period of the planned economy, and contacts with the advanced economies of the world were reduced to a minimum within the autarkic CMEA community. As a result, Czechoslovakia's relative economic level fell, the structure of production stagnated and a widening technological gap appeared.

Comparisons undertaken within the European Comparison Project, organized by United Nations bodies in cooperation with Eurostat, show that by 1990, Czechoslovakia's economic level had fallen to half that of Austria. Czech per capita GDP, calculated from comparable baskets of goods and services, was 54 per cent that of the Austrian level. Austria, in turn, exceeded the average western European level by roughly 5 per cent. Moreover, as Table 4.1 indicates, Czechoslovakia retained only a modest lead over the other economies of east–central Europe.

Table 4.1 GDP per capita in the central European countries in 1990

	Purchasing power parity	Exchange rate	Purchasing power parity	Exchange rate
	In thousand Austrian schillings		Austria = 100	
Austria	232.4	232.4	100.0	100.0
Czechoslovakia	115.7	32.6	49.8	14.0
Hungary	88.2	33.6	38.0	14.4
Poland	71.0	19.1	30.5	8.2

Source: Auer and Müller, 1993, p.682.

Thus, while the Czech economy had been playing a leading role as the 'engineering works and forge' within the closed CMEA community, it paid dearly for the loss of contacts with the developed world.

Structural stagnation was clearest with the sheer scale of heavy industry, the sector that expanded most rapidly to help the industrialization of the Soviet bloc in the 1950s. It was left with a high material and energy intensiveness, using low-quality raw materials, especially from the former USSR. Moreover, its scale and the technology used contributed to an immense burden of environmental damage, especially in northern parts of Bohemia and Moravia. The Czech Republic is now the linchpin of the so-called 'black triangle' of central Europe, alongside the former East Germany and Poland.

This relative decline of the Czech Republic closely mirrors that of the former GDR. Comparisons of the indicator net material product, as calculated by the Statistical Commission of CMEA, showed the GDR with only a modest lead in the late 1980s. It was probably less than 10 per cent above Czechoslovakia's economic level. In view of the higher level of the Czech Republic within the Czechoslovak federation, and also in view of the greater upward distortion of GDR statistics, it is reasonable to assume that there was no substantial difference between the two countries.

Distortions in the structure of production — meaning a structure that appears outdated in comparison with the advanced market economies — were also analogous. Both economies suffered from excessively large industrial sectors and a strong bias towards heavy industry. In both cases, the service sector was small in comparison with market economies at a similar level of development. There were also some differences. Steel, heavy engineering and some branches of light industry dominated in the Czech Republic, while chemicals and precision engineering were relatively more developed in the former GDR. In both cases, however, this reflected the division of labour established in the autarkic CMEA system. In both cases, moreover, the technical level was low by western European standards.

The orientation towards the eastern market was, however, exceptionally high in the former Czechoslovakia. Indeed, of all the CMEA countries it was surpassed only by Bulgaria. More than two-thirds of foreign trade was linked with centrally-planned economies. The newer Slovak enterprises, especially, were likely to be totally dependent on eastern markets. Products exported to the former Soviet Union were the lifeblood of the mechanical engineering industry in both the Czech lands and Slovakia. Every year, Czechoslovakia exported to the Soviet Union hundreds of locomotives and trams, thousands of heavy terrain trucks and capital equipment for major projects. The same market also took standardized products of light industry, including tens of thousands of ready-made garments, millions of pairs of mass-produced shoes and large quantities of glass and china. This one-sided orientation was a major contributor to the sharp fall in production after the disintegration of the CMEA market in 1990 and 1991.

The massive export of investment equipment in the past does provide some possibilities for a renewal of the export of spare parts and for the modernization of existing equipment. Nevertheless, a full return to an economy based on such heavy reliance on investment goods, or on standard simple products of light industry, would be impossible, even assuming a full recovery across eastern markets. Those markets have changed, too, and Czech products now face competition from the rest of the world. Thus, there is no future for the Czech Republic without a substantial restructuring of production and a new orientation towards higher-quality products.

THE TRANSFORMATION CRISIS

The decline in output in the early 1990s led, across east–central Europe, to a further fall in the countries' economic level in relation to western Europe. In the Czech Republic, per capita GDP had fallen to 44 per cent of the Austrian level at the time of the breakup of the federation at the end of 1992, equivalent to less than 49 per cent of the EU average. Table 4.2, based on recent Austrian calculations, shows the Czech Republic in a better light and Slovakia and Poland in a worse light than previous estimates. This may partly reflect an overestimation of the Slovak share in GDP prior to the breakup of the federation.

In a number of respects, the Czech Republic did enjoy better starting conditions for the transformation both in economic terms and in the broader social and political sphere. The slightly higher economic level was associated with a generally better position in terms of macroeconomic equilibrium, as shown by a lower monetary overhang on both the domestic consumer-goods and the semi-manufactured-goods markets. It also enjoyed a relatively well-balanced state budget, when taken over the long term, and a considerably lower level of foreign indebtedness. The extent and significance of this advantage is shown in Table 4.3, below, which compares across the members of the Central European Free Trade Area, henceforth CEFTA.

Table 4.2 GDP per capita in CEFTA countries in 1994

	Purchasing power parity	Exchange rate	Purchasing power parity	Exchange rate
	in US dollars		Czech Republic = 100	
Czech Republic	9,490	4,419	100	100
Hungary	6,537	4,403	69	100
Poland	5,477	3,124	58	71
Slovakia	6,749	3,240	71	73

Source: Extrapolated from Rittenau, 1995, p.703.

Table 4.3 Gross external debt in CEFTA countries in 1989

	Gross debt in $billion	Gross debt as percentage of GDP	Gross debt as percentage of exports	Debt service as percentage of exports
Czechoslovakia	7.9	14.9	108.7	18.8
Hungary	20.4	71.3	239.8	40.6
Poland	41.5	58.8	475.8	44.5

Source: OECD, 1994.

In the social sphere, the transformation quickly revealed a higher level of adaptability from the population and a greater willingness to make temporary sacrifices in the standard of living. Behind this lay a clear perception of the aim of gradually regaining the country's former position among the developed economies of the world. These factors were more influential in the Czech than in the Slovak Republic. The difference lies in their past histories, as Slovakia had not enjoyed the status of an advanced area within the Austro-Hungarian monarchy or in the inter-war period. Its rapid economic development was concentrated primarily into the post-war years. That, alongside a slightly sharper impact of the transformation on the Slovak Republic — it was more affected by the decline of central planning and the collapse of the CMEA markets — contributed to the political processes that culminated in the breakup of the Czechoslovak federation and the establishment of independent Czech and Slovak Republics in January 1993. Since then the Czech Republic has established an exceptional reputation for political stability. The same coalition government established after the June 1992 elections held a firm grip on power until narrowly losing its overall majority in elections in June 1996.

Despite these differences in starting conditions, there were strong similarities in the policies pursued across the countries of east–central Europe. However, in the former Czechoslovakia, and later in the Czech Republic, the aim of liberalization was applied with more consistency and determination than elsewhere. Indeed, the progress of the reform was consistent with the government's scenario prepared after the first free elections in June 1990. The price liberalization in 1991 included a wide range of products and services. Significant areas of controlled prices have remained only in the housing, energy and public transport spheres. Opening the economy to world markets was achieved rapidly, leaving hardly any protection, although reference will be made later to the strongly undervalued exchange rate of the Czechoslovak crown. The average tariff level was lower in 1991 than the European Community countries' level towards third countries. An import surcharge on consumer goods was used only temporarily and abolished after one year. Privatization has also been very rapid in the Czech Republic, even though with some problems, as discussed in Chapters 5 and 6. There is a clear contrast here with the Slovak Republic where, following the division of the old federal state, there have been repeated delays and modifications to the original conception.

There were differences within the Czechoslovak, and subsequently within the Czech, government, but the dominant direction was set by federal Finance Minister and subsequently Czech Prime Minister Václav Klaus. His stated intention was the creation of a market economy 'without adjectives'. His narrowly economic approach meant a rejection not only of the term 'social market economy' as such, but also of any consistent recognition of the place for broader ecological, industrial or pro-export policies generally. All the emphasis was placed on market forces alone which, it was believed, could solve all problems that might emerge.

There were, however, inconsistencies within this 'free market' approach. The need to maintain a social consensus made it impossible in practice to ignore entirely the social acceptability of the transformation. Consequently, pragmatic solutions were sometimes adopted which appeared inconsistent with radical liberal proclamations. It was thanks to these elements of pragmatism that the government was able to maintain a social consensus around which it could press ahead with other aspects of its reform programme. Examples of compromises here include the maintenance of rent controls, in conflict with standard free market theory, the setting of a minimum wage and the subsidization of some large enterprises which could otherwise have faced collapse.

Nevertheless, these appeared as adjustments rather than as integral parts of a coherent government strategy. Indeed, an important implication of this conception of reform is that there was no place for what could be termed a medium-term economic strategy. This was rejected *a priori*. There are serious questions here as to whether inadequate state support for the cultivation of various factors of production and conditions of economic development may not lead to the appearance of bottlenecks in the medium term. The priorities chosen may have contributed immediately to achieving macroeconomic stability. There may, however, be a heavy price to pay for the severely restrictive policies which allowed a decline in the education system and health service, a breakup of the research and development base, an effective suspension of housing construction and a general decline and deterioration across the social and economic infrastructure.

More immediately, however, the stabilization measures adopted were a major cause of the deep decline in output during the transformation period. The low point in GDP in 1992 saw an overall fall of one-fifth, with industrial output down by one-third against the level at the start of reforms in 1989. These figures are actually very similar to those for Poland and Hungary, although in the latter case the decline was more gradual while in Poland it took place sooner and was overcome more rapidly. The figures in Table 4.4 suggest that the economic recovery that started in the Czech Republic in 1994 was not as impressive as in Poland, Slovakia or even, for that matter, Slovenia. The GDP growth rate reached only 2.6 per cent, with industrial output up by 2.1 per cent.

The consistency of the fall in output across east–central Europe, and its coincidence with the policies of macroeconomic stabilization, point to the presence of a causal relationship. The conventional transition strategy may involve a built-in downward pressure on production levels, leading to the destruction of capacity that might otherwise be viable. One reason could be the monopolistic environment, under which monetary and fiscal restrictions do not so much curb inflation as lead to a reduction in output.

Adjustment takes place through quantity rather than price changes. The shape of the aggregate supply curve is a well-known topic of fierce macroeconomic controversy. It appears that in the transitional economies of east–central Europe, only the agricultural market is competitive and flexible. This is the only substantial area in which producers' prices were clearly held in check by the low level of demand.

Nevertheless, there are unmistakable differences between countries. Macroeconomic stabilization policies have undoubtedly brought greater success in the Czech Republic than in other transitional economies. As Table 4.4 indicates, it enjoys the lowest rate of inflation, the most stable currency, the lowest budget deficits and the lowest rate of unemployment across east–central Europe. To some extent, these elements of macroeconomic stability reinforce each other, with the high level of economic activity supporting a high level of taxation so that public expenditure at about 44 per cent of GDP in 1995, a figure close to the European average, is still consistent with a balanced budget. Even the external debt position still remains comfortable, with central external reserves covering more than eight months' imports. The Czech Republic is in credit with the IMF and introduced full convertibility of the Czech crown on the current account, in line with Article VIII of the IMF Agreement, in October 1995. Most elements of the capital account were deregulated at the same time. This aura of stability helped the Czech Republic's acceptance as the twenty-sixth member of the OECD from the start of 1996. It was the first transitional economy to be accepted, although others are expected to follow shortly.

To a great extent, these indicators of a relative success should be seen as the results of the favourable starting conditions referred to above. They may also reflect some policy differences with the very strong Czech prioritization of anti-inflationary rather than pro-growth policies. A stable macroeconomic climate is often considered a

Table 4.4 The main indicators of the CEFTA countries, 1990–1994

Indicator	Year	Czech Republic	Slovakia	Hungary	Poland
GDP growth rate in constant prices	1990	–1.2	–2.4	–3.5	–10.2
	1991	–14.2	–14.5	–11.9	–7.0
	1992	–6.4	–7.0	–3.0	2.6
	1993	–0.9	–4.1	–0.8	3.8
	1994	2.6	4.8	2.9	5.0
	1990–94	–19.4	–22.1	–15.9	–6.6
Industrial output rate of growth	1990	–3.3	–3.8	–8.1	–26.4
	1991	–21.6	–19.3	–18.5	–13.6
	1992	–7.9	–9.5	–9.4	2.9
	1993	–5.3	–3.8	4.0	5.6
	1994	2.1	4.8	9.2	13.1
	1990–94	–32.5	–29.2	–23.1	–19.8
Rate of unemployment end of year	1990	0.7	1.6	1.7	3.5
	1991	4.1	11.8	8.5	11.6
	1992	2.6	10.4	12.3	13.6
	1993	3.5	14.4	12.1	15.7
	1994	3.2	14.8	10.9	16.0

Indicator	Year	Czech Republic	Slovakia	Hungary	Poland
Annual average rate of inflation	1990	9.1	9.9	28.6	533.2
	1991	56.6	61.3	35.0	70.3
	1992	11.1	10.0	23.0	45.3
	1993	20.8	23.2	22.5	36.9
	1994	10.0	13.4	18.9	33.2
	1990–94	20.3	22.2	25.5	95.5
Budget surplus as percentage of GDP	1991	–2.1	–3.8	–5.0	–3.8
	1992	–0.2	–3.3	–7.0	–6.0
	1993	0.1	–6.8	–5.6	–2.8
	1994	1.0	–5.9	–7.4	–2.7
Percentage rise in exchange rate against dollar	1991–93	0.1	–4.6	–26.9	–71.1
	1994	1.3	–4.0	–12.5	–22.3
Debt ratio	1994	83.6	58.0	314.5	206.1

Note: The debt ratio indicates gross foreign debt as a percentage of exports.

Sources: OECD, 1995; United Nations, 1995; World Bank, 1994; Bulletins of Central European Cooperation in Statistics; Eurostat.

necessary precondition for stable economic growth. It was, however, beyond the reach of economies suffering from persistent financial disequilibrium and an inheritance of substantial internal and external indebtedness. As the Polish experience suggests — with inflation and external disequilibrium even under conditions of strongly negative growth in 1990 and 1991 — it may be impossible to achieve macroeconomic stability even under conditions of stagnation. With this starting point, they may have no option but to support an acceleration of growth even at the risk of creating still larger imbalances. Nevertheless, this apparent handicap has its positive side because, as is frequently argued, a higher rate of inflation can be accompanied by a more rapid adjustment process both for relative prices and for the structure of production.

Table 4.5 Balance of payments of the Czech Republic in convertible currencies in $million, 1992–1995

	1992	1993	1994	1995
Current account	–305.1	433.1	289.8	–1,448.4
Trade balance	–1,901.6	–609.2	–849.6	–3,815.5
Exports	8,448.4	10,163.0	11,675.6	14,916.5
Imports	10,350.0	10,772.2	12,525.2	18,732.0
Balance of services	1,485.9	1,040.7	1,035.6	1,852.2
Transport	854.9	532.8	501.0	672.0
Tourism	659.3	1,032.8	891.5	1,245.0
Others	–28.3	–524.9	–356.9	–64.8
Balance of income	5.6	–128.4	–20.5	–94.5
Unrequited transfers, net	105.0	130.0	124.3	609.4
Capital account	1.9	2,639.0	2,445.4	7,546.7
Direct investment	982.9	516.6	841.5	2,526.1
Portfolio investment	–26.0	1,059.1	819.3	1,615.1
Other long-term capital	319.7	528.4	859.5	3,172.6
Short-term capital	–1,274.7	534.9	–74.9	232.9
Change in reserves (– indicates an increase)	80.1	–3,029.3	–2371.6	–7,458.1
Errors and omissions	223.1	–42.8	–363.6	1,359.8

Sources: SR, 1995 and Czech National Bank.

There are, however, possible limitations to the Czech strategy as adopted to date. These were indicated by the emergence of a $3.8 billion trade deficit in 1995. Although it is covered partly by a surplus on the invisibles account and partly by a substantial surplus on the capital account, as shown in Table 4.5, this deficit cannot be allowed to continue indefinitely. Figures for the whole of 1995 point to a current account deficit of $1.9 billion, including transactions in non-convertible currencies, balanced by a capital account surplus of $8.4 billion, compared with the current account surpluses in 1993 and 1994 and the much smaller capital account surpluses. Thus, the current account deficit did not appear as a cause for panic, not least because its appearance can be related to some extent to a revival of investment in modernization and restructuring which has been accompanied by a resumption in productivity growth, reaching 9 per cent in industry in 1995. For the whole economy, however, the figure is only 3 per cent, due to the influence of the rapidly growing share of the service sector which has experienced a lower rate of productivity growth.

Table 4.6 The predicted economic prospects of CEFTA countries in 1995 and 1996

	Czech Republic		Hungary		Poland		Slovakia	
	1995	1996	1995	1996	1995	1996	1995	1996
Real GDP rate of growth	4.8	5.4	1.1	2.5	7.0	5.5	7.4	6.0
Index 1989 = 100	85	89	85	87	99	104	84	87
Rate of inflation, annual average	9	9	28	22	28	20	10	8
Rate of unemployment, end of period	2.9	3.5	10	14	15	15	13	12

Sources: Pöschl, 1995, and Czech Statistical Office, estimates from May 1996.

Thus, despite the growing balance of trade deficit, there are still powerful arguments for policies aimed at achieving an acceleration in growth. Integration with the EU requires some equalization of economic levels, as well as rates of inflation and other macroeconomic indicators. A widely accepted view is that a rate of economic growth of at least 5–6 per cent annually will be necessary for the second half of 1990s. As was rightly recognized by Jeffrey Sachs, a renowned supporter of the stabilization policies adopted across east–central Europe, at the International Conference on Transformation and Investment in Prague in October 1994, only if this is achieved will the stabilization phase have proved itself in the long term. Current forecasts suggest that, for the next few years at least, this may just be achievable. As Table 4.6 indicates, the Vienna Institute for Comparative Economic Studies assumed that the rate of growth of GDP would be more than 5 per cent in 1995 and 1996 in the Czech Republic and the results for the first of those years confirmed the expected acceleration. There are, however, major uncertainties, with the possibility of both higher and lower figures. A crucial factor is whether the resources available in the economy for investment and growth can be utilized in the most effective way.

FINANCING INVESTMENT

All of the former CMEA countries have suffered from a weak investment climate. There were, however, clear signs of a change in the Czech Republic in 1994 when the investment rate, measured by the share of gross fixed capital formation in GDP, reached 30.0 per cent, climbing to 32.2 per cent in 1995. This is above the levels recorded in Hungary or Poland and substantially above the west European average, which fell to about 20 per cent in the 1980s. Nevertheless, even this relatively high rate of investment appears inadequate when set against estimates of the extent of reconstruction and modernization needed. Industry is 'undercapitalized' and unable to modernize plant and equipment rapidly without foreign capital inflows.

There is some scope for financing investment from new internal sources across east–central Europe. Wages have lagged even further behind than labour productivity, compared to EU members. Thus, GDP per worker in the Czech Republic is 40 per cent of the Austrian level, while for average wages the figure is about a third, measured in purchasing power parity. This difference creates one of the potential sources of internal savings and of a higher investment rate. It is, however, still only a potential. The figures in Table 4.7 are encouraging, suggesting that the revival in Czech economic growth from 1994 onwards was heavily dependent on investment growth. The expansion of private consumption, although still providing a substantial stimulus, was slipping into a supporting role.

Table 4.7 Annual percentage growth rates of components of GDP in the Czech Republic, 1993–1996

	1993	1994	1995	1996, forecast
Private consumption	2.9	5.3	6.4	7.0
Public consumption	–0.1	–2.3	–4.3	–2.0
Fixed capital formation	–7.7	17.3	16.1	14.6
Domestic effective demand	–0.8	6.9	7.2	7.8
Exports of goods and services	7.5	0.2	7.9	8.7
Aggregate effective demand	2.3	4.2	7.4	8.2
Imports of goods and services	10.4	7.8	19.2	11.8
GDP	–0.9	2.6	4.8	5.4

Source: Czech Statistical Office, estimates from May 1996.

This is an important and significant change, as private consumption had clearly been the driving force of growth in the preceding years. Its pre-eminence stemmed from a number of factors, some of which should be of lasting importance while some were only temporary. In the former category was the relatively high rate of increase of real wages after 1991, which have gradually been catching up with their pre-transformation level. Among one-off influences was the restructuring of total consumption in favour of its private part, at the expense of public consumption, which has fallen in real terms, and the boost to consumption following voucher privatization and restitution, whereby property was returned to pre-1948 owners. Small shareholders have sold about a third of their shares, often spending the money immediately, as do the restituents with their real estate.

Thus, the rate of growth in personal consumption can be expected to decline. Personal incomes are also unlikely to become a major source for the financing of investment. Published figures suggest that savings relative to disposable personal incomes reached 10–11 per cent in the Czech Republic in 1995, a figure similar to the German or Austrian level. This, however, depended on the inclusion of the proceeds from the sale of assets, such as shares acquired from voucher privatization and real estate derived from restitution. When these are excluded the savings rate is probably about 1–2 per cent.

There is more potential for financing investment from the non-financial enterprise sector, for which the rate of profitability measured as a percentage of costs reached 4.4 in 1995. There have, however, been complaints from the enterprise sector that the capitalization of these profits is limited by Corporation Tax of 43 per cent in 1994, albeit falling to 41 per cent in 1995 and 39 per cent for 1996. It has also been argued that the calculation of capital stock depreciation was not valorized after the price liberalization. This has had the effect of decreasing registered costs and increasing the volume of taxable profit. Thus, it can be argued, taxes are higher than they should be when set against the real costs of production.

A still more important problem is the distribution of profits between enterprises. This is strongly biased towards those which have been able to exploit their monopoly positions. That means particularly the energy sector. The emerging capital market is not functioning efficiently enough to allow reallocation of these resources into other sectors that desperately need them. The significance of the allocation problem becomes even clearer from figures derived from national accounts which point again to a relatively satisfactory level of domestic savings, reaching 24 per cent in 1995 compared with the long-term EU average of only 20 per cent.

As Table 4.8 indicates, this is far more important than foreign sources in providing resources for investment. The current account deficit in 1995 reached 4 per cent of GDP and this was the first year in which it could have provided a significant contribution to gross domestic capital formation. The predominance of domestic saving as a source could be seen as a guarantee of the sustainability of high economic growth rates, assuming that resources can be allocated into the right projects. The implication for policy would be the desirability of supporting long-term domestic and foreign capital at the expense of short-term capital.

Table 4.8 Gross domestic savings and gross capital formation in the Czech Republic, 1992–1995

	Gross capital formation	Balance of current account	Gross domestic savings	Gross domestic savings as percentage of GDP
1992	214.1	–8.6	205.5	26.0
1993	163.9	3.3	167.2	18.4
1994	213.0	–1.4	211.6	20.4
1995	338.9	–50.2	288.7	23.9

Note: All figures are in Kč billion, current prices, unless otherwise stated.

Source: Czech Statistical Office.

THE FOREIGN CAPITAL INFLOW

The net foreign capital inflow into the Czech Republic, at $3.0 billion in 1994, is the highest among the CEFTA countries. The gross inflow is greater in Hungary, but it is absorbed by debt service. The 1994 figure is equivalent to 8.4 per cent of GDP. This is an extraordinarily high figure, as can be indicated from a comparison with the peak years in Chile (8.1–10.6 per cent of GDP in 1990–92), Egypt (8.5 per cent in 1991) and Mexico (7.8–9.9 per cent in 1991–92). An even greater inflow was experienced in Thailand (12.6 per cent in 1991) and probably in the current period in Peru. The highest inflow in Spain — a European country with which the Czech Republic could reasonably be compared — was equivalent to only 3.8 per cent of GDP in 1987 and 1989. In 1995, the inflow into the Czech Republic reached $8.4 billion, an all-time world record proportion of GDP. Some comfort can, however, be drawn from the evidence in Table 4.5 of a welcome tendency in 1995 for the share of long-term capital to increase at the expense of short-term capital.

The most frequently cited factor encouraging the different forms of capital inflow is the stable political and macroeconomic environment, leading to the favourable investment rating of the Czech Republic. The authoritative business advisers Moody's and Standard and Poors have both set the Czech Republic clearly ahead of the other east–central European countries. A relatively well-educated, skilled and cheap labour force is also of great importance for foreign direct investment. For short-term capital, the undervalued exchange rate and the interest-rate differentials referred to below play a significant role. Part of the inflow is of an openly speculative nature, with 'hot money' estimated at nearly $2 billion, equivalent to slightly less than one-ninth of the total foreign exchange reserves.

The key open question is how far this capital inflow has been, or can be, used for modernization and restructuring in the Czech Republic. It is impossible to give an absolutely unequivocal answer, although it is clear that macroeconomic policies, aimed at holding in check credit creation as an anti-inflationary measure, could have operated against the productive use of at least a part of the resources available. Indeed, this appears as a clear case of a possible conflict between the continuing emphasis on anti-inflationary policies and the needs of a pro-growth policy. Policies aimed at credit restriction have succeeded in holding the growth in domestic credits close to the growth in nominal GDP since 1992, with a ratio of total credits to GDP of about 75 per cent, falling slightly below this level in 1995. This, however, has been achieved on the basis of nominal interest rates that remained about 13 per cent during 1994 and 1995, leading to a differential compared to the EU of about 5 per cent. Although real interest rates were not high, this, in the context of a stable nominal exchange rate, has created an obvious and strong incentive for the inflow of foreign speculative capital.

The government's reaction to this had the effect of further restricting the scope for banks to grant credits and in turn made it less likely that this part of the foreign capital inflow could find a productive use. Thus, in 1994 and 1995, sterilization policies were applied to curb the possible inflationary impact of the resulting expected money supply growth. Key elements were increases in interest rates and in compulsory minimum reserve levels for banks. The first of these, however, had the effect of increasing the incentive for speculative capital to move into the Czech Republic. Further measures were therefore adopted in August 1995 to regulate the acceptance of foreign obligations by commercial banks. The steps taken were not unusual for a country experiencing a sudden inflow of foreign capital, but their continuation into a second year is unusual. Their impact on the money supply is as yet uncertain. Figures point to growth in M_2 of 20.5 per cent in 1993, rising to 21.5 per cent in 1994 and falling slightly to 20.2 per cent in 1995. It is, however, far from clear that this is an important factor in domestic inflation, a topic discussed at the end of this chapter.

Table 4.9 Direct and portfolio investment and financial credits in 1994 and 1995 in convertible currencies, net increase in $billion

	Direct investments	Portfolio investments	Financial credits to enterprises
1994	0.84	0.82	1.40
1995	2.53	1.62	1.54

Source: Czech National Bank.

However, as Table 4.9 indicates, the largest element in the inflow was accounted for by direct financial credits to enterprises. It can be added that foreign direct investment has also been growing very rapidly, as discussed in Chapter 6. Thus, there is every likelihood that, despite the possible negative effects of sterilization policies, a substantial proportion of this inflow of financial capital is being transformed into an inflow of real productive capital. That would be consistent with the high rate of growth of fixed investments, within which the machinery and equipment category grew four times as rapidly as the construction category, together with the share of machinery in imports, reaching 35.6 per cent in 1995.

Nevertheless, open questions remain on the regulation of the capital inflow and on whether policies adopted to date are creating the best possible conditions for its productive utilization. There is also a continuing doubt over the adequacy of its volume. The net contribution of foreign direct investment and of long-term foreign financial credits to non-financial enterprises reached about one-tenth of gross fixed capital formation in 1994, increasing further during 1995. The incremental contribution was higher in 1994, reaching about 40 per cent, at the expense of domestic credits restricted by the sterilization policies. However, the inflow of foreign capital cannot be compared to the shifts of financial resources into eastern Germany. There is still a strong possibility that the Czech Republic will be left lagging behind the advanced countries of western Europe for a long time to come. This point can be amplified around the following discussion of exchange rate policy.

THE POLICY OF DEPRECIATION

All the countries of east–central Europe devalued their currencies early in the transformation. If stabilization policies are to be judged a success, then it should be possible to show that this has created an environment supporting a desirable restructuring of enterprises and of the economy generally. Some helpful comparisons can be made across east–central Europe, as there were differences in the extent to which the exchange rate was undervalued relative to its purchasing power parity. As Table 4.10 indicates, Czechoslovakia went the furthest, with an Exchange Rate Deviation Index (henceforth ERDI) reaching 2.9 on the basis of the US dollar, or 3.55 on the basis of the Austrian schilling or the German mark.

In the course of the first five years of transformation the nominal exchange rate of the Czechoslovak crown, or the Czech crown, has hardly changed at all, despite substantially more rapid inflation than in western Europe. As Table 4.10 shows, the currency experienced an average real appreciation against the US dollar of 3.4 per cent over the period 1991–1994, as indicated by the GDP deflator. A rapid increase in the Real Effective Exchange Rate (henceforth REER) occurred after price liberalization in the course of the first months of 1991, and further after a tax reform that introduced a value-added tax in early 1993. This increase in the REER, as indicated by consumer prices and the GDP deflator, continued into 1994, in which year it amounted to 10.5 per cent against the US dollar and 7.9 per cent against the German mark.

Table 4.10 The Exchange Rate Deviation Index and appreciation of currencies in the CEFTA countries 1990–1994 against the US dollar

	Exchange rate deviation index (ERDI)		Average annual rate of real effective exchange rate (REER) percentage growth
	1990	1994	
Czech Republic	2.9	2.54	3.4
Hungary	2.1	1.52	7.7
Poland	3.0	2.01	9.5
Slovakia	2.9	2.40	4.6

Sources: Calculated from Auer and Müller (1993), and Rittenau (1995).

Table 4.10 shows that the smallest initial undervaluation of the exchange rate across the CEFTA countries was in Hungary. That country also experienced rapid real appreciation in the period 1991–1994 with a 7.7 per cent annual average against the US dollar. Devaluations of the nominal exchange rate lagged substantially behind the inflation differentials over that period. Consequently, Hungary reached a relatively low deviation between the internal and external purchasing power of the forint in 1994, when the ERDI coefficient on the US dollar basis was 1.5. Thus, it was by then at the level of the less-developed west European market economies, such as Portugal when that country entered the EC in January 1985, and beneath the level of the least-developed OECD countries, such as Turkey.

Slovakia, together with the Czech Republic, finds itself at the opposite extreme. The REER in Slovakia increased at 4.6 per cent annually between 1990 and 1994 as a result of inflation differentials, partly compensated by a 10 per cent currency devaluation in July 1993. The ERDI was the second highest among the CEFTA countries in 1994, at 2.4 against the US dollar. This degree of undervaluation of the Slovak currency has contributed to a relatively successful export performance in 1994 and 1995.

Slovakia has been helped in comparison with the Czech Republic by other measures apart from the 1993 devaluation. The complex system for financing trade between the Czech and Slovak Republics, established at the time of the breakup of the federation, has enabled Slovakia to devalue its currency against the Czech crown alone. Slovakia has also adopted more openly protectionist measures, including the introduction of a surcharge on imports and various requirements for certificates for certain categories of imported goods. Its high rate of unemployment, as indicated in Table 4.5, has contributed to holding back the rate of inflation. Indeed, in 1995 the rate of inflation in consumer prices in the Slovak Republic, at 10.0 per cent, was surprisingly close to the Czech figure of 9.1 per cent.

Poland has been as successful with exports as the Slovak Republic. Its ERDI reached 2.0 to the US dollar in 1994, which was slightly below the level of the Czech Republic. In 1995, monthly devaluations of the nominal exchange rate of the złoty amounted to 1.2 per cent until July, when they were reduced to 1 per cent per month. Nevertheless, the rate of devaluation of the nominal exchange rate is less than the inflation differential, pointing to a real appreciation of the złoty.

In general, however, the setting of a heavily undervalued exchange rate cannot on its own ensure a desirable economic restructuring. In the Czech case it helped to maintain macroeconomic stability in the short run, making it possible to shift exports from eastern to western markets. A high 'monetary cushion' in the initial period of the transformation at the turn of the years 1990 and 1991 helped — together with the rapid cut in domestic demand — to establish equilibrium on the trade balance and even to create a considerable trade surplus of Kčs 25 billion in 1991, despite the need to reorient exports.

The longer-term implications are less favourable. The undervalued exchange rate supports and stimulates an export structure which is in conflict with the countries' long-term comparative advantage. Thus, it has been argued that Czech enterprises were 'spoiled' by the highly undervalued exchange rate at the beginning of the transformation. They were under little pressure to undertake investment-intensive modernization or deep changes in their production structures although, it should be added, the evidence in Chapter 6 points also to serious obstacles in the lack of finance.

Thus, an undesirable side-effect of the undervalued exchange rate is the increasing share in exports of raw materials and basic products alongside the declining share of machinery and equipment. While the share of the latter fell from 44 to 26 per cent between 1989 and 1995, the share of SITC groups 2–6, meaning raw materials, chemicals and semi-manufactures, grew to 54 per cent of total exports. That is the second highest share among CEFTA countries, behind only Slovakia, and well above the European average. In the case of more sophisticated consumer goods, machinery and equipment, and higher-quality components, price competitiveness generally plays a secondary role. Moreover, institutional barriers to foreign trade are also very strong, including the power of well-known trademarks, established distribution networks and internal trade between branches of multinational companies. Nevertheless, in order to exploit the existing industrial tradition and comparative advantage of a well-educated and skilled labour force, there will have to be a switch at some point towards exports of more sophisticated products.

However, comparisons of exchange-rate policies across east–central Europe do indicate the dangers in an approach of limiting devaluation. The most significant point to note is that Hungary was not successful in maintaining its relatively mild exchange-rate undervaluation. In March 1995, following balance of payments problems, the forint was devalued by 9 per cent, followed by monthly devaluations of 1.9 per cent until June and then by 1.3 per cent every month. Over 1995 as a whole, the extent of devaluation of the forint was very close to the inflation rate of 28 per cent. Hungary has accepted the need to counter a relatively serious external disequilibrium with more dramatic devaluations. The original 'Hungarian way' of a relatively small undervaluation of the exchange rate has proved impracticable. That, of course, does not mean that, especially when combined with other policies, a gradual revaluation of the Czech crown might not be desirable. It cannot, however, be achieved at once without an accompanying improvement in product quality to a level that would enable the Czech Republic to compete in much more than price-sensitive raw materials and similar products.

The Czech Republic, too, started to experience a balance of trade deficit from June 1994, as indicated in Table 4.5, and this can be related to the faster GDP growth rate and to the acceleration in the real appreciation of the Czech crown from 1994 to 1995. This led to considerable debate and indecision among Czech policy makers. They came under strong pressure from exporters for devaluation, although the general case against this in terms of longer-term structural changes has been made clear above. A partial single smaller devaluation was a possibility and could have brought short-term benefits, as shown by the experiences of Slovakia and Poland. The case, however, was weaker in the Czech Republic, partly because the surplus on the capital account, as shown in Table 4.5, pointed rather to a case for revaluation and partly because the Czech Republic has not been burdened with high unemployment that could justify immediate measures to stimulate exports.

The dilemma for policy makers was further complicated by the importance of the large deviation in price levels as a major contributory factor to Czech inflation. The final section in this chapter points to a number of factors that are likely to rule out a reduction of the rate of inflation below 6–7 per cent in the foreseeable future. Indeed, even to reduce the ERDI to 1.5 on the US dollar basis over approximately 10 years would require an annual rate of appreciation of the Czech crown of between 4 and 5 per cent. This could hardly be achieved by the inflation differential alone, as it implies a reduction in inflation before the changes in the ERDI that are themselves expected to influence the inflation level. There would, therefore, have to be some appreciation of the nominal exchange rate, the approach generally preferred by the IMF.

Revaluation, however, would have conflicted with the immediate interests of exporters, especially in view of the 1995 trade deficit. There were therefore strong arguments for a continuous moderate devaluation over the coming years. Amid the uncertainty and debate over how to proceed, the decision was taken to allow movements of up to 7.5% above or below a fixed nominal rate. The system came into operation on 28 February 1996 and the first months saw the rate generally close to the fixed nominal rate.

The dilemmas discussed here point to a further aspect in the relationship between stabilization and growth-promoting policies. A substantial revaluation, necessary for reducing the rate of inflation, would be incompatible with external equilibrium. It therefore presupposes the creation of a new and stronger export potential around those more sophisticated products that, thanks to the undervalued exchange rate, much of Czech industry may currently have little direct incentive to produce. The problem, then, cannot be resolved by exchange-rate policy alone.

The transition to a fully convertible Czech crown on the current account will show the demand for and the supply of the domestic currency more realistically and, should this lead to revaluation rather than devaluation might, as a side-effect, strengthen pressures for restructuring industrial production. Nevertheless, a failure to bridge the increase in currency value of their currencies with adequate improvements in quality and the technical level of products would ultimately lead to a stunted and partial transformation. The seriousness of this warning can be amplified by a more detailed account of how the exchange-rate regime has affected the development of foreign trade.

TRENDS IN FOREIGN TRADE

The most dramatic change in the foreign trade structure has been the reorientation towards new markets. The share of countries with a centrally-planned economy in the foreign trade turnover of the Czech Republic varied around two-thirds before the transformation. In 1995, 65 per cent of imports to the Czech Republic and 60 per cent of exports were accounted for by the developed market economies. Germany has now taken over the position previously held by the USSR as the main trading partner, accounting for 32 per cent of exports to, and 26 per cent of imports from, the Czech Republic in 1995.

There are, however, persistent traces of the autarky of the past. The export quota, calculated as the export of goods and services as a proportion of GDP, reached 52.4 per cent in the Czech Republic in 1994, which is considerably more than in the comparable small developed market economies. In Austria this share was 37.9 per cent in 1993. In Holland it was 50.6 per cent. Only in Belgium did it reach a higher figure of 68.7 per cent. There are, however, even larger differences in exports per capita, but in the opposite direction. Thus, the Austrian figure is four times, and the Belgian figure nearly ten times, the Czech level. However, as Table 4.11 indicates, the Czech and Slovak Republics stand out as the CEFTA countries with the highest level of exports, both per capita and in relation to GDP.

Table 4.11 Export quotas of the CEFTA countries in 1993

	Czech Republic	Slovak Republic	Hungary	Poland
Exports per capita in $	1,240	1,026	864	360
Imports per capita in $	1,219	1,186	1,214	440
Exports as percentage of imports	102	87	71	86
Exports CEFTA per capita = 100	197	163	137	57
Export quotas CEFTA = 100	141	142	133	66

Note: GDP figures are calculated by purchasing power parity as in Table 4.1.

Source: Calculated from Karasz, 1995.

The shift in commodity structure in individual countries is also strongly influenced by their past, as shown by comparisons across east–central Europe. All the countries have moved towards the less-processed and simpler products, meaning raw materials and semi-finished products. In light industry and in mechanical engineering, manufacturers have taken on simple tasks from western firms, often under short-term agreements. As discussed in Chapter 7, and as indicated in Table 4.12, the Czech Republic has maintained its strong

Table 4.12 The relative specialization of central and eastern European exports to the EU in 1993

	Bulgaria	Romania	Czech Republic	Slovakia	Hungary	Poland
Food & agriculture	182	47	45	32	174	109
Raw materials	49	96	122	193	4	130
Chemicals	135	52	118	123	120	80
Textile, clothing, leather	133	204	66	94	100	95
Wood, paper, glass	69	57	132	158	64	102
Metallurgy	82	59	113	164	70	109
Machinery	56	43	128	76	117	95

Note: Figures are percentages of the average for all countries listed.

Source: Lemoine, 1994.

representation in mechanical engineering, but its exports of raw materials are also high, surpassed only by Poland and Slovakia.

In the Czech case, the rate of growth of exports of goods reached an annual average level of about 11 per cent, using current prices, in the period 1991–94. The growth rates for imports were higher, averaging 14 per cent. In both cases there were large fluctuations in individual years. Since mid-1994, however, the rate of export growth has slowed down, falling to 10 per cent in 1995, while the growth in imports has accelerated, reaching 29 per cent in 1995, leading to the $3.8 billion trade deficit in 1995. As Table 4.5 shows, it is impossible to cover such a high deficit in the balance of payments with the surplus on services. It can only be covered with the substantial surplus on the capital account, emerging as a consequence of the inflow of foreign capital.

Table 4.13 Exports and imports of goods and services, 1991–1995

	1991	1992	1993	1994	1995
Current prices					
Exports	412.3	447.9	516.6	544.2	619.8
Imports	363.5	444.9	496.3	548.6	682.9
Net exports	48.8	3.0	20.3	–4.4	–63.1
Constant 1984 prices					
Exports	239.0	255.2	274.4	274.9	296.5
Imports	208.8	254.8	281.4	303.3	361.6
Net exports	30.2	0.4	–7.0	–28.4	–65.1

Note: All figures are in Kčs billion or Kč billion.

Source: Czech Statistical Office.

Tables 4.13 and 4.14 show the development of the trade balance and the rates of growth of exports and imports of goods and services, pointing to a widening gap between imports and exports since 1992.

The acceleration in imports follows the exhaustion of the effects of the devaluations and the dramatic restriction of domestic demand in 1991. Thus, the large surplus created in the first year of price liberalization was progressively whittled away, leading ultimately to the inevitable conversion of the surplus into a deficit. The gap between the growth of imports and exports is lower when expressed in current prices but, as Table 4.14 indicates, the trend is clear in both cases.

Table 4.14 The growth rates of exports and imports of goods and services, 1992–1995

	1992	1993	1994	1995	1992–5 average
Current prices					
Exports	8.6	15.3	5.3	13.9	10.7
Imports	22.4	11.6	10.5	24.5	17.0
Constant 1984 prices					
Exports	6.8	7.5	0.2	7.9	5.5
Imports	22.0	10.4	7.8	19.2	14.7

Source: As Table 4.12.

The most obvious explanation for the growing trade deficit is the economic recovery plus the real appreciation of the Czech crown, making imports cheaper and increasing the cost of exports. These causes are supplemented by a specific impulse from the foreign capital inflow which, as suggested in the previous section, was transformed predominantly into reserves in 1994, but in 1995 took the form of an increase in real capital and other real expenditures. These factors can be followed in some detail including, most obviously, the effects of the economic recovery.

The income elasticity of imports, meaning the increase in imports related to the increase in GDP, has been rising progressively with the acceleration of economic growth. This phenomenon is wellknown in market economies and was also true in the period of central planning. It is amplified by the accumulated demand for foreign goods which had previously not been available. Especially those with higher incomes are keen to buy more prestigious imported cars, which are claiming a greater share in the domestic market. There is a similar effect with delayed investment plans for modernization and the restructuring of production, but consumer goods are still the main component of import growth. That can easily be explained in the light of the minimal level of protection for the domestic market, apart from the weakening impact of the undervalued exchange rate. Moreover, there are determined efforts by foreign and multinational corporations to penetrate domestic markets, in which there is a preference for their goods, even when they are neither better nor cheaper.

Economic recovery also stimulates demand for domestically-produced goods. The pressure to export is thereby weakened. In some cases, exports had represented the sole possibility of sales after the drastic restriction of domestic consumer and investment demand in 1991. Now, however, domestic demand for goods of both 'long-term' and 'short-term' consumption has been recovering. Thanks to a combination of panic buying and hoarding in anticipation of price rises, and the reduction of disposable incomes that followed price liberalization in 1991, domestic sales of some products of light industry fell dramatically with, for example, footwear recording a 35 per cent fall in one year. The collapse was even greater for bed linen and household equipment. Disposable incomes grew every year after 1991, reaching rates of 6 per cent in real terms in 1993 and 7 per cent in 1994. Thus, domestic demand has been increasing, not least also because some purchases cannot be postponed any longer.

Exports probably have been held in check by the real increase in the value of the Czech crown. The exclusive reliance on an under-valued exchange rate must ultimately reach its limits. Exports based on price-elastic raw materials and semi-manufactured goods are restricted ultimately by the simple exhaustion of reserves. Their exploitation is also limited, albeit slightly less rigidly, by strengthening criteria for protection of the environment. It is impossible to rely permanently on exporting whole hills of basalt, such as the vanishing

Tlustec Hill in northern Bohemia, to western Europe. It is impossible indefinitely to transport wagon-loads of kaolin, which are in some cases deposited in disused German mines as a long-term reserve. Exports of cement and other building materials, the production of which can seriously damage the environment, ultimately find their limits. Nor can the country rely on raw-material and energy-intensive exports of steel.

The exhaustion of the possibilities for growth in exports of those items is a major factor slowing down overall export growth. If it is assumed that some sort of absolute limit is being approached, then that could help explain the reduction in export growth in 1995. It points again to the case for an export strategy, based on high-quality commodities with a longer-term perspective, although the problems of developing new products mean that this could not be seen as a short-term task.

THE ROOTS OF INFLATION

An analysis of the factors behind Czech inflation also points to the general conclusion that macroeconomic stabilization cannot be considered as an achievable objective without active steps to encourage a more general restructuring of the economy. The course of inflation in the transition period is given above in Tables 4.4 and 4.6. Since 1993, there have been no 'exceptional' influences, such as the general price liberalization of 1991 or the tax reform in January 1993 in which the introduction of value-added tax led to an 8.5 per cent jump in prices in one month. The annual rate of inflation, measured by the consumer price index, has since stabilized at about 9 per cent.

Progressive deregulation of prices in fuel, public transport and housing increases consumer prices by 1–2 per cent annually. Once the influence of price deregulations and the tax reform have been excluded, the underlying growth of consumer prices has been stable in the Czech Republic in the last four years and is less than 8 per cent annually. Inflation among western European neighbours has decreased significantly to about 2.5 per cent in the last few years. The inflation differential therefore remains a clear indicator of a divergence from the economic behaviour of the developed market economies.

Nevertheless, the gap between the domestic and world price levels remains high and the ERDI, estimated at 2.2 in relation to the US dollar in 1995, remains one of the main sources of the higher domestic inflation. As argued above, the appropriate time for dampening inflationary pressures through a revaluation has been missed and the best hope now would be for a gradual reduction in the gap in price levels over a ten-year period. Even that assumes an improvement in product quality, without which it would appear difficult to reduce the ERDI and hence the inflation differential.

Another important source of a higher rate of inflation is the continuing gradual process of prices on newly-created markets moving towards their world levels. This is most visible still with prices of factors of production, such as wages, amortization of tangible investment property and the prices of different categories of land. A market for housing is also yet to take firm shape. A part of the previous price distortions is being removed by price deregulation, including the ending of wage regulation in July 1995. This adaptation process involves increases in some prices and is not fully compensated by a slower growth in others. The net effect is therefore to increase the overall price level in relation to the world level.

Inflationary expectations, incorporated into wage trends and into producers' prices, are another important factor preventing speedy harmonization with the average rate of inflation in EU countries. The Hungarian and Polish experiences, where the rates of inflation seem stuck close to 30 per cent, seem to confirm this. The gradualist nature of the reform in Hungary carried forward inflationary expectations formed in the 1980s. There was also, for a time at least, a lack of faith in the stability of the currency. The Czech and Slovak Republics were in a more favourable position in this respect, thanks to the firm progress of the transformation and to the rapid establishment of faith in the stability of the currency. Nevertheless, an increase in the price level of 9 per cent has now been established as a stable expectation in the Czech case. It is taken into account by both trade unions and employers when setting wage increases. It would, therefore, be unrealistic to expect an annual decrease in the rate of inflation of more than 0.5 to 1 percentage points over the coming years.

The rate of inflation in the Czech Republic is now very near to that of Greece and only double the Spanish and Portuguese levels. Nevertheless, the gradual equalization of price levels is likely to occur with a domestic rate of inflation at least three times the average rate in the EU countries, with no realistic hopes for a decline to less than twice their level. It will be very difficult for the Czech Republic to fulfil the original criteria of the Maastricht Agreement, notwithstanding the fact that its rate of inflation is the lowest of all the east–central European countries.

The general conclusion is that the stabilization policies adopted in east–central Europe, despite some significant differences in the details of the measures and in their precise impact, have not created a macroeconomic environment familiar in the more advanced countries of the European Union. There continues to be higher inflation, exchange-rate weakness and the persistent threat of balance of payments difficulties. Growth has been resumed, but its foundations cannot be considered fully secure. The Czech Republic, thanks to more favourable starting conditions and possibly also the consistency with which policies have been pursued, may have a more stable base than others in the region. Nevertheless, the case seems strong even there for combining macroeconomic policy measures with appropriate intervention at the micro- level to ensure an improvement in productivity and the quality of products. Without that, the benefits so far reaped from stabilization measures may themselves increasingly come under threat.

5. An Incomplete Transformation?

All the radical reform steps have now been taken. The transformation will now continue with the further development of the model into a fully functioning market economy. (Josef Tošovský, Governor of the Czech National Bank, 18 November 1993)

We are hearing from a number of sides, both at home and abroad, that the macroeconomic results of the transformation process in the Czech Republic are good. We hear, however, that the situation is different and adaptation slow at the level of the enterprises or at the microeconomic level. There are phenomena like excessive indebtedness, over-employment and the like. There are then claims that a microeconomic, or if you like structural, or even industrial policy is needed. Each of the critics who uses these terms defines them as they wish and then puts the argument that this or that government policy is needed. (Karel Dyba, Minister for the Economy, *Hospodářské noviny*, 17 March 1995)

These two quotations introduce the themes for this chapter. On the one hand, Josef Tošovský was putting the view as long ago as 1993 that the key reform measures had been implemented. The implication, as frequently emphasized by Czech Prime Minister Václav Klaus, was that the hardest part of the systemic transformation had already taken place. This has obvious attractions for politicians wishing to impress both a domestic and a foreign audience, with the latter particularly relevant to enhancing the prospects of early admission into the European Union. It also, as the quotation from Karel Dyba suggests, can play a role in policy debates. If the economic transformation has been broadly successful, then there is no need for new policies. The approach, based on little more than macroeconomic stabilization and privatization, would seem to have been successful. Calls for a coherent industrial policy can, therefore, be dismissed as efforts by powerful lobbies to gain softer conditions for themselves, just as they did under central planning.

This chapter pursues these issues around the question of whether the Czech transformation really can be considered 'complete'. It centres on five key areas: the broad sectoral structure, the changing organizational forms of business activity, the transformation of ownership, the reorientation of foreign trade and the shifting geographical location of economic activities. The conclusion is that a massive change has taken place since 1989. It is, however, clear that the process is, in a number of key respects, distinct from the changes that have taken place over recent decades in western Europe. The Czech economy today, at least in terms of these indicators, still retains strong imprints from its past. It is in the midst of a long and complex transformation that cannot yet be considered complete. The policy implications of this can only be touched on at the end of the chapter.

Each of the five areas allows for some comparison with western European economies. Thus, the shift in employment away from manufacturing towards services has been a general trend across advanced market economies since the 1960s. It was delayed in east–central Europe during a long period of structural stagnation, after the industrial structure, with its strong emphasis on heavy and extractive industries, had taken shape in the 1950s and 1960s. It would, therefore, be encouraging to find a process of very rapid change in broad sectoral structures with east–central Europe moving quickly towards the western European pattern.

Changes in organizational structure and in ownership, meaning above all the twin processes of privatization and the emergence of new enterprises, clearly appear as a movement towards a more familiar western European pattern. There are, however, signs again of an 'incomplete' transformation, both in terms of the role of new owners in larger privatized enterprises and in the nature of the newly-emergent small firms. Similarly, both the reorientation of trade and the shifting geographical pattern of economic activity show similarities to, but also differences from, analogous trends in western Europe. The specificity of these processes needs to be understood before a definite conclusion can be reached on the appropriateness or otherwise of any industrial policies to which Karel Dyba was referring in the quotation above.

THE NEW SERVICE SECTOR

Table 5.1, showing the changes in the broad sectoral structure of the economy, would seem to confirm expectations of a very rapid process of 'catching up' with advanced market economies. The figures for Slovakia show that the Czech Republic is by no means an exceptional case. Indeed, when put into a crude comparative perspective, both parts of the former Czechoslovakia could be said to have jumped from a structure similar to West Germany in the early 1960s to one remarkably similar to that country in 1983 — 5.4 per cent in agriculture, 41.1 per cent in industry and construction — in the course of six years.

Table 5.1 Comparisons of percentage shares in employment in main economic sectors

	Czech Republic		Slovakia		Germany		United Kingdom
	1989	1995	1989	1995	1989	1992	1992
Agriculture	11.1	5.3	15.0	9.1	3.9	3.7	2.2
Industry and construction	47.4	41.9	44.0	38.8	40.2	39.1	30.2
Services	41.5	52.8	41.0	52.1	56.0	57.2	67.5

Note: The standard ILO definitions apply for all figures. German figures refer to West Germany only in 1989.

Sources: SR, 1994, *Bulletin ČSÚ*, 1994, No. 12, and Eurostat, *Labour Force Survey*, 1989 and 1992.

The service sector is, of course, very diverse, as are the reasons behind its expansion in advanced market economies. Table 5.2 gives some indication of the fortunes of its different parts. Some can become a major earner of outside revenue, as in the case of finance in the UK. Others are dependent on growth in demand from other parts of the domestic economy. In the Czech case, the dominant factor appears to have been expansion of small-scale personal services, such as retail trade, repair and catering. The implication of evidence later in this chapter on the growth of new small businesses is that most of this expansion should be seen as a process of catching up from a low base level rather than a response to any post-1989 rise in living standards. Living standards were already adequate to justify a larger service sector, but its growth had been stifled under central planning. Any further expansion is likely to be more gradual.

Table 5.2 Comparisons of percentage shares in total employment in subdivisions of the service sector

	Czech Republic		Slovakia	Germany	United Kingdom
	1990	1995	1995	1992	1995
Trade, repair	9.8	12.7	10.5	16.3	16.7
Hotels, catering	1.7	3.2	2.7	*	5.9
Transport, storage, communication	6.9	7.7	7.6	6.1	6.0
Finance and insurance	0.5	1.9	1.4	8.1	4.4
Property, research, enterprise services	7.1	4.9	4.5	*	12.3
Public administration, defence	1.8	5.2	6.3	8.7	6.2
Education	5.9	6.3	7.9	18.1	8.4
Health	5.2	6.0	6.8	*	11.3
Other services	3.8	3.6	4.3	*	4.6

Note: The growth in the public administration category in the Czech Republic after 1990 followed the exclusion of officials of federal agencies from earlier figures for the Czech Republic. * Included in the category above.

Sources: As Table 5.1, plus *Annual Abstract of Statistics*, 1996.

Table 5.2 also points to a growth in some services for businesses, such as finance, but a decline for the category including property, research and services to enterprises. The principal reason was the decline in research while the other categories have grown, reflecting the demands of a developing market economy. Comparisons with Germany and the UK could imply potential for further growth here. It is, however, unlikely that they will become major export sectors, although some foreign currency earnings have already come into Czech consultancy firms.

The full significance of the change that has taken place here can be amplified with reference to changes in the overall level of employment. The remarkable feature of the Czech transformation has been the extraordinarily low level of unemployment, at about 3 per cent, stimulating the accusations referred to in the quotation from Karel Dyba at the start of the chapter of a stunted transformation with enterprises refusing to shed surplus labour. The evidence in this section goes some way towards refuting those fears by pointing to the mobility of labour between broad sectors. Table 5.3 sets this in the context of the relative stability of overall employment levels, showing that the Czech working population of productive age was higher in 1995 than in 1989.

There had been job losses, especially in agriculture and some sectors of industry, but much of the brunt of this was borne by working pensioners. Even the proportion of women in the labour force remained remarkably stable, at exactly 45.8 per cent in both 1989 and 1995. Thus, the massive job shedding in some sectors was fully made good by rapid expansion in others. The comparison with Slovakia indicates that this is not typical across east–central Europe — the Slovak figures are more in line with those from other countries — but the Czech specificity is clearly due to the rapid creation of new jobs rather than to a delayed process of job loss in declining sectors.

Indeed, figures from labour force surveys point to a high level of labour mobility in the Czech case. In mid-1995, only 43 per cent of the workforce had been in the same job for five years. The lowest figure in any region was 35 per cent, in Prague, while the highest was 49 per cent in North Moravia. There was clearly considerable mobility even over shorter time periods, with 15 per cent holding the same permanent job for one year or less — compared with figures of 13 and 11 per cent in the UK in 1989 and 1991 — while 8 per cent were on temporary contracts.

Table 5.3 The Czech and Slovak labour forces

	Czech Republic		Slovakia	
	1989	1995	1989	1995
Working population of productive age	4,660	4,850	2,247	2,159
Working pensioners	518	240	194	49
Registered unemployed		190		327
Population of productive age	5,996	6,292	3,027	3,195
Working population of productive age as percentage of population of productive age, unemployed excluded	77.8	77.1	74.2	67.6
Unemployed included	77.8	80.1	74.2	77.8

Note: Figures are in thousands unless otherwise stated.

Sources: SR, 1991, and *Czech and Slovak Labour Force Surveys.*

NEW AND OLD FIRMS

This shift towards the service sector has been accompanied by enormous changes in the organizational structure of the economy, reflecting changes within the state sector, privatization of parts or all of state enterprises and the growth of new private firms. Figures for 1989 showed 65,202 individuals with the right to undertake private business activity, 430 state-owned industrial enterprises, 1,024 agricultural cooperatives, 290 other cooperatives and 2,600 other kinds of organization operating in the Czech economy. Table 5.4 shows the changes in the size of industrial enterprises while Table 5.5 shows the changes in the organizational forms of economic units.

There are two striking features. The first is the appearance of small and medium-sized industrial enterprises, although that should not be exaggerated. In 1989, 94 per cent of industrial employment was in enterprises with more than 1,000 employees. The comparable figure was still 59 per cent in 1993 and 50 per cent in 1995. The old structures had not been wiped out in total and the enterprises that had dominated the Czech economy before 1989 were still there, albeit in reduced size, and still playing important roles.

Table 5.4 Size structure of Czech industrial enterprises

Average employment	1989	1990	1992	1994
25–100	na	na	na	1,801
101–500	48	459	1,765	1,608
501–1,000	84	207	299	337
1,001–2,500	175	250	245	176 (–2,000)
2,501–5,000	74	74	79	108 (2,001+)
5,000+	49	29	28	
Total	430	1019	2,416	4,024

Sources: SR, 1990, 1993 and 1995.

This is a clear point of contrast with the east German experience, and may have important implications for the future. Thus the giant Škoda–Plzeň heavy engineering combine, which had employed more than 45,000 in the early 1980s, faced a collapse in its markets and possible extermination. The government, with a general commitment to maintaining the core of the economy inherited from the communist past, was actively involved in finding a solution. Škoda–Plzeň, with slightly fewer than 19,000 employees at the end of 1995, has re-emerged as a powerful force in the Czech economy, regaining export markets, acquiring other Czech companies and expanding its operations abroad with joint ventures or subsidiaries in Russia, the USA, Germany and China. One of the key questions for industrial policy is whether these survivals from the past should be regarded as a bonus or rejected as an irrelevance, or even as so much ballast to be swept aside to allow for a completely new start.

The second striking feature is the appearance and growth of very small enterprises. There are, however, difficulties in interpreting the significance of the 'individual entrepreneurs' category. The published figures show the number of individuals who have received permission to undertake a certain specified form of business activity, but by no means all have taken up the opportunity and even for those that have, this need not be the principal source of income. This, then, is very much a feature of a specific legal framework, making an international comparison possible only with Slovakia.

Table 5.5 Forms of business organization in the Czech economy

	end 1990	end 1991	end 1994
State enterprises	2,945	3,760	1,522
Commercial companies	3,034	25,522	88,424
Cooperatives	2,856	4,070	5,226
Individual entrepreneurs	310,653	902,797	846,285
Individual farmers	127	7,533	91,936
Others	17,219	26,750	85,141
Total	336,834	97,0432	1,118,534

Sources: SR, 1991 and 1992, and *Bulletin ČSÚ*, 1994, No. 12.

The figures in Table 5.5 point to very rapid growth into 1991 followed by stagnation at a level equivalent to about 10 per cent of the population, or 20 per cent of the labour force. Slovakia experienced a somewhat more gradual growth, leading to a total equivalent to about 6 per cent of the population. Figures for individual districts — of which there are 76 in the Czech Republic and 38 in Slovakia with an average population of 137,000 — point to some variations in density across the Czech Republic, with the percentage of individual entrepreneurs per capita varying from about 16 in Prague to about 7 in some rural or mining districts. In Slovakia the range is from more than 9 in Bratislava, a figure itself less than the Czech average, to barely 3 in many more remote rural, and some industrial, areas. Regressions, however, show no strong relationship in either republic between individual entrepreneurs and unemployment. Nor is there a significant relationship to likely stimulants on the demand side, such as retail spending or tourist activity. In the Czech Republic the only clear conclusion is that the density is high in Prague and low in mining areas (Myant, 1994).

Figures on the sectoral distribution of individual entrepreneurs show broadly similar patterns across the two republics, with manufacturing, construction, trade and repair and property services and consultancy each accounting for about 20 per cent. Figures at the district level relate only to the total number of individual entrepreneurs. There could be substantial variations between districts in the kinds of activity undertaken, but limited available evidence does not confirm this, with the exception of the unique case of Prague, which is referred to below.

Some alternative sources, while not providing so detailed a geographical breakdown, indicate how many entrepreneurs are self-employed and how many also have additional employees. Thus, the 1992 household survey showed 6.1 per cent of all Czech and 3.7 per cent of Slovak households dependent on entrepreneurship as their principal source of income. This corresponds to roughly half those registered as entrepreneurs. More recent labour force survey data confirm this figure, although the proportion seems to have been rising slowly, despite a stagnation in the number of registered entrepreneurs. Nevertheless, the figures in Table 5.6 showing the relatively small proportion of entrepreneurs with an employee, would seem to confirm that these are mostly very small businesses. There is strong evidence that they are very severely limited by the lack of access to sources of finance, meaning that the small business sector is largely restricted to activities which need little startup capital (Myant, 1994).

The figures in Table 5.6 also point to a similar geographical distribution to that indicated by the figures on registered entrepreneurs and to a similar contrast with Slovakia. Again, the highest density is to be found in Prague, with the lowest level in the Czech Republic in the mining area of North Moravia, although that is still above the average for Slovakia as a whole. Even the breakdown by activities is very similar, with Prague particularly well represented in property and consultancy services, construction, transport and, to a much lesser extent, consumer-oriented services. The clear implication is that Prague should be considered as a quite special case. Across the rest of the country, much of the initial growth in self-employment reflected the emergence of small-scale personal services to satisfy pre-established demand levels. It is, however, unclear whether the relatively small variations between districts should be related to different demand conditions or to some other factors that may have better-equipped individuals in certain areas for initiating and undertaking entrepreneurial activity.

Table 5.6 Czech self-employed as a percentage of total employed labour force

	Czech Republic		Prague	North Moravia	Slovakia
	1993	1995	1995	1995	1995
Self-employed with no employee	6.8	7.5	11.7	5.7	4.4
Self-employed with one or more employee	2.7	3.8	4.6	3.2	2.0
Total	9.5	11.3	16.3	8.9	6.4

Source: Czech and Slovak Labour Force Surveys.

Indeed, it appears possible that high levels of demand, rather than stimulating larger numbers of entrepreneurs to appear, may be reflected in higher incomes per entrepreneur. This at least is hinted at from household survey figures from various years, used in Table 5.7 to show how income inequality has been influenced by individual enterprise. Up to 1992, it had made no significant difference to the pattern of Slovak inequality. Individual enterprise was undertaken by people on very low incomes with very small returns, to broadly the same extent as it was undertaken for large sums by individuals with higher incomes. In many cases, then, private enterprise was probably a response to poverty and unemployment. In the Czech Republic,

Table 5.7 Percentile distribution of per capita incomes of households measured as percentage of median

	Slovakia				Czech Republic			
	1980	1988	1992	1992	1980	1988	1992	1992
10 per cent	58.3	62.7	64.5	64.8	59.2	64.2	67.7	70.0
25 per cent	76.4	79.0	80.3	80.5	75.8	78.0	80.1	82.5
75 per cent	131.2	130.1	121.5	121.0	134.3	132.8	127.1	126.1
90 per cent	170.0	165.0	149.7	147.7	172.0	168.1	170.1	163.4
95 per cent	193.0	189.5	175.3	172.5	187.8	—	208.0	198.4

Note: The second set of 1992 figures excludes income from entrepreneurship.

Sources: Calculated from household surveys, 1980, 1988, 1992, from *HSR*, *SR*, 1994, and Štatistický úrad Slovenskej republiky, 1994.

however, earnings from enterprise have been one of the factors increasing inequalities during the 1990s. It can be added that 13 per cent of the top 5 per cent in Slovakia were entrepreneurs, compared with 23 per cent in the Czech Republic.

Further international comparisons can put this in a slightly different perspective. The rate of self-employment in Poland is very much higher because of its exceptionally strong representation in agriculture, a sector which in the Czech and Slovak cases is dominated by enterprises that have grown out of the former agricultural cooperatives. Even excluding agriculture, the self-employed in Poland increased from 4.9 per cent of the labour force in 1989 to 10.8 per cent in 1992 and 11.2 per cent in 1994. Thus, growth in numbers was somewhat slower than in the Czech case, suggesting that there may have been a slower pace of new job creation. There is also a stronger indication of an end to expansion.

This still leaves open the explanation for the difference in entrepreneurial activity between the Czech and Slovak Republics, which started from a very similar base in 1989. This could help explain the extent of new job creation in the Czech case. The most obvious is the direct stimulus from tourist demand, although district data suggests that that accounts for relatively little. It would have to be postulated that the impact of tourist spending was somehow spread beyond the main tourist centres. There could also be a stimulus to enterprise-oriented services and to small construction firms from the needs of a faster pace of systemic transformation and from a higher level of economic activity which, of course, could be partly stimulated by tourist activity. There could be institutional differences, for example in the availability of credit, but no evidence supports that. A final explanation is a different 'enterprise culture' in the two republics. That notion is notoriously difficult to define, let alone measure (Burrows, 1991), but it is a popular explanation that can be linked to an account of state-led Slovak economic development in the post-war period. A reservation is that this is not supported by evidence from opinion polls, which show just as many Slovaks as Czechs wanting to set up a business (*Lidové noviny*, 18 June 1992).

Despite this, there are a number of clear limitations to the process whereby these new, small firms have emerged in the Czech Republic. Above all, they have had to get by with extremely limited capital, with banks generally heavily committed with loans to larger enterprises. The author of one survey conducted in the spring of 1993, having confirmed the extreme difficulty of obtaining any outside finance, concluded that access to funds often depended on 'exceptional favours' from bank officials (Hálek, 1993).

There have been cases of growth beyond the scale of a small entrepreneur, but the more typical case is of an extremely small business. A telephone and a desk are often enough to set up a travel agency, while some chairs and tables in a garden are enough to set up a pub in the summer months. These 'firms' can exist in a very specific situation in which the service sector was historically very weak and has yet to be dominated by larger corporations. Their fate must be uncertain as larger firms enter the field. In the meantime, of course, they provide the benefits of a broadening of service provision alongside considerable job opportunities.

THE SUCCESS OF PRIVATIZATION

Privatization has been proclaimed as the great success story of the Czech transformation, putting the country ahead of others in east–central Europe and backing up claims to have achieved a modern market economic structure. Raw figures can certainly look impressive. The non-state sector accounted in 1994 for 56.9 per cent of industrial output, 90.2 per cent of construction output and 86.4 per cent of retail trade, encouraging leading government figures to claim that about 60 per cent of GDP was coming from the non-state sector.

This was more than the 52.2 per cent claimed for Poland at the time, with all firms included that had a majority private ownership. There are, however, two reservations to Czech claims. The first is that a significant proportion of the enterprises included were still not fully privatized. The 60 per cent figure depended on including the state's share in enterprises that had been converted into joint-stock companies and transferred to the National Property Fund, the body administering the transfer of state assets into the private sector, but not yet transferred into full private ownership. National Property Fund officials have in fact accepted that they are still many years away from completing their task.

The second, and more crucial, reservation is that privatization has not necessarily transformed the behaviour of enterprises into that desired for a successful market economy. In some cases, particularly where a large foreign share is concerned, changes have often been substantial. In those where privatization relied heavily on the voucher method, the situation is less clear. This section, therefore, outlines how voucher privatization operated, leading to an assessment of its results. Similar conclusions are reached from somewhat different evidence in Chapter 6.

The voucher method was the one most clearly in harmony with the dominant underlying assumption behind Czechoslovak, and subsequently Czech, government policy. This was the familiar neoliberal view that a private firm is more efficient than a state-owned firm primarily because, and in so far as, an identifiable, 'active' owner can keep a check on management and weed out inefficiency. This, it should be added, was not the only thinking that played a role in shaping privatization policy for larger enterprises. Some key firms were transferred in part or in whole to foreign ownership. The most important early example was the sale of ultimately a controlling share in the Škoda car manufacturer to Volkswagen. The thinking there was that managerial expertise, new technology, finance for investment and access to a sales network would help overcome the enterprise's business problems and lead to the spread of good management practice through a large part of the engineering industry (Myant, 1993). There was much more to this than the simple view derived from neoclassical, or even more clearly neoliberal, economic theory that owners exert pressure on managers. There was an acceptance that expertise and finance are necessary preconditions for Czech enterprises to adapt to the modern market environment.

Nevertheless, the core of the Czechoslovak privatization policy was the voucher method, and this accounted for 64 per cent of the value of assets in joint-stock companies transferred out of state ownership up to mid-1995. It clearly dominated over alternative methods such as direct sale to domestic or foreign owners, meaning that the 'typical' larger Czech privatized company is under the majority ownership of former voucher holders.

The method had overwhelming attractions for those who believed that simply finding private rather than state owners was the key aim. It was not difficult to prove that, in view of the limited level of domestic savings, the 'standard' method of selling shares to the public would be exceedingly slow. Thus, from early 1990, Václav Klaus, then Minister of Finance in the federal government, started to suggest schemes whereby each citizen would receive a number of voucher points which could then be exchanged for shares, enabling the speediest possible transfer of state property into private hands. Apart from, in his view, creating the essential precondition for economic efficiency, he was impressed by the likely political impact of involving much of the population in benefiting directly from the privatization process.

Voucher privatization was carried through in two waves. In the first, shares in 1,491 enterprises — 943 Czech, 487 Slovak and 61 federal — were on offer, equivalent to 12 per cent of the country's fixed assets. The detailed preparations reflected a recognition on the part of the scheme's architects of the need to water down some of the original conceptions. Instead of simply offering shares in all existing businesses, enterprises were required to work out their own privatization plans, which could include reorganization, total or partial sale to a foreign firm, partial or total sale for vouchers, sale by auction or direct sale to a named buyer of all or part of the business. Any other party could also present a proposal, and many individuals and groups did so. The newly-established Ministry for Privatization had time only for a very superficial look at each project before reaching a decision, and made no serious effort to assess the viability of alternative business plans. In practice, the conceptions put forward by managements generally dominated the outcome.

Public participation in the scheme depended on citizens buying voucher books for the nominal fee of Kčs 1,000. When these books first went on sale in the autumn of 1991, there was only limited interest. The big change came in early 1992 with the appearance of investment privatization funds. The original privatization law had made a small reference to the possibility of such bodies, in which citizens could invest their voucher points. The fund, with its investors as shareholders, would then invest their voucher points.

The success of the funds followed an offer by one to pay Kčs 10,350 at a set future date to any investor who subsequently wanted to withdraw. In the end, nearly 77 per cent of the adult population bought voucher books and 70 per cent of all points were invested through a total of 264 funds. During the spring of 1992, bidding took place in successive rounds for shares. For those with a strong excess demand, the price was increased in the following round. For those with excess supply, the price was reduced. After five rounds, 92.8 per cent of shares set for this first wave had been sold. Shares were in the hands of the public on 24 May 1993, after which they could be traded.

For the second wave, 861 Czech enterprises were on offer, amounting to about 5 per cent of total fixed assets. Bidding started on 12 April 1994, with 74 per cent of the adult population taking part. One hundred and ninety-five investment privatization funds from the first wave sought to attract voucher points, alongside a further 158 investment funds which offered only a share in profits and no rights as shareholders in the fund. After six rounds of bidding, 96.3 per cent of property on offer had been allocated, with 70 per cent to various kinds of investment funds. Shares were distributed in March 1995. With this, voucher privatization ended, although a number of major enterprises in transport, utilities and parts of manufacturing remained in state hands. Another 28 per cent of the shares in joint-stock companies was still in the hands of the National Property Fund in mid-1995. Thus, privatization was clearly not over, although it was to continue by the 'standard' method of selling shares. Eventually, then, shares distributed by the voucher method should be in the minority.

The decision not to press ahead with a third wave has been surrounded by minimal controversy. It could be seen as an implicit recognition from within the government that there are serious drawbacks to the voucher method. In fact, the whole idea of vouchers was surrounded by controversy from the very start. It had been advocated in Poland before its adoption in Czechoslovakia, but governments there shied away from its speedy implementation, eventually adopting a substantially more cautious method. Hungarian governments gave a firmer rejection, although voucher privatization was never far from the agenda, at least for discussion. In Slovakia, the 'second wave' has still to take place. In the Czech Republic, Miloš Zeman, the chairman of the Social Democratic Party and hence of the most influential opposition force, used to describe voucher privatization as 'the fraud of the century', even adding that the Czech Republic may be 'the first state that has succeeded in almost completely robbing itself' (*Práce*, 5 April 1993).

There was a great deal of serious debate in Czechoslovakia during 1990, and many of the same points have resurfaced in discussions across east–central Europe in subsequent years. In general terms, the most persistent themes have included a refusal to believe that private ownership alone, without an accompanying industrial policy and without reference to who the private owner was to be, would be enough. There was also a deep suspicion towards this new and untried method which, by giving access to shares to the whole adult population, was clearly not creating the structure of a 'typical' market economy. The most important practical points can be summarized around five key themes.

The first relates to the danger of instability at the macroeconomic level. Citizens, presented with the windfall gain of shares, might sell them quickly, strengthening inflationary pressures or harming the balance of payments in so far as they bought imported goods. In practice, despite estimates that about a third of owners have sold all their shares from the first wave, this has not led to excessive inflationary pressures. As discussed in Chapter 4, the sources of inflation are not primarily to be found on the demand side. The extra purchasing power probably has contributed to the growth in imports but again, for reasons explained in Chapter 4, this has not yet become a serious threat to the economy.

The second theme relates to the danger that, while creating formal private ownership, this form of privatization would not lead to the emergence of a functioning capital market without which many of the benefits of private ownership would not be felt. Thus, for example, share prices would be depressed by the rush to sell, thereby making it practically impossible to raise finance by new share flotations. There are problems in following share prices, as many are sold outside any formal system. It is, however, clear that prices on the formal systems have tended to fall since trading started in May 1993, with the index down from 1,000 to less than 600 by March 1995, then falling towards 400 after shares from the second voucher wave went on sale.

There have been a few cases of share price rises, including a few banks and energy suppliers which have attracted foreign portfolio investors, but most share values have fallen, with some worth less than 10 per cent of valuation at the start of the voucher privatization process. It therefore does seem safe to conclude that new share flotations offer poor prospects for raising finance for investment. In this respect, something is missing from a fully-formed modern market economy.

The third theme relates to the difficulty of conceiving of voucher privatization leading to the emergence of 'active' owners. Power would be dispersed among huge numbers of individuals, meaning that management would be even less controllable than in the past. In practice, dispersion of ownership has been mitigated by the position of the investment funds. Although this was somewhat attenuated until early 1996 by a rule that prevented any single fund from holding more than a 20 per cent share in any enterprise, there were cases of funds clubbing together to gain full control over firms. In general, however, research does not confirm claims of an active role (Klvačová, 1994 and 1995; Hejkal, 1994; Oswald, 1994). When questioned on whether they are involved in improving management, a number always respond positively, or reply that they invested so wisely in the first place that there was no need to do anything. They are, however, far less convincing when asked to specify exactly what they have done.

Investigations have pointed to a possible division into broadly three types of funds. The first, set up by large banks, may have shares in several hundred firms and representatives on many boards: with the same representative on possibly up to 40 companies, their active role is very small. A second group have aimed to achieve a 20 per cent share in a small number of companies, and this may lie behind much of the share dealing that has taken place. Even they, however, lack the expertise to influence managements. A third group are interested only in taking the 2 per cent commission allowed by law for fund managers.

Moreover, even in those cases where funds have played an active role in shifting enterprise strategy, they have tended to press for the immediate payment of dividends rather than devoting resources to higher wages or to investment. This could reflect the desire of funds to keep their own shareholders happy, although they, too, should have little reason to fear so dispersed and fragmented a group. It is, however, worth repeating that their influence must be small, as real wages have been rising steadily from 1992 onwards and the over-whelming majority of enterprises were reported to be paying no dividends in 1995. The conclusion would therefore seem to be that active owners have not emerged and the existing management has remained dominant. This, of course, could be judged very positively as, despite neoliberal thinking, there are powerful arguments — for example, in the historical studies by Chandler (1990) — that business success in a large firm depends more on good, expert management with considerable freedom to develop a long-term conception of the firm's strategy rather than on meddling by owners with very little knowledge of the business. That view is supported by the discussion in Chapter 6.

The fourth theme in the debates over voucher privatization is an argument that it would make the task of restructuring inefficient enterprises more difficult. A number of reasons have been quoted. It would miss an opportunity to raise finance that could be used for investment and modernization. It would restrict the potential for direct foreign investment if shares were dispersed among domestic owners, and it would make harder rationalization across sectors, which could better be achieved by an active, selective industrial policy.

There is an enormous body of research that has looked at adaptation at the enterprise level across east–central Europe, often looking directly for a possible effect from privatization. It points, however, towards rather ambiguous conclusions (Carlin et al., 1994). On the one hand, it is absolutely clear that substantial changes have taken place in practically all enterprises studied. These frequently include reductions in labour, changes to products and the establishment of an independent distribution structure. More substantial adaptation, including significant new investment, has been rare, with exceptions to be found in firms that enjoy significant sources of finance, usually from a foreign partner. On the other hand, privatization does not appear to have been the central factor in determining these kinds of restructuring. It may be more important for what has been termed 'ambiguous' restructuring, in which reorganization and the hiving-off of parts of existing enterprises may further the interests of particular individuals rather than contributing to improvements in overall efficiency. It is, of course, also important when linked with access to sources of finance.

Czech research is broadly in line with these general conclusions. Surveys point to a great deal of change at the enterprise level, but relatively few cases of significant changes in production methods.

Moreover, firms privatized by voucher show no particular signs of dynamism (cf. Zemplínerová and Laštovička, 1994, and Oswald, 1994). Voucher privatization may even for a time have been counter-productive by causing a period of uncertainty described as 'pre-privatization agony', during which enterprises could not formulate any long-term plans as they awaited the arrival of new owners. They then had to face the disappointing realization that the new owners have nothing new to offer. The conclusion here is therefore again somewhat ambiguous, with the clear impression that voucher privatization has not as yet been a key factor in encouraging enterprise restructuring.

The fifth and final theme in the debates is the claim that voucher privatization would create immense scope for corruption which, in more apocalyptic versions of the argument, might threaten public confidence in new institutions generally. There have been accusations of corruption over specific privatization decisions, but proven cases are not enough to justify accusations that the whole operation has been a fraud. The fairest assessment is that there is simply no way of knowing whether the 'right' decisions were taken and how far officials were influenced by misconceptions or even bribery. Voucher privatization, it was always and with some justification claimed, was less susceptible to corruption than direct sales to private individuals or foreign companies, as decisions about ultimate ownership were taken through a random process and did not depend on individual state officials.

These five points do not point towards any simple conclusion on voucher privatization, or indeed on Czech privatization in general. In terms of transferring state property into private hands it has been very successful. It has probably also been extremely important in allowing the emergence of smaller and medium-sized enterprises which have often been formed out of the subdivision of larger units. It has not, however, guaranteed the speedy transformation of the former large state-owned enterprises into powerful engines for the creation of a modern market economy. This point can be amplified with a discussion of foreign trade performance, which points again to the same picture of substantial transformation alongside signs of persistence of past weaknesses.

A NEW EXPORT STRUCTURE

The changes in organizational and ownership structure of the Czech economy have coincided with the massive reorientation of trade towards western European markets. The European Union accounted for 54.9 per cent of Czech exports in 1994 compared with 18.3 per cent for Czechoslovakia in 1989, leaving no doubt that much of the loss of markets in the East has been covered by the gain of new markets in the West. The commodity structure of trade has shifted somewhat, with a particularly sharp decline for the machinery and transport equipment category — down from 44.4 per cent in 1989 to 25.8 per cent in 1994, with the latter figure excluding exports to Slovakia — but this has been compensated by higher exports of raw materials and of other categories of manufactured goods. This suggests a rapid process of structural change alongside integration with advanced market economies. The open question is how far this can be linked to a more profound transformation of the economic system.

The most obvious reservation, as indicated in Chapter 4, is the worsening commodity structure of exports, although that point should not be exaggerated. There has been no major change in commodity structure of exports to the European Union alone. Thus, exports of machinery and transport equipment have remained roughly constant with a share of about 25 per cent, suggesting a substantial growth in absolute terms, even if one insufficient to cover for the decline in machinery exports to the East. It would probably have been unrealistic to expect a much better outcome in this respect, as the kind of heavy capital equipment exported to the East was never likely to find a market in western Europe. The expansion of exports to the latter market therefore points to a considerable degree of adaptation in terms of the kinds of products sold.

Nevertheless, evidence from highly disaggregated figures on exports to the EU of both basic products and raw materials points to the fragility of the Czech Republic's position, much of which is based on very small footholds in markets won by selling low-priced and technologically unsophisticated products. This can be illustrated with the results of an empirical investigation of Czech and Slovak exports to the European Union, covering the two broad sectors of basic iron and steel products (7201–7207 in the EU foreign trade classification system) and road and rail transport equipment (8602–8716). Both are areas of past industrial strength, leading to at least some past presence in western European markets, and of more recent export achievement. There is also scope for a contrast between a case of a basic product for which very little product adaptation was necessary, and a sector of manufacturing in which competitive advantages depend to a great extent on product quality.

The two indicators used here are the share in total EU imports and the kilogram price of imports into the EU from Czechoslovakia, in 1989 and 1992, and from the Czech Republic and Slovakia in the first nine months of 1994, corrected where appropriate to give an estimate for the whole year. Kilogram prices are used as an approximate indicator of product sophistication, with the assumption that a higher price per kilogram points to a more sophisticated product.

There are reservations to the use of this indicator. In particular, it gives no indication of the costs involved in production or the sophistication of the production process. Thus, a cheap and simple product could be made in a highly sophisticated way, while a more complex product could be made using an enormously expensive method. In these cases the kilogram price would not be telling the whole story. Nevertheless, the measure is useful when comparing broadly similar sectors, particularly of manufacturing industry in which the quality of the product is frequently a key element in competition. It can be used both as a rough indicator of the sophistication of a product and, when set against an appropriate standard, as an indicator of the relative sophistication of products from different countries. That is achieved here by using the kilogram price of all imports into the European Union as a standard.

It should be possible, with the data on market shares and relative kilogram prices, to shed light on the growth in exports into the European Union after 1989. This could have been achieved by expanding from existing footholds, or it could have been due to the penetration of markets with completely new products, such as ones that had previously been sold to the East. It could have been accompanied by an improvement in product quality or, conceivably, by a decline, as enterprises were forced by the depressed state of demand to export goods that were no longer saleable either domestically or on former CMEA markets. Thus, the results would give some indication of the extent and nature of any restructuring that might be under way in industry.

Table 5.8 Indicators of Czech and Slovak export performance in steel products

	Total number of categories	Categories with Czechoslovak representation	Percentage of EU imports	Quality indicator
1989	76	26	1.32	0.51
1992	76	47	5.56	0.47
1994	88	38	7.06	0.59
Czech Republic	88	34	5.55	0.54
Slovakia	88	20	1.51	0.86

Note: The quality indicator in the price per kilogram of imports into the EU from Czechoslovakia divided by the price per kilogram of all imports into the EU.

Source: Calculated from Eurostat figures.

Table 5.8 shows the results for steel products. The biggest growth had come by 1992, with an increase in value terms of 233 per cent over the 1989 level, and was based primarily on the expansion of exports in categories that Czechoslovakia had been exporting before. Categories exported for the first time contributed little more than 15 per cent of the growth in exports although, as Table 5.8 indicates, the number of categories in which Czechoslovakia was represented had grown substantially. The relative kilogram price over the whole product group was well below unity in both years, due partly to a bias towards less sophisticated steel products and partly to low relative kilogram price levels among those more sophisticated product categories in which Czechoslovakia had some representation.

The last column in Table 5.8 indicates a slight fall in the relative kilogram price but, in general, figures for relative kilogram prices show no major changes. There was no statistically significant relationship between product quality and market shares and no clear evidence of a quality improvement in any category of product. Some did rise, as had been expected on the Czechoslovakia side, where barriers to trade were believed before to have been limiting the prices they could charge, but the aggregate figure was pulled down especially by the prominent position of the ungraded and unsorted waste and scrap category, which increased from 24.3 per cent of Czechoslovak steel exports to the EU in 1989 to 38.3 per cent in 1992, and enjoys an exceptionally low absolute kilogram price.

The year 1994 saw a fall of nearly 30 per cent in the total value of exports in this group of products, with the sharpest decline in those that had not been exported in 1989. The market share held up well, thanks to the overall decline in EU imports, and the relative kilogram price increased significantly. This, however, was due largely to a sharper decline in exports of some categories with low absolute kilogram prices. There is no sign of a significant improvement in product quality in any specific category. Indeed, the dangers of relying on the kilogram price indicator alone are illustrated by the comparison between Czech and Slovak figures from 1994. Slovakia's relative kilogram price is considerably more respectable, but its market share is less than could have been predicted on the basis of the size of its economy relative to that of the Czech Republic. Slovakia was poorly represented in exporting scrap, but quite well represented in a very few categories, such as ferro-chromium, with reasonably high absolute kilogram prices. There is, of course, no way of knowing how far these differences between the Czech Republic and Slovakia were present before the breakup of the federation, but it seems reasonable to assume that relative strengths had already been established before 1993.

Transport equipment presents a slightly more complicated picture. Czechoslovakia was never as well placed here as in steel products. It enjoyed a range of tiny footholds across, as Table 5.9 indicates, almost half the product categories followed by Eurostat. The only real success story was the class of agricultural tractors with a power between 37 and 59KW (8701.90–25) in which Czechoslovakia accounted for 30.8 per cent of imports at a relative kilogram price of 0.67. Apart from that, there were only footholds spread apparently at random across the full range with statistical tests revealing no bias towards goods with either high or low absolute kilogram prices.

Table 5.9 Indicators of Czech and Slovak export performance in transport equipment

	Total number of categories	Categories with Czechoslovak representation	Percentage of EU imports	Quality indicator
1989	224	109	0.80	0.41
1992	224	180	1.94	0.39
1994	249	160	2.64	0.42
Czech Republic	249	156	2.20	0.42
Slovakia	249	72	0.44	0.44

Note: The quality indicator is defined on Table 5.8.

Source: As Table 5.8.

The year 1992 saw more than a tripling of Czechoslovak exports in these categories over the 1989 level. This was achieved primarily by an expansion in categories that were already being exported. This, however, proves very little, as Czechoslovakia had a foothold in 1989 in almost all significant categories. The year 1994 saw a fall in the value of exports of 40 per cent despite the increase in market share. A disproportionate share in that decline in the absolute level of Czech exports was accounted for by categories which were exported for the first time in 1992. Kilogram price figures point to no categories in which there is evidence of a clear improvement in Czech product quality. Moreover, there is again no statistically significant relationship between market shares, or their growth, and kilogram prices for individual product categories. The one reservation to that is the general absence of representation in the small number of categories with very high absolute kilogram prices.

Table 5.10 provides a further breakdown of the export expansion up to 1992, indicating that it was largely due to three broad categories. The first are relatively unsophisticated finished products with no source of independent power, such as railway wagons, containers, trailers and railway passenger coaches (8605, 8606, 8609 and 8716). In some of these categories the Czech Republic had by 1994 grown from scratch to become virtually the only source of imports into the EU, so that its relative kilogram price was, inevitably, close to unity. This success followed linkups with major western firms giving access to markets. No significant change to product sophistication was needed, as indicated by extremely low absolute kilogram prices.

Table 5.10 Percentage shares of various product categories in Czech exports of transport equipment to the European Union

	1989	1992	1994
Cars	52.3	46.7	61.2
Coaches and trailers	4.1	10.7	27.4
Parts	7.5	13.1	25.8
Goods vehicles	4.4	13.4	2.7
Tractors	24.0	9.8	7.5

Note: The broad categories used are explained in the text.

Source: As Table 5.8.

The second are passenger cars (8703), reflecting the success of Škoda cars. The share of imports into the EU increased from 0.73 per cent in 1989 to 6.27 per cent in 1992 and 9.1 per cent in 1994 for the category of passenger cars with an engine capacity between 1,000 and 1,500cc (8703.22-19). This cannot be attributed to the reunification of Germany, as Škoda had a very weak position in the East German market in the late 1980s. The overall increase was accompanied by an increase in relative kilogram price from 0.55 in 1989 to 0.73 in 1992 and 0.66 in 1994, following the introduction of the Favorit model, which had been developed prior to 1989. This, then, was a case of a finished product that underwent little adaptation, but there clearly were immediate benefits in terms of image and sales potential from the linkup with Volkswagen.

The third broad category accounting for the export expansion is parts and components for a wide range of transport equipment (8607, 8708 and 8714), which grew from 7.5 per cent of exports in 1989 to 25.8 per cent in 1994. This grouping covers parts for railway or tramway vehicles, motor vehicles, motor cycles and bicycles. Components can be quite sophisticated products, but the Czechoslovak kilogram prices have been particularly low and have declined, in some cases quite dramatically, suggesting a concentration on the least sophisticated kinds of product. This is slightly surprising as there have been press reports of major German manufacturers opening new production facilities for motor industry components in the Czech Republic. These may lead to the appearance of higher-priced exports in future. Up to 1994, however, it is reasonable to hypothesize that the export of components was coming either from substantial Czech engineering firms that could no longer sell their finished products or from new smaller firms that had split off from larger parent companies.

Table 5.10 also indicates the fate of two other important categories. Sales of tractors (8701) have remained remarkably steady in value terms. This is a case in which no firm linkup has been made with a partner in western Europe and nor has there been much change in the Czech product. Goods vehicles (8704) saw a sudden jump to 1992, followed by a dramatic decline. Again, attempts to find foreign partners proved unsuccessful, although relative kilogram prices, at 0.51 in 1989 for general goods vehicles, do not point to a relative product quality much below that of passenger cars. The great success in 1992 was in diesel-engined goods vehicles with a gross weight of more than 20 tonnes (8704.23–91) which rose from 2 per cent of EU imports in 1989 to account for nearly 12 per cent in 1992, falling back to 2.9 per cent in 1994, in all cases with a relative kilogram price of about 0.4.

Figures for the year 1994 reveal a further, obvious point. The Czech Republic has done much better than Slovakia in terms of overall market share and in terms of representation across categories. That presumably reflected a position established by 1992, as a result of the kinds of activities inherited from the past. The Czech Republic enjoyed the advantage of a number of finished products that could easily be exported with little adaptation. It also appears to have done substantially better than Slovakia at exporting parts and components, accounting for 84 per cent of total Czechoslovak exports in this category in 1994. This points to a possible higher level of adaptability from existing engineering enterprises. That conclusion appears even more acceptable in the light of evidence on the changes in the geographical location of economic activity covered in the next section.

THE ABSENT REGIONAL PROBLEM

Prior to 1990, Czechoslovakia, and especially the Czech Republic, was renowned for the small differences in income per head across the country. Either industry itself, or the effects of industrialization, had spread over effectively the whole country. This relative geographical equality has persisted through the transformation, as indicated by unemployment levels. The lowest in any of the 76 districts was 0.3 per cent in Prague in December 1995. The highest was 7.3 per cent in Most, a North Bohemian mining district. Some specific job creation measures have helped areas experiencing the greatest job loss, but even in their absence the peak unemployment rates would only have been about 14 per cent in a few districts.

It would appear, then, that the Czech transformation, despite the absence of much of an explicit regional policy, has been accomplished, while maintaining both low unemployment and a reasonable level of equality in conditions across the country. This is a substantial success when set against the record of other east–central European countries. Thus, in both Poland and Slovakia, unemployment levels range up to almost 30 per cent in some agricultural areas alongside manageable levels in big cities.

The differences can be related to a favourable geographical situation today, with the close proximity to Germany, and to a different heritage from the past (Myant, 1995). This Czech 'specificity' can be illustrated around four general themes that typified eastern European regional problems. The first, that can be passed over very quickly, is the persistence of rural underemployment. This was simply not a substantial problem in the Czech Republic, although it certainly persisted in parts of Slovakia and elsewhere in east–central Europe.

The second is the dependence of some whole areas on coal-mining and steel-making, sectors that were expected to experience rapid decline. This clearly has been a problem for the Czech Republic, especially for North Moravia and parts of North Bohemia. In practice, however, the employment decline has been similar to that in large enterprises in other branches of industry, partly because of the relative export success of raw material sectors. There are, however, two specific features associated with these regions. The first is the weakness of new growth, either in new and small manufacturing enterprises or in the service sector. This is fairly typical of experience in western Europe, reflecting partly the impossibility of adapting the product or production process to fit in with new market needs and partly the nature of the employees in these sectors whose long experience in large single-product enterprises has generally deprived them of a background in entrepreneurial and other skills that would enable them to shift into very different sectors.

A second specific feature of mining areas is a level of unemployment well below what could be expected from net job loss figures. That is due partly to a past history in which large numbers of miners and steel workers commuted from neighbouring districts or, in the case of parts of North Moravia, from Slovakia, and partly to the availability of new job opportunities in neighbouring districts. Thus, for example, the coal and steel town of Kladno experienced a 20 per cent fall in employment from 1989 to 1994, but an unemployment rate of less than 5 per cent. There were plenty of vacancies in nearby Prague.

The third general theme is the dependence of a number of smaller towns on one single industrial employer. This was a feature of economic growth under central planning, in which completely new enterprises were set up in previously undeveloped rural areas. They were often, as was typical under central planning, largely autarkic, producing as far as possible all the components they would need, and they frequently supplied the CMEA market with a new finished product. These were often the only substantial employer in the area, so that closure could threaten a total economic and social disaster for the whole district. The problem was particularly serious, as the enterprises had often been the sole providers of a range of social and other facilities for the whole community. The most extreme cases in the former Czechoslovakia were in the electronics and armaments industries, especially in Slovakia.

At first sight this movement of manufacturing into rural areas could appear similar to a well-documented trend in advanced market economies. The difference, however, is that western European rural areas were more likely to be colonized by small firms or branches of larger companies. It therefore brought diversity and more variation in the forms of integration into a larger economic entity. In fact, the striking point about the Czech Republic was that it was somewhat closer to the western European model than was typical in east–central Europe. Thus, thanks to its earlier industrialization, there were relatively few cases of towns that were excessively dependent on a single employer. Moreover, even in those cases, transport links often made it easy to take employment in a neighbouring district.

The fourth general theme was the dependence of some districts on branch factories serving larger enterprises. These were often nominally independent, but they were in practice tied totally to one major customer. Again, the clearest cases in the former Czechoslovakia were in Slovakia, reflecting that country's more recent industrialization. Many such companies faced extreme problems when the Czech manufacturer of the final product reduced output and cut previously established links. In other cases, however, a different kind of branch factory emerged, where large enterprises spread their activities out from a city into the immediately surrounding countryside, or where smaller branches were set up in areas that already had some diversity of economic activity. This was the case especially for the engineering industry which spread, often by means of relatively small production units, across the Czech countryside and into practically every district. Thus, again, the relatively high level of development of the Czech Republic at the start of central planning, with a number of well-established major enterprises in larger cities and a relatively small number of areas completely untouched by industry, led to a pattern of industrial location that was somewhat untypical of east–central Europe.

This degree of specificity of the Czech Republic in eastern European terms points to a partial explanation for the economy's adaptability. By way of comparison, development in Slovakia appears in a sense to have been more straightforward (Myant, 1995). The level of unemployment in a Slovak district depends closely on the fall in employment, a relationship which, as argued above, is rather weak in the Czech case. Moreover, the fall in employment in Slovak districts has been especially large in more remote and predominantly agricultural districts, which is fully in line with the sharp decline in agriculture. There has also been a drop in employment across industrial areas, with only Bratislava recording any increase, one of 4.5 per cent between 1990 and 1994.

In the Czech case, changes in the net employment levels appear as a more complex outcome of a set of conflicting tendencies. The point can be illustrated by reference to the figures in Table 5.11, which shows the structure of employment in eight districts, selected as extreme cases of particular points. Prague, with a clear increase in its level of employment, has become a centre for services with a retail trade turnover per capita 3.6 times the national average in 1993. There is no other comparable centre either across the Czech Republic or in Slovakia. It also has the highest percentage of employment in finance. Like other big cities, it has experienced a decline in the already exceptionally low level of industrial employment which, by way of contrast, has increased in the neighbouring Prague-West district, an area in which total employment has also grown.

Český Krumlov is a sparsely populated district on the Austrian border which is highly attractive to tourists. The share of employment in hotels and catering is the highest in the country, while employment in trade and repair is also slightly above average. A comparison with districts with no significant tourist activity points to the tentative conclusion that tourism may be contributing directly about 10 per cent of total employment in this district. It also has a substantial indirect effect on sectors such as construction and parts of manufacturing. Indeed, the decline in the share of manufacturing employment in this district, albeit in the context of rough stability of the total employment level, is somewhat surprising, as other frontier areas have benefited from close links with western firms. In fact, the fall may well be reversed following the announcement in late 1995 of inward investment from the motor components industry.

Table 5.11 Percentage of labour force active in selected sectors in sample of Czech districts in 1994

| | Industry | | A | F | T&R | H&C | U | E |
	1990	1994						
Prague	22.5	18.4	0.3	3.1	20.3	4.1	0.3	5.7
Prague-West	25.6	31.2	6.3	0.3	13.7	3.2	0.7	5.4
Český Krumlov	32.4	29.7	11.0	1.2	13.2	7.1	3.4	−1.3
Tachov	24.7	27.2	14.1	1.4	13.1	2.1	4.7	−7.2
Třebíč	37.8	38.2	15.6	0.9	11.9	1.0	5.3	−11.3
Plzeň-South	25.0	29.0	22.1	0.6	11.0	1.3	1.0	−6.4
Jablonec nad Nisou	59.7	53.7	2.2	1.2	8.4	2.1	0.9	−10.2
Karviná	60.8	52.8	1.1	0.8	9.8	1.9	6.6	−7.1
Czech Republic	40.1	35.2	6.5	1.4	12.8	2.3	3.1	−3.2

Key: A: Agriculture. F: Finance. T&R: Trade and repair. H&C: Hotels and catering. U: Unemployed. E: percentage change in employment from 1990 to 1994.

Source: Czech Labour Force Survey, summer 1994.

Tachov is another frontier district, this time bordering western Germany. It has suffered an above-average decline in employment because of enormous job losses from agriculture which accounted for 29.4 per cent of employment in 1990. These losses have, however, largely been replaced by jobs in services and, most remarkably, industry. This includes some major investment by a German car component firm attracted by the geographical location and, for a time, by the plentiful labour supply. Třebíč, however, presents a rather different picture. As an area with substantial agriculture somewhat further from a frontier, new growth has not been sufficient to compensate for the decline in agricultural employment. The drop in the total employment level has been well above the national average and unemployment is relatively high.

Plzeň-South, the district with the country's highest proportion of agricultural employment, clearly has seen enough industrial growth to keep the unemployment level low. This has almost entirely been in smaller enterprises and, although published statistics do not make possible a more detailed sectoral breakdown, it may be significant that much of the industry previously established was based on the production of components for the giant Škoda–Plzeň heavy engineering combine. The district has also benefited from its proximity to Plzeň, with the expanding service sector typical of cities, which has ensured that unemployment remains low despite significant net job losses.

The last two cases exhibited the highest proportions of industrial employment in 1990 and 1994. Karviná is strongly dependent on coal-mining while Jablonec depends on light industry and engineering. Karviná shows the least sign of new growth in any sector, but unemployment has been held in check partly by the previous dependence on inward commuting, especially from northern Slovakia. The employment decline in Jablonec was also made bearable by the previous use of foreign workers. The proportion of employment in trade and repair in these districts is the lowest in the country, while the share in hotels and catering in Karviná, an area with hardly any tourist activity, is not far above the minimum as exhibited by the figure for Třebíč, the lowest in the republic.

This, then, is a picture of new growth alongside decline and of mobility between districts. The striking contrast with Slovakia is the maintenance of employment levels even in rural areas, as a result partly of the strength of the service sector, especially when stimulated by tourist demand, partly of the possibilities for finding work in neighbouring districts and partly of the growth in new industrial employment. Statistical tests confirm that this has been most pronounced in those districts with no large town in which industrial employment was previously low (Myant, 1995). In some cases there have been new greenfield developments by foreign firms, but statistical data shows that the tendency for manufacturing employment to grow is not dependent on significant outside investment.

Indeed, the growth in employment is largely accounted for by units with fewer than 100 employees. It would seem likely that at least a part of this rural growth could be associated with the export of relatively simple components, as discussed in the previous section.

A GUIDE TO POLICY?

The discussion of these five areas of structural transformation leaves a number of open questions as to the exact nature of changes in the Czech economy. They can be put together into a rough tentative framework, starting with a crude division into opposing tendencies of decline and growth. Decline is most visible for agriculture and for 'old' manufacturing, based on giant enterprises exporting machinery. In the Czech case these were often based in sizeable cities. These firms have tried to maintain roughly their previous production profiles, but clear success is possible only in close association with a foreign partner, as shown above all by the Škoda car manufacturer. Another kind of 'old' industrial enterprise is, of course, able to survive on its own. Producers of basic materials, such as coal or steel, could find new markets without needing to change their final products, without the need for major internal reorganization and without needing to gain access to a western firm's distribution network. Changes in organizational or ownership structures were therefore of little relevance and these firms were still, in fact, mostly in state hands in 1996.

'New' growth can be seen in both the industry and the service sectors. In the latter case it is associated especially with very small-scale personal services, which grew very rapidly at the start of the transformation. The extent of the potential for further growth is unclear, although figures on self-employment do suggest that some expansion is continuing. The finance sector is something of a special case, with a clear concentration into larger cities, and it is conceivable that it could expand its export earnings, which are currently still very modest. New industrial growth has also largely centred on small firms, often exporting simple products. Changes in organizational structure and privatization may have been important here in giving smaller units greater independence for developing links with new western partners.

One possible conclusion is that this is the best that could have been expected. There might then be no grounds for arguing with the quotation from Karel Dyba at the start of the chapter as, despite possible interpretations of the structural transformation as still incomplete, a stage of this sort could lead on without further policy intervention to the full development of a modern, high-tech market economy. Links so far established with western firms could gradually become firmer and associated with the transformation of technology, a process that has started to take place in a number of cases. That would not rule out a different case for a more systematic approach to industrial policies elsewhere in east–central Europe, but the Czech Republic, thanks to its fortunate geographical location, its major tourist attractions and its reasonably good transport network, might be able to do very well with its free market approach.

There are some obvious reasons for treating too rigid a *laissez-faire* approach with some scepticism. Thus, for example, some special measures might be desirable to give mining areas the same chances as the rest of the country. The real question, however, relates to the acceptance of the division into decline and growth, which has dominated up to now. Thus, integration into the wider European economy seems to have been achieved by a 'destructuring' of much of what existed before. Old networks have been broken down as firms have switched to producing simple components for export rather than contributing to complex Czech production processes. A fully successful Czech economy may depend crucially on the success of its own large firms and on the integration of smaller firms around them. So far, large Czech enterprises have been dependent either on foreign ownership or on state assistance, given to ward off collapse rather than as part of a systematic strategy to facilitate full revival and growth. One of the key industrial policy questions is whether these 'old' enterprises should not be accorded a more important role in a revival of Czech economic fortunes. This point is taken up again in the concluding chapter, after a discussion of developments within the Czech enterprise sector.

6. Transforming Czech Enterprises

The most obvious and noticeable signs of transformation in the Czech enterprises are the change in the size of the organizational units and the privatization of the units responsible for the bulk of output in the commercial sector. These, as referred to in Chapter 5, were not in themselves enough to ensure the emergence of a fully developed, modern, market economy. They were only one aspect, albeit a very important one, of a dramatic process of change at the enterprise level.

Perhaps paradoxically, this was accompanied by a high degree of continuity from the past which was most obvious in the technological level of much of the economy. It was also partly true of the organizational forms themselves, with the economic transformation depending on the conversion of enterprises that had up grown under central planning. Their development depended on managerial personnel inherited from the past and on their ability to formulate new strategies and create new organizational forms for their firms. Subdivision and changes in ownership could not completely overwhelm this element of continuity.

This chapter, therefore, provides a survey of the experience of larger and medium-sized enterprises, concluding with two case studies which illustrate some of the points referred to throughout the chapter. The evidence on which the arguments are based is generally derived from the intimate involvement of the consultancy firm, Management Focus International, in advising about 200 of the larger Czech firms throughout the whole transformation period. It is, therefore, in effect a summary distilled from experience across almost all sectors of the Czech economy.

The chapter starts with a discussion of some key problems inherited from the past, including the levels of enterprise debt and the practices and modes of thought that persisted from the old system. That is followed by a discussion of the transformation itself, showing differences between sectors and between firms, depending on how they were privatized. This leads into a discussion of the changes in management practices and of the impact of cooperation with foreign firms. A conclusion briefly considers what policy alternatives might have been available to the government.

FINANCIAL PREPAREDNESS

The role of money and the financial system generally is one of the most important differences between a centrally-planned and a market economy. Under the latter system, firms are assumed to have an independent financial existence. They can earn their own revenues and use them as they wish. They can raise further finance for their own purposes from various sources, including banks and the stock exchange. Under central planning, however, financial indicators were used purely as a means of checking whether an enterprise was complying with regulations. At the end of each year, enterprises transferred the great bulk of profits to the state budget. Investment was frequently financed not from the firms' retained earnings but by credits following decisions at higher levels in the hierarchy. Thus, the enterprise had no real financial autonomy. Nominally, however, it could be carrying a heavy burden of debt and its costs were increased by the payment of interest. This financial dependence both limited the experience of formulating long-term strategies and meant that enterprises typically had minimal financial resources at their disposal at the start of the transformation.

They were then hit by the effects of the post-1989 depression. The fall in domestic demand, the collapse in trade with the CMEA and the suspension of payments by many foreign customers inevitably created immense difficulties for many Czech enterprises. Table 6.1 shows the breakdown of profitability, measured as pre-tax profit as a percentage of total revenue, for selected sectors. The slight rise in profitability in 1991 was the result of substantial price increases in some sectors. As the figures indicate, this was not possible in agriculture because of competition between dispersed producers at a time of falling demand. It was also impossible in some sectors of industry, but relatively easy in those with monopoly positions and secure domestic markets. The real fall in profitability had taken full effect by 1994 although, again, some sectors were far less affected than others. The point is taken up for branches of industry in more detail later.

Table 6.1 Profitability of selected sectors of the Czech economy 1989–1994

	1989	1991	1994
All	9.62	9.93	3.43
Agriculture	7.27	-8.49	–2.57
Industry	9.75	15.64	3.49
Construction	3.48	3.61	4.15
Transport	–6.66	–15.21	–3.22
Communication	85.08	26.54	21.87

Note: Profitability is measured as pre-tax profit as a percentage of total revenues.

Source: SR, various years.

Privatization could in some cases provide an escape route, but it was often actually accompanied by a worsening of the situation, a point that is elaborated later. The situation was most severe in enterprises privatized in the form of direct sale. Most new owners were unable to pay the purchase price in cash and had to cover its payment with another credit, creating a further burden and another addition to costs. Some enterprises acquired a capital structure in which outside capital, in other words credits, constituted a clear majority. The law laid down a minimum level of Kč 100,000 to be provided by the firm itself. Many firms had no more than this, while credits could amount to more than one hundred times as much.

In many cases, the burden of these costs has worsened firms' competitive positions, limiting scope for investment and modernization and even threatening their solvency. Repayment has therefore become increasingly difficult. There have even been a number of cases of a failure to keep up payments to the National Property Fund, the holding company for state-owned firms on their way to privatization, to which bills have in the first instance to be paid. In the last months of 1995, legal action was taken to reclaim property from some of the biggest debtors. The total outstanding debt through 1994 and 1995 fluctuated around Kč 7 to Kč 8 billion, but had fallen to Kč 6.1 billion by the end of the period.

Although this figure is not in itself catastrophic when set against a total of Kč 90 billion worth of property privatized by direct sale up to June 1995, it can be interpreted as an extreme manifestation of a more widespread problem. It is, of course, not universal across all enterprises as in those privatized by voucher no new debts were acquired, but nor was there any new capital inflow providing new resources for restructuring.

These financial difficulties were further exacerbated by the behaviour of the banking sector, in which a mechanical approach to the granting of credits has persisted. In view of their lack of financial resources, Czech enterprises inevitably continued to rely heavily on credits for most of their investment. Indebtedness, therefore, remained high, still equivalent to about three times the level of investment undertaken in 1994. Banks, however, insist on a maximum four-year credit period and demand what for enterprises appear to be excessively high rates of interest — between 13 and 14 per cent — and over-stringent guarantees to ensure repayment. In short, they have been unwilling to shoulder any of the burden of risk involved in individual projects.

A cautious approach from banks is, of course, not unusual. In this case, however, they appear to have been extremely cautious in a situation in which other factors make the financial conditions facing enterprises especially difficult. Moreover, banks would have no strong case for claiming a lack of resources. They have been paying a rate of interest of about 7 per cent on time deposits, leaving a very comfortable difference from the rate on credits. Their wealth is clearly visible in the renovation and expansion of their buildings and in the high salaries of employees. Average pay in the finance sector increased from a level about the average for the economy as a whole in 1989 to a level 75 per cent above that average in 1994.

The combination of these factors led to what was described as primary insolvency in many enterprises. They simply could not pay their bills. This was gradually accompanied by the so-called secondary insolvency, whereby enterprises cannot pay for goods received, because they have not been paid by their own customers. This started in enterprises affected directly by a suspension of payments from the CMEA countries and by the reduction in armaments production. It spread gradually as a chain covering almost all enterprises. Governments have made various efforts to solve the problem by arranging for a pooling and mutual cancellation of inter-enterprise debt. Such efforts have never proved very effective. Various figures have been produced to indicate the extent of payment arrears in the economy, with an estimate for mid-1995 from the Ministry of Industry and Trade of Kč 120 billion, representing little change on the position a year earlier. Estimates from the Czech Statistical Office have been higher, reaching Kč 222 billion for the start of 1995, equivalent to more than 20 per cent of GDP.

Some enterprises cannot even pay bills for water, heat and power deliveries. The most serious case has been the Poldi steel producer of Kladno, to which energy deliveries were suspended at various times in late 1995. More generally, a number of firms have on occasion had to seek solutions through barter arrangements or by suspending deliveries to non-paying debtors. This seemingly logical solution can have a paradoxical effect, as an enterprise may have found markets for products that cannot be manufactured because it has no financial resources with which to buy the necessary raw materials.

Various partial steps have been found, including the effective elimination of some of the burden of past debts and help to some individual enterprises in particularly serious difficulties, but no complete solution to the problem of secondary insolvency has yet been found. It continues to present a barrier to restructuring in many enterprises. More generally, the habits that have been formed and reinforced in relation to interenterprise relations have led to a significant decline in what could be termed business ethics. Managers can look back with nostalgia to a time when payment of bills seemed to be automatic. At least under central planning the financial system seemed to enterprise managements to work satisfactorily from this point of view. Nowadays, even if an enterprise has the resources for payment, it may prefer to join the widespread trend and delay for as long as possible.

MANAGEMENT AND WORKERS

Despite their financial difficulties, it has frequently been maintained that Czech enterprises inherited the clear advantage of a skilled and qualified labour force that should ultimately give them good prospects for the future. The qualification level of manual workers, medium-level technical employees and a large proportion of professional engineers is up to the western European level. Moreover, wages are low in Czech enterprises not only when compared with western Europe, but also in comparison with some former CMEA states. The precise figures vary somewhat with fluctuations in exchange rates, but a common estimate is a level of total labour costs in the Czech Republic of about 10 per cent the German level. This suggests an area of opportunity for Czech enterprises if they can achieve an increase in productivity and gross output and especially if they can find markets for their products.

Even before 1989, productivity in Czech enterprises was lower than in comparable west European enterprises, with estimates pointing to a level between 25 and 50 per cent of the Austrian or German figure for manufacturing as a whole. Many enterprise managements believed the gap to be smaller, suggesting that calculations often ignored the breadth of activities undertaken by Czech enterprises. Thus, as was common in centrally-planned economies, they were typically responsible for transport, repairs, and a range of other services that western firms might buy in from outside. Nevertheless, the productivity gap was certainly very substantial, stemming both from obsolete technology and from poor organization of work. With the possible exception of some sectors of light industry, such as imitation jewellery, footwear, clothing and textiles, a substantial proportion of employees could already have been surplus to requirements in 1989 if production had been properly organized even around very much the same technology.

After 1989, the reduction in the number of employees was at first substantially slower than the reduction in output. Although the two had broadly come into line by 1994, it can be assumed that there are still large reserves of labour in many enterprises, especially labourers and administrative workers, which could be used for increasing the volume of production. This maintenance of 'disguised' unemployment, meaning the payment of wages for employees who contribute extremely little, was a further aspect of enterprise behaviour that worsened their already severe financial difficulties.

At the same time, some large enterprises, for example in the footwear industry, in coal-mining and in some parts of the construction industry, have been suffering from labour shortages. These are most severe for some forms of monotonous or extremely difficult manual work and also for some categories of work requiring a high level of qualification, such as knowledge of foreign languages, financial or marketing expertise and even some forms of highly-skilled manual work. Workers with skills in high demand are often recruited from manufacturing into the service sector or to enterprises that can afford to pay high wages. This frequently means firms under full or partial foreign ownership. Small and newly-established firms have also enjoyed the advantage of not being constrained by regulations limiting wage growth, which were not finally abandoned until July 1995.

It can be added that employment problems are worsened by a very low labour force mobility. This stems partly from the conservatism of employees, and partly from the fact that no full housing market as yet exists. An employee is therefore bound practically for a whole lifetime to his or her place of residence and thus often also to his or her enterprise.

This contradictory position in the potential of the labour force as a whole is matched by the situation with respect to management preparedness. In the technical and technological areas, the qualification level of the top and medium-level management is generally quite high. This is true at least for those sectors in which the Czech economy is strong. It may also soon be true in some areas of electronics and information technology in which the Czech level could rise rapidly. It may not be so clear in other areas of advanced technology in which isolation of the Czech economy from contacts with the most developed states of the world in the post-war period and the departure of many skilled employees to foreign countries have left severe weaknesses.

There are also serious weaknesses in the spheres of accounting, financial management and marketing which affect all sectors of the economy. Indeed, marketing and sales activities were exceptionally poorly developed before 1989, as they were of little relevance to the activities of an enterprise in a centrally-planned economy in which the demand constraint was weak. This is an area of current rapid development, but Czech managements have as yet not fully appreciated the place and importance of marketing in their activities. Reaching the western European level requires training a very large number of employees. It will require time and substantial financial outlays to build up adequate domestic and foreign distribution networks. There is also a long way to go in mastering the methods and instruments of accounting and of financial activity in general, including the functioning of financial markets and of the stock exchange.

Alongside these fairly specific gaps in past practices, managements also inherited a reputation for a low level of innovativeness. This remains a major problem. Despite a huge number of researchers employed directly in enterprises, and in sectoral nationwide research institutes — for 1989 the figure was more than 300,000 employees — the rate of scientific and technological development was extremely slow. At present, the fastest rate of innovation is taking place in the service sector, where it is less dependent on sophisticated technology and expensive equipment. Prime examples are the rapidly changing tourism industry, hotels, banking and some areas of administration. Many new products have also been developed in light industry and there have even been signs of 'higher-order' innovations in the key mechanical engineering branch, including the heavy engineering giant Škoda–Plzeň, and among suppliers of components to the motor industry.

It is impossible to quantify these developments precisely, but the systemic changes, while in certain respects encouraging innovativeness, have still left many managements under strong pressure to be as cautious as possible. Thus, the pressure of competition should lead enterprises to seek innovations to improve their competitive positions. In many branches, however, monopolies or oligopolies still dominate. The highly profitable telecommunications and electricity industries are examples. Moreover, even where competitive conditions prevail, the financial insecurity of enterprises and uncertainties over the future in general, including the unpredictability surrounding the possible consequences of currency convertibility or accession to the European Union, have tended to encourage firms to maximize short-term profits, rather than facing the risks that inevitably accompany major innovative activities. In this area, then, the short-termism at the enterprise level that was familiar from the old system has to some extent been reproduced.

There is, however, still great potential in some sectors for relatively minor innovations. With most enterprises burdened, or maybe blessed, with surplus fixed assets, there are substantial reserves available that could enable enterprises to expand production very rapidly. They are ready and waiting to take on contracts for new production from western Europe.

Overall, then, the enterprises inherited from the past and transformed in various ways still retain important vestiges of their former position under central planning. In terms of overall efficiency, the level remains by western European standards relatively low. This is a result both of the effects of the transformation itself, which led to the fall in output and worsening financial conditions in many enterprises, and of the continuation of many past practices with managements still oriented primarily towards production activities, with less attention to financial and marketing issues. It is worth repeating that this is not the 'fault' of the present managements, or indeed of the present enterprises at all. It is rather a consequence of the former centrally-planned management system and of the complexity of the transformation process which coincided with the difficult situations on eastern and western markets and the growing competition from producers in the Far East.

There are differences between sectors, as discussed in the next section, but an even greater differentiation between managements of enterprises has been taking place. In some cases, managements have by now emerged that are able to manage enterprises effectively under hard market conditions. This, however, is not yet the general picture. With good management, many enterprises could convert this low level of efficiency into high levels relatively quickly. The preconditions include privatization into the right hands, success in the search for markets corresponding to the capacity of the enterprise, a qualified management that can introduce modern techniques of production, and financial control and an improvement in marketing activities.

An objective assessment of the enterprises inherited from the past would therefore include a combination of both strong and weak points. Some of the latter may be overcome fairly quickly, while others may prove to be more long-lasting. A fairly similar conclusion was reached for the economy as a whole in a study by the International Institute for Management Development in Lausanne under the title *World Competitiveness Report 1994*, which received extensive coverage in the Czech media (*Hospodářské noviny*, 8 September 1994). It noted 'strong' points in the stable political and social climate, the existence of a basic industrial infrastructure, including in domestic energy sources, in the skilled labour force, in low wage levels and in the number of research workers. It was, however, negative on the sophistication of the financial sector, on the telecommunications network, on the level of productivity and on a whole range of factors relating to human resources and management practices. These included the attention to training and retraining of employees and managerial weaknesses in information technology, the organization of work, the orientation towards customers, foreign experience and the implementation of strategic plans. In short, the weaknesses were in areas that require the creation of a sophisticated institutional infrastructure and a more substantial reorientation of practice and thinking within firms themselves. They are issues that could not be resolved immediately by privatization alone.

DIFFERENTIATION BY SECTOR

Despite these underlying weaknesses across the whole economy and the importance of individual managements in determining the success of an enterprise, there clearly are differences in prospects depending on the precise sector. The contrasting fates of various branches of industry are shown in Table 6.2, which indicates the continuing fall in output across almost all sectors after 1991. Unfortunately, the figures may exaggerate this as they refer only to larger enterprises employing 100 or more up to 1991 and 25 or more in 1994. In both of those years, about 12 per cent of total industrial output was estimated to have come from firms smaller than the specified size. It is also impossible to construct fully comparable figures covering all branches, because of changes in the methods of classification.

Table 6.2 Changes in output and productivity in branches of Czech industry, 1989–1994

	Output		Labour productivity	
	1991	1994	1991	1994
All industry	73.2	58.4	84.9	101.5
Coalmining	88.4	72.0	97.6	114.4
Food	80.8	70.5	90.7	89.4
Textiles and garments	62.6	45.5	75.0	92.4
Leather	65.1	54.1	73.4	99.4
Woodworking	73.8	51.8	84.5	75.0
Paper	80.9	86.2	92.2	129.9
Chemicals	65.9	58.9	81.6	108.2
Rubber	76.0	71.0	75.4	99.3
Metals and metalworking	68.0	53.1	76.9	99.6
Mechanical engineering	69.4	44.3	81.0	84.0
Electrical engineering and electronics	56.2	41.2	71.7	104.4

Note: All figures are percentages of the 1989 level. Figures for 1989 and 1992 refer to enterprises with 100 or more employees. Figures for 1994 are for enterprises with 25 or more employees.

Source: SR, various years.

Nevertheless, it is possible to see the transformation dividing into two stages. In the first, up to 1991, practically all sectors were hit hard. In the subsequent years they could begin to adapt in various ways. The most obvious were a stemming, or even reversal, in the fall in productivity, achieved by shedding labour, and a sharp rise in exports as a share in total sales. This latter point, as shown in Table 6.3, was of crucial importance in raising profitability, as one effect of the low exchange rate has been to make exports especially lucrative in terms of Czech currency.

Table 6.3 Percentage of sales exported and profit rates in Czech industry, 1989–1994

	Exports as percentage of sales			Profit rate
	1989	1991	1994	1994
All industry	15.1	18.3	25.6	3.43
Coalmining	0.5	8.2	28.0	2.09
Food	5.6	8.8	9.3	3.73
Textiles and garments	26.7	35.6	45.4	1.94
Leather goods	30.5	36.3	37.7	1.40
Woodworking	23.8	32.3	44.2	−1.71
Paper	15.2	23.0	23.0	4.56
Chemicals	19.5	20.3	41.3	7.50
Rubber and plastics			32.4	2.15
Metals and metalworking	13.7	18.6	40.5	1.09
Mechanical engineering	26.7	33.4	37.0	−2.09
Electrical engineering and electronics	22.0	20.5	25.1	0.46

Note: Profit rate is measured as pre-tax profit as a percentage of revenues.

Source: SR, various.

Firms with a secure monopoly position and safe domestic market, such as electricity and telecommunications, had few worries. The food industry also did slightly better than average as it never had been export-oriented and, despite the appearance of foreign competitors, still dominated on the domestic market. Producers of some basic products, such as the chemical, petrochemical and pharmaceutical enterprises, have either resisted the large drop in output experienced elsewhere or been able to increase exports dramatically enough to achieve a high level of profitability.

The picture is less rosy in the coal- and ore-mining enterprises, which were hit initially by the drop in demand from machinery and metallurgy customers and by a decline in overall energy intensiveness. Coal, however, has a secure position as a major domestic energy source and both the share in sales going for export and the absolute level of exports have increased. Coal mining has also been able to adjust employment levels relatively easily, as mining always suffered from labour shortages. It has, therefore, been able to achieve a very significant improvement in labour productivity. Some other producers of basic products, such as cement and quarrying, have also profited from export opportunities. Enterprises in the metallurgy sector suffered a sharp drop in output at the start, but many of them, too, have survived and prospered, thanks to export growth.

The transformation process has hit hardest the export-oriented enterprises in mechanical and electrical engineering, electronics and consumer light industry such as textiles and footwear. The subsequent success of these sectors in adapting to the new circumstances has proved to be highly variable. Most enterprises in mechanical engineering and electrotechnics reacted in what could be termed the worst way. Many have not managed to adapt their production programmes, and face extremely severe financial problems. For mechanical engineering, although the share of exports has risen, the absolute volume is down considerably and the sector had not returned to profitability even in 1994. It can be added that these figures conceal a substantial structural change within the sector, with the manufacture of investment goods, the traditional export to the East, performing especially badly, while the success story has been the Škoda car manufacturer. Many consumer goods enterprises have also responded very quickly, with the establishment of cooperation relations with western European enterprises, the implications of which are discussed below. Thus, although output in the textile and garment sectors has fallen, the growth in the proportion exported has helped maintain a positive rate of profit.

In the initial stages, construction enterprises were also hit hard following a reduction in housing construction and an overall decline in investment activity. The dramatic extent of this is indicated by

Table 6.4, which points to the likelihood of a depression in total activity continuing for some time as the number of new starts has remained at a very low level over a number of years. This has further implications for economic development as a factor restricting geographical labour mobility. The construction sector, however, was able to find new markets relatively quickly. Demand soon began to revive, especially around the development of the infrastructure and the reconstruction and conversion of existing buildings. Overall, although Czech statistics show the low point of the depression in construction in 1993 at 59 per cent of the 1989 peak, compared with a drop to 66 per cent for industry, there have since been signs of a reasonably rapid recovery. The years 1994 and 1995 saw growth rates of 5.4 and 8.5 per cent respectively. The official figures derived from 1984 prices probably substantially overstate the extent of the fall. Recalculation in 1990 prices points to a drop in output up to 1993 of less than half as much.

Table 6.4 Housing construction in the Czech Republic, 1990–1994

	1990	1991	1992	1993	1994
Finished flats	22,000	21,000	22,000	18,000	15,000
Initiated flats	36,000	8,000	4,000	4,000	4,000
Flats under construction	170,000	144,000	98,000	76,000	60,000

Source: SR, various.

Two other broad sectors stand out. Agriculture was hit hard by the drop in domestic demand and a growth in imports. Its output fell by 28 per cent in the 1989–1994 period, with the decline continuing into 1995. It would, however, not be fully accurate to argue that the sector has not adapted at all. It may be almost unique in its failure to achieve a turnaround in production, but it cut employment from 629,000 in 1989 to 338,000 in 1994. It is therefore quite outstanding in terms of productivity growth, with a figure over that period of 33 per cent.

The second outstanding case is the service sector, which has benefited from the growth in tourism and the appearance of completely new activities in the financial field. This was the most rapid element in the transformation, powered forward both by changes within existing enterprises and by the emergence of new firms. It is less easy to relate this to changes in productivity when the activities covered by the term 'services' are so diverse and so many new enterprises have been started from scratch. An indication of the transformation is the extent of employment growth as referred to in Chapter 5.

THE EFFECTS OF PRIVATIZATION

A second important dimension of differentiation among enterprises is a combination of factors derived from the form of ownership, the method of privatization and the extent of accompanying enterprise reorganization. Generalizations have obvious dangers and there are differences that may relate rather to sector than to form of owner-ship. Thus, much of heavy and extractive industry remained for longer in state hands so that the overall behaviour of state-owned enterprises would be biased by their specific circumstances.

It is not possible to follow this precisely from published Czech statistics, which do not give a breakdown by ownership forms across branches of industry. It is possible to compare only broad sectors with the data presented in Table 6.5. Even this, however, can be misleading for three reasons. The first is that the category 'private' includes enterprises with a continuing share of state ownership. The second is that the figures were calculated before the completion of the second wave of voucher privatization and therefore understate the size of the private sector. The third is that they apply to enterprises with 25 or more employees, which again means that they understate the significance of the private sector. Nevertheless, one point stands out that will be referred to later, and that is the higher level of productivity in foreign-owned and mixed enterprises while, if anything, productivity would appear to be lower in private than state-owned industries. This last point should not be taken too literally, as the figures relate to gross output which is likely to give an appear-ance of higher productivity to raw material producers. The use of a value-added indicator could change the picture substantially.

Table 6.5: Percentage shares of output and employment by ownership, 1994

	Industry		Construction	
	Output	Employment	Output	Employment
Private	28.6	34.5	70.4	69.1
Cooperative	1.2	3.2	0.8	1.6
State owned	40.2	41.9	11.6	14.4
Foreign owned	11.3	6.9	17.2	14.9
Mixed foreign and domestic ownership	18.7	13.5	*	*

Note: Figures refer to enterprises with 25 or more employees only. * Construction firms under mixed ownership are included in the 'private' category.

Source: SR, 1995.

Table 6.6 Property approved by the Czech government for privatization up to 30 June 1995

	Total	Industry only
Value in Kč billion	950.5	448.9
By method of privatization, percentages		
Auction	1.0	0.4
Public tender	3.3	4.4
Direct sale	9.5	8.8
Joint-stock company	80.6	84.8
Free transfer	5.6	1.5

Source: SR, 1995.

Nevertheless, in general, state enterprises and joint-stock companies with a dominant share of state ownership have characteristics that appear almost entirely negative. They are typically characterized by obsolete products and services, bad payment discipline, low productivity and efficiency, an excessive number of employees and a low level of interest from top management in the implementation of radical changes. Indeed, managements often seem interested primarily in activities that may worsen the situation of the enterprise, such as the preparations for selling off parts that can be done in such a way as to bring personal gain to the managers. These are also very likely to be enterprises carrying a large burden of debt from the past. Again, that need not be entirely a consequence of state ownership. It is also partly a reflection of the fact that enterprises with such characteristics were the hardest to privatize.

The second element of differentiation considered here is the method of privatization. Table 6.6 shows the breakdown as of 30 June 1995 in terms of the volume of property approved by the government for privatization. Not all of this had been disposed of at that point. The largest item was the transformation into joint-stock companies, and this was particularly true for industry. The auction method was used mostly for shops and other small businesses, sometimes when separated off from larger units. Table 6.7 shows the breakdown for the disposal of shares in joint-stock companies, up to 31 December 1994. The most striking feature is the dominance of distribution by voucher. Perhaps as remarkable is the extremely small share allocated for direct sale to foreign firms. This, however, was not the only means for foreign firms to buy into Czech companies, as they could enter through direct sales or public tenders or, very frequently, by establishing a joint venture with a Czech company.

By way of contrast, joint-stock companies and limited liability companies in private ownership have often shown a keen interest in adapting to the new conditions. They have often achieved substantial improvements in productivity and have proved themselves to be flexible and adaptable. The most frequent problem, however, is the continuation of financial difficulties stemming from debts incurred during the privatization process. They therefore often cannot implement what might appear to be very promising business strategies. Indeed, in some cases it appears that limited liability companies may have been privatized in a way that gave them no real chance at all. It is as if they were intended for bankruptcy.

Table 6.7 Methods of disposing of shares in joint-stock companies, by percentage of total, up to 31 December 1994

Intermediated sale	3.67
Vouchers	50.71
Domestic direct sale	4.92
Foreign direct sale	2.12
Free transfer	7.23
Restitution fund	3.15
Permanently with the National Property Fund	9.79
Temporarily with the National Property Fund or other public funds	18.41

Source: SR.

Small private firms, often set up by enthusiastic entrepreneurs and with a low burden of debt, appear to be the most dynamic element in the economy. They, however, feel themselves constrained by the complicated regulations over taxes and accounting procedures. A small business is the least well equipped to handle the complex practices required from a modern economy. They also face a serious financial barrier, which means that they can rarely compete with, let alone replace, larger enterprises in manufacturing. Their main strength is in the service sector.

Larger firms are more typically under the predominant ownership of funds, following privatization by the voucher method. Although, as indicated in Chapter 5, this may give them some influence, their representatives typically have no great knowledge or understanding of the enterprise they are involved with. Moreover, their efforts to press enterprises into paying dividends have made them a source of pressure on enterprises to stick with a short-term view and to siphon any profits they can into dividend payments. This obviously limits the scope for modernization, investment and the development of new sales and distribution networks. Thus, funds have often been a source of pressure, hampering rather than aiding restructuring at a time when enterprises really need freedom from short-term pressures and every encouragement to formulate and implement long-term strategies.

THE EVOLUTION OF MANAGEMENT

The most striking feature of the position of enterprise management since 1990 has been the de facto absence of any superior authority. Managements have been left to manage themselves following the effective collapse of the power of central bodies. Boards of Directors and Supervisory Boards, the two bodies established under Czech company law to oversee management, have thus far played only a secondary role in most enterprises and have usually been effectively subordinate to management while, as outlined above, new owners have begun to play a role only during the course of 1994 and 1995, and even then their influence is often small.

This relative autonomy of enterprises has meant both that the manager's personality has become an extremely important factor in deciding the fate of an enterprise and that many decisions may not reflect a full and objective analysis of the best way forward for enterprises in general. Thus, a trend towards the formation of an excessive number of subsidiary joint-stock companies appears often to have been the result of fashion rather than business logic. There is every reason to expect some enterprises to return more to their former divisional structures.

A more important, and probably longer-lasting, trend is the continuing adaptation of the internal structure of management, with an increasing emphasis on the role of marketing and financial issues. This process is slow, partly because of the shortage of qualified employees and partly because of the persistence of the traditionally dominant style of thinking in production units, as exemplified by frequently heard views that 'the main thing is material production' and 'technology can solve everything'. Development towards more business-oriented rather than purely production-oriented organizational forms is likely to show up the lack of logic in some of the fragmentation of organizations previously undertaken. It may also prove important in the clarification of the relationship between management, Boards of Directors and Supervisory Boards.

The case for larger organizational forms may also become clearer if firms are to revive, or even establish for the first time in a serious way, a meaningful interest in research and innovations. This is more dependent than any other change on government help, as practically no enterprise has the resources to finance a more extensive modernization and restructuring, the introduction of 'higher-order' innovations or even the establishment of distribution networks on its own. State support in the area of innovation has been exceptionally weak, falling foul of the government's restrictive macroeconomic policies.

There could also be organizational implications of a revival of the sort of large-scale manufacturing exports that typically required government help, meaning in particular heavy investment goods that usually have to be sold with the help of credits. So far, the government has a record of dragging its feet over the implementation of pro-export policies. A number of major export projects were finally given some assistance in 1995. A full revival here would strengthen the position of the large, heavy-engineering combines and could strengthen the case for some organizational reintegration.

In many cases, however, the process of subdivision of large firms may be irreversible, especially when it has led to the complete break-up of larger units into fully independent firms. This was for a time given considerable encouragement, and many of the resulting small enterprises were supported from both domestic and international sources, including help from European Union programmes. The motivation behind this, and its justifiability, varied widely. It was often linked to the laudable aim of breaking up the monopolies. In many cases, however, more subjective factors played a major role, including efforts to be free of former superiors, or to become independent, in the hope that this would bring advantages for particular managers irrespective of its impact on the development of an effective organizational structure. Overall, however, the process should be evaluated positively. Smaller, more flexible enterprises with more transparent finances and more clearly defined responsibility for their own further development came into being, and with this competitive conditions were created. In some cases, however, links that do have a clear business logic have been impaired, common research and development has been reduced and some distribution networks have been cut off from manufacturers that had used them in the past.

Across practically all enterprises, one clearly positive feature has been the background of social peace. In practice, this means that managerial autonomy has not been threatened from within the enterprise any more than from without. The term 'strike' is hardly ever heard. A fifteen-minute strike was held in the Škoda motor factory on 17 October 1994, but it was essentially to do with supporting the Czech government during some difficult negotiations with Volkswagen. A nationwide fifteen-minute strike in support of trade unions' demands relating to government proposals on pensions on 21 December 1994 was also essentially a demonstration of opinion on an issue of national policy and probably no more than 10 per cent of employees actually stopped work. It may reflect a worsening of relations between the government and the Czech trade union centre, but it need not have any implications for labour relations within workplaces.

Indeed, the relations between management and trade unions are in most enterprises good, because the former have generally been able to grant increases in real wages since 1991 and have rarely had to impose compulsory redundancies. The only possible blemish, emerging throughout 1995, was a wave of militancy in parts of the public sector, especially among doctors, teachers and railway workers. The last of these groups were on the point of a crippling strike in June 1995 following the government's plans for a restructuring of the railway system and the erosion of their relative pay level. Again, however, this does not appear to presage a change in industrial relations across the economy as a whole.

ENTERPRISE STRATEGIES

Thus, the key force in the restructuring of enterprises remains the management. If they are to resolve the problems of long-term development, of the transition to new manufacturing programmes, and of success in securing new markets, then they need to develop clear long-term strategies. In practice, many have failed to do this. They are even adept at thinking up justifications for their own inaction. The following quotations can be taken as typical:

'So far we have lived without any strategy, we will survive without one in the future as well' — a comment that reveals a lack of understanding of the fundamental changes that have occurred in the economy.

'How can we elaborate any strategy not knowing what will come tomorrow?' — a remark that reveals an inability to work and forecast under conditions of uncertainty.

'We have no time for the elaboration of a strategy, we have to concentrate on immediate problems' — a comment that points to a lack of understanding of the necessity of fundamental changes in the activity of an enterprise and a lack of understanding that even short-term decisions must be made on the basis of a long-term strategy.

'A strategy is a fabrication of theorists. Our strategy is clear. We do not have to write it down. It is there in our heads' — a justification that conceals a superficial and incomplete approach. The inadequacies of a strategy of this sort, which inevitably will be vague and incomplete, will always be revealed at some point.

'We have no money for the implementation of strategic plans' — a comment that reveals a failure to understand that money is more likely to be raised on the capital market if there is a good strategy.

'The government will not dare to abolish our traditional enter-prise' — a view that demonstrates a lack of understanding that an inefficient enterprise is not abolished by the government in market economy, but by the market.

These and similar arguments have ensured that only enterprises with the most far-sighted managements have elaborated their strategies on the level accepted for successful firms under western European conditions. These 'enlightened' enterprises are the ones that can now pass from the original strategy, aimed at survival, to the elaboration of a new strategy, oriented towards growth and innovation. In many cases, these are enterprises that have benefited from close links with major western firms.

INTERNATIONAL LINKS

International cooperation at the enterprise level took off almost at once after the political changes at the end of 1989. It was an immediate and positive benefit of the effective delegation of wide-ranging powers to managements. The first links were oriented predominantly towards the developed market economies, especially Germany and Austria, and generally began with cooperation agreements for the delivery of spare parts, components, or semi-finished products made to precise orders from the foreign partner. This was especially common in the engineering industry, while in the textile and garment sector, and also in some parts of engineering, there was a rapid development of the subcontracting of the production of complete final products following documentation supplied by the western partner.

The immediate attraction of these types of cooperation for the Czech enterprises was that they enabled economic survival for those that had lost their former domestic, or foreign, customers. There were more general implications for the economy as a whole, as these early forms of cooperation brought with them the potential to learn a great deal about accepted western business practices. Thus, the Czech partners had to comply with western European quality requirements, leading to the introduction of total quality systems and certification in line with ISO standards. They also became more aware of west European business thinking and methods while the terms of cooperation agreements typically forced the Czech partner to develop the invaluable habit of keeping to the agreed commitments.

Nevertheless, the potential gains from this lowest form of cooperation were exhausted relatively quickly. It could not provide the basis for a complete transformation of Czech enterprises into modern, internationally-competitive firms. They have, therefore, been keen to move towards higher forms of cooperation, including the formation of joint ventures. Many of these enterprises function well, and it is reasonable to assume that this organizational form will become a normal form of economic activity in the Czech Republic in the coming years. Indeed, the time could come when a clear majority of larger enterprises in the Czech Republic have a foreign co-owner.

There have, however, been a number of problems which relate above all to misunderstandings as to what can be achieved and as to what each partner is offering, with a general tendency towards excessive expectations on both sides. The western European side has often been guilty of exaggerated hopes of cost savings, reflecting an overestimation of the importance of the low Czech wage levels. Indeed, many joint-venture agreements were successfully negotiated but then never implemented once the foreign partner had appreciated the problems stemming from the lower level of Czech labour productivity and the high share of overhead costs in some enterprises. From the Czech side, on the other hand, there has often been an expectation that they would be helped by a capital inflow, after which they could look forward to a more secure and comfortable existence. They have been less eager to appreciate the need for major changes to bring about an improvement in productivity and product quality. In some other cases, the two partners seem to have misunderstood each other's intentions. Thus, both parties have been known to expect the other to ensure markets for the newly-formed joint venture's output.

Problems have also arisen from quite basic misunderstandings, for example over terminology, and these have been exacerbated on occasion by ignorance of languages. A more general form of misunderstanding has been a tendency by the foreign partner to underrate the qualification level of Czech specialists and to send young, inexperienced or second-rate employees to take leading positions.

These, it should be noted, are the kind of problems that should not recur as firms on both sides get to understand each other better. Moreover, even where faced, they have frequently been overcome. The most obvious evidence for this is the rapid growth both of foreign participation in Czech firms and of firms with foreign partners. Moreover, these firms appear to be particularly dynamic in the introduction of new technology and modern management methods. In the most successful cases, an established joint venture has become a seed for the proliferation of further joint ventures. Thus, for example, the Škoda motor manufacturer initiated the formation of a further 42 joint ventures at its Czech suppliers. In a further 17 cases, foreign firms built new plants on greenfield sites in the Czech Republic. These enterprises supply in total about one half of all components for final Škoda products. Thanks to the links to Volkswagen and to foreign partners, they have been provided with the necessary financial means, managerial expertise and development capacities to reach the level required for the western European motor industry.

Table 6.8 Foreign direct investment by country of origin, cumulative to June 1995

	$ million	Percentage of total
Germany	1,349.6	36.3
USA	699.1	18.8
France	527.9	14.2
Austria	254.5	6.9
Belgium	202.5	5.5
Switzerland	155.7	4.2
Others	525.0	14.1
Total	3,714.3	100.0

Source: Czech National Bank.

The figures in Tables 6.8 and 6.9 show the breakdown of direct foreign investment by country of origin and broad sector. There have been some changes over the years in sectoral structure, which are partly the result of particularly large investment projects dominating in individual years and partly the result of clear trends. The first big investment came with Volkswagen buying into the Škoda car manufacturer from 1991 onwards. During 1993, the emphasis was on consumer goods and tobacco, construction and machinery. A major part of this was due to the US tobacco firm Philip Morris, which bought the Tabák enterprise of Kutná Hora. Interest in 1994 returned to the key area of transport equipment, due in particular to further investment in the Škoda car manufacturer which is now majority owned by Volkswagen. There was also growing interest in the financial sector, followed by construction. Nevertheless, any Czech specificity was in the early interest in the well-established engineering industry, with investment in the infrastructure coming somewhat later.

Table 6.9 Foreign direct investment by sector, cumulative to June 1995

	$ million	Percentage of total
Transport equipment	772.0	20.8
Consumer goods and tobacco	692.4	18.6
Construction	480.6	12.9
Banking and insurance	411.7	11.1
Food industry	325.0	8.8
Chemicals	278.5	7.5
Others	754.1	20.3
Total	3,714.3	100.0

Source: Czech National Bank.

When broken down by country of origin, foreign direct investment shows broad stability. The extent of German domination is rather exceptional in east–central Europe and can again be related to the particularly favourable circumstances of the close links between the Czech and German engineering industries. The big new developments in 1995 were agreements for the sale of a 27 per cent share in the telecommunications company to a consortium of Dutch and Swiss firms, and an agreement for foreign investment in petrochemicals involving a consortium of Agip, Conoco and Shell.

The sums involved are very substantial and will alter both the sectoral structure and the pattern of countries of origin. It is, however, still noteworthy that there has been little interest in some sectors, most obviously agriculture, paper and timber. Nor has there been significant outside investment in high-technology branches. Indeed, the level of foreign ownership in the Czech economy, as indicated in Table 6.5, is still relatively low for a European country at that level of development.

HAS THE GOVERNMENT HELPED?

It is fair to say that most Czech enterprises have overcome the shock of the transition from the planned to the market economy. Despite substantial differences, depending on the circumstances of individual branches and between individual enterprises within each branch, most firms appear to be ready to move into a phase of development and expansion. There are, however, clear weaknesses and problems and it is worth asking whether different government policies could not have led to a more favourable outcome in the past and whether some policy changes now might not stimulate more rapid and lasting growth.

Any such assessment is inevitably difficult, not least because, in comparison with other east–central European countries, a number of features of Czech development appear to be rather favourable. Thus, a simple comparison with other economies in the area does not point to any obvious scope for improvement or ideas that could be lifted. The most positive features are the stable political, social and macroeconomic climates, the wide-ranging delegation of powers to enterprises and the rapid pace of privatization. More specific points, such as the liberalization of imports, the breakup of foreign trade monopolies, the subdivision of large domestic monopolies and a high level of taxation on wage costs undoubtedly also helped by putting enterprises under strong pressure to improve efficiency levels.

In a number of respects, however, government actions have not helped the transformation of Czech enterprises. Examples that are often quoted by managements are the precipitate abandonment of the 'eastern' markets, an excessive reduction of armaments production, generally weak support to science, research and innovation projects, the failure to solve the problem of secondary insolvency, allowing excessively high interest rates and extremely rigid requirements from banks, insufficient support to exporters and weak anti-dumping policies in some branches.

In some cases, hesitant steps are being taken to find solutions. Thus, means are being created to help with export credits and at least some consideration is being given to better ways of supporting science. Progress, however, is slow, and in a number of other areas painfully slow. Notable examples are the possible need for special policies for agriculture or housing, areas which, as argued above, have suffered extremely severe difficulties and typically rely on various forms of government support in advanced market economies.

Above all, enterprise managements would benefit from the elaboration of some strategic thinking from the government on these and other issues. It is an open question whether at the moment, in view of its past ideological attachment to a strictly non-interventionist approach and in view of the turbulent political climate, it is realistic to hope for any such reappraisal of the strengths and weaknesses of past policies.

CZECH ENTERPRISE CASE STUDIES

1. ABC Enterprise

This study of the history, present condition and likely future development of the ABC company is a typical case of a firm that did try to develop a strategy and to respond to the changed circumstances, but was severely handicapped by financial problems. The firm is based in Jablonec nad Nisou, traditionally the largest production base of artificial jewellery in the world, with a strong export orientation. The firm's greatest strength has been in the production of Christmas decorations. The domestic market is small, but it has been expanding across the world in recent years and can be expected to experience further growth. This points to the need to maintain competitiveness and product quality by rationalization and flexibility of production and by improvements in the quality of service to customers. There are already signs of intensifying competitive pressures, particularly from the newly industrialized countries of the Far East. Although the Czech Republic ranks among the ten largest exporters in the world, its share in world trade has been decreasing, and the industry based around Jablonec cannot regard its position as secure.

The transformation
The ABC Enterprise was established on 1 December 1990 from the subdivision of a larger combine. In 1991 it was still a state-owned enterprise. It had a highly diversified production programme covering Christmas decorations, metal parts for artificial jewellery, artificial jewellery itself, light fittings, blinking eyes for dolls, glass eyes for toys, devotional articles, gilded and loose beads and pins. Of these, Christmas decorations accounted for the majority of the enterprise's revenue. Exports, sold through a foreign trade enterprise, accounted for 75 per cent of production.

The enterprise had 800 employees, of whom 75 per cent were home workers, 8 per cent white-collar employees, 0.5 per cent management and 16.5 per cent manual workers. Wages were a substantial part of costs, as is normal for this kind of low-tech light industrial activity. Table 6.10 shows the breakdown of various categories of cost in both 1991 and 1994. A noteworthy point is the low level of interest payments in 1991, the change in which is taken up below. Total costs amounted to Kčs 69 million. Total revenues amounted to Kčs 86.6 million, with Kčs 83.2 million coming from the sale of products, leaving a pre-tax profit of Kčs 17.6 million.

The firm was privatized on 1 November 1992, following a public tender in which three interested parties had made bids. The winner was a limited liability company made up of officials of the former state enterprise, ABC. They were immediately faced with the difficult task of overcoming a number of weaknesses, stemming partly from the firm's past as part of a larger unit and partly from the method of privatization. The first of these problems meant that it did not have a management team prepared for the full range of activities required in a fully independent firm. There was no sales team, no supply team and no accounting and finance departments. In view of the market situation, these weaknesses had to be remedied quickly. Thanks to a crash programme of seminars and short- and longer-term training, a reasonably well-qualified medium-level management team took shape within six months.

Table 6.10 Breakdown of costs by category in ABC Enterprise in 1991 and 1994.

	Percentage of costs	
Category	1991	1994
Consumption of material	38	20
Consumption of fuel and energy	2	2
Repairs and maintenance	4	1
Wages and other employ-ment costs	37	32
Transport costs	2	na
Services	8	12
Interest	2	18
Miscellaneous	6	15

Source: Management Focus International.

This, however, still left the problems deriving from the method of privatization. As ABC had offered more than the book value of the firm in the public tender, it had had to take out a bank loan, the repayment of which represented a substantial burden. Privatization also left some bad feeling, as the firm had had to fight with a strong local lobby which had wanted to divide the firm and separate off one lucrative part. As a result, partly of the uncertainty surrounding privatization and partly of the subsequent financial difficulties ruling out wage increases, the firm experienced a rapid decline in the labour force, including the loss of some valued employees.

By 1994, ABC was a limited liability company. The production programme had become far more specialized, with a clear emphasis on Christmas decorations and chains. Moves were under way to end the production of pins and glass eyes, which was to be transferred to the toy industry in which they are used. There had also been a strong reorientation towards exports, the share of which in total production had risen to 98 per cent. The number of employees had been cut by 600, leaving only 200. The percentages of different categories of employee were absolutely unchanged in comparison with 1991.

Earnings, at Kč 54 million, had declined by 38 per cent as against the year 1991, with earnings from sales of the firm's own production down to Kč 42.6 million. When set against the rate of inflation, this suggests a drop in output of more than 60 per cent. This, however, could be considered a good result in view of the reduction in the labour force, which rather suggests a slight improvement in real productivity. Earnings from the sale of tangible and intangible fixed assets amounted to Kč 3.8 million, while earnings from sale of stocks amounted to Kč 4.1 million. The breakdown of costs, as shown in Table 6.10, indicates above all the dramatic rise in the share of interest payments. With total costs of Kčs 61 million, the firm made a loss of Kčs 7 million. Total interest payments were roughly Kčs 4 million greater than this. Even without them, the financial position would have deteriorated significantly since 1991, but at least there would have been some profit. The other factors worsening the firm's position were the increases in the share of services and in the miscellaneous category. It is, however, also noticeable that wage costs increased relative to the consumption of materials, reflecting the pressures to raise payment levels.

The strategy
A strategy was worked out by the management in early 1991, while the firm was still under state ownership. Three possible production

programmes were elaborated, with the differences depending on different possible extents of privatization. The key element, which won confidence within the firm, was the concentration on, and expansion of production of, Christmas decorations, aided by the use of computer technology. The strategy, however, was based on two erroneous suppositions.

The first related to the consequences of privatization. Because of the high price paid for the firm, insufficient financial resources remained to allow for the planned expansion of production or to establish a satisfactory distribution network. The second error related to the level of unemployment in the region which, it was assumed, would be high enough to enable the firm to recruit and retain the necessary qualified manpower without facing pressure on wage costs.

Over the following three years, the firm undertook a major restructuring. This involved changes in organizational structure and relations with customers, specific measures to overcome problems with the labour force and the introduction of new technology. The organizational changes amounted to a subdivision into smaller units controlled by the top management of the company. Efforts have also been made to restore links with former customers, which had been disrupted in the course of privatization. This was particularly important as the practice in the past had been for payments to be made to the firm throughout the whole year even though sales were strongly biased towards the period around Christmas. The breakdown of stable relationships had left outstanding debts to the firm of Kč 9.5 million, of which Kč 7 million could effectively be written off.

The main development with the labour force was the reduction in the number of employees, but with it came dangers of a worsening structure because of the large number of pensioners among the home workers still employed. The management set about trying to recruit new employees, who were qualified, efficient, and able to devote their free time to the firm. Moreover, it had to improve the qualification level of some highly specialized manual workers, such as glass-blowers. It tried to stimulate its employees partly through higher wages, but also with opportunities for greater independence and personal development, and with the attractions of cooperation with foreign countries. Broadly speaking, despite the low level of unemployment in the area, the management solved the problem of stabilization of its workforce at least to the extent that this was not the major barrier to future success.

Together these changes in the labour force helped the management of the firm to reduce its cost level, although that was only possible in the third year after privatization. The reduction in labour costs was achieved above all by rationalization of posts for technical and economic employees, by the retirement of employees who were then not replaced and by the elimination of unprofitable production programmes.

The key technological improvement is the preparation of a new method for dyeing beads in an air-conditioned room to replace the established method which depends on the weather and the air humidity. The management also wanted to replace the technologies of dyeing and silver-plating beads, which were harmful to the environment with the drained silver killing all micro-organisms in water. It also wanted to use modern software to save labour inputs and, above all, to reduce the time needed to complete an order. All of this, however, costs money.

A final element in restructuring was the selling off of superfluous buildings and equipment. Much of this was bought by very small private entrepreneurs. This added a further element of flexibility for the firm as they could contract out work to these individuals when big orders were won. As the figures referred to on the firm's revenue indicate, the sales themselves were not particularly lucrative, although any income is obviously welcome for a firm in financial difficulties.

The future

The ABC company has set targets for improving quality and reducing costs through a deepening of specialization. It hopes not only to keep up with current fashions, but even to set new trends. It is, however, under threat from two directions. The first is the development of competition. Domestically it faces small private manufacturers, who are able to adapt themselves very flexibly to requirements of the market and have minimal overhead costs. Competition abroad comes especially from the Far East, where manufacturers offer goods that are similar, but much cheaper, because they are made from plastics. Moreover, ABC is still struggling to overcome the recent disruption of links to customers.

It has retained the services of one export firm, but has been trying to come to an agreement with another which may give access to further markets in Russia and Japan.

The second threat comes from the pressure on costs, partly due to pressure for higher wages and partly from the possible revaluation of the Czech crown. Evidently, the only solution is to increase productive efficiency and continually innovate its products. Under current labour market conditions, with extremely low unemployment across the whole Czech Republic, it is very difficult to see a future as a low-tech enterprise relying for its competitive position on low wage levels. It must be better than the competition that already exists and that may yet appear. This, however, is made extremely difficult by the firm's financial situation, especially in view of the need to repay the debt from privatization.

This, then, is a firm that could have benefited from different government policies and that would welcome more active help to exporters now. Possible steps in the past could have been support for firms suffering from the failure of former customers to keep up payments and a different privatization method that would have involved sale at a price corresponding to the real market value of the assets. Today the firm would benefit from tax concessions on exported goods, from more favourable export and investment credits and possibly from currency devaluation. It would, however, benefit most of all from measures enabling it to undertake substantial investment and modernization which could to some extent be seen as an alternative to devaluation. Without that its prospects are not encouraging.

2. *Stavby silnic a železnic Praha*

Stavby silnic a železnic Praha (SSŽ), Construction of Roads and Railways of Prague, was established under its current name in 1951 and remained under full state ownership until 30 April 1992, when it was converted into a joint-stock company. It is an example of an enterprise that suffered a major drop in its market followed by some recovery. It was able to survive the worst period and even build a base for future success, thanks to a linkup with a foreign partner.

The transport construction sector was hit hard after 1989 by cuts in the state budget and by the instability, and frequently insolvency, of prospective customers among the larger Czech enterprises. New transport construction fell sharply and, despite an urgent need for the development of the infrastructure, has recovered only very slowly. The sector has also suffered from rising prices of building materials, machines, means of transport, fuel and energy. As in other sectors, there are shortages of highly qualified employees.

Overall, a hard competitive environment has been created in this sector of the construction market. There have, however, been clear signs of revival in the market from 1993 onwards, with rising demand for road and rail construction and for work to overcome ecological damage. This includes cleaning up waste dumps and work to restore the landscape in former mining and military training areas.

The transformation

The major changes began in 1990, with a thinning down of the enterprise's organizational structure within the framework of what was described as demonopolization. In practice, this meant the separation from the enterprise of two independent plants, the shedding of an educational establishment and the splintering off of activities such as electrical engineering, catering, the part of the design department concerned with bridge building, part of the transport section and the enterprise's legal professionals. Many of these activities were hived off as separate units under the small privatization programme.

Meanwhile, from autumn 1989 until September 1990, the management worked out its so-called 'Starting Strategy of SSŽ'. This represented the first experience of strategic thinking for the firm's top management. The basic idea was the formulation for the coming two-year period of a strategy for coping with the expected stagnation in transport construction. At the same time, preparations were to be made for an expected recovery, and that meant maintaining the basic orientation of the enterprise and taking steps to strengthen the firm's capital position to enable modernization of its equipment. This was done with the help of a foreign partner. Following a selection procedure during 1991, carried out by the Vienna consultancy firm Creditanstalt Investment Banking, the recommended partner was included in the business plan approved by the government in April 1992.

It was also assumed that there would have to be changes in the management system and organizational form in line with the emerging market conditions. The firm had to choose between the various possible legal organizational forms of an association, a holding company or a classical joint-stock company. The management went for the last of these combined with, during 1990, a progressive slimming down of the internal structure, amounting to the maximum of decentralization into separate organizational units which roughly corresponded to existing plants. The number of head-office staff was reduced from more than 300 to 30. Some units providing necessary activities were converted into profit centres. A flexible organizational structure was thereby created, including a clear separation into four production programmes of roads, railways, bridges and earthwork.

Another problem was a fundamental change in the competitive conditions. The management, however, saw no alternative to its orientation towards domestic customers. It was still heavily dependent on orders from central, regional and local government bodies and, to a smaller extent, from major industrial enterprises such as power stations and the large heavy-engineering combines. The proportion of output going to exports was small and made up largely of building parts, such as bridge beams, semi-finished products, such as precoated bituminous mixtures, and various steel structures.

It was also assumed that active steps would be needed to create the basis of a stable, qualified staff team. In 1989, the firm had about 8,300 employees, of which about 2,000 were white-collar employees. Following the separating off of various parts, the joint-stock company SSŽ had 3,979 employees in May 1992, of which 917 were white-collar employees. As Table 6.11 shows, there has been little further shedding of labour. The table also indicates the changes in broad outline in productivity and output from 1990 onwards. The effects of the drop in demand in 1991 are very clear. In view of an increase in prices of construction output of more than 40 per cent over this period, the real fall in output appears to have been almost 50 per cent. That figure cannot be taken literally, as the fall in the firm's total output was due in part to the splitting off of parts of the enterprise. The figure for labour productivity points to a fall in real terms of about 37 per cent.

Table 6.11 Changes in labour force, productivity and output for SSŽ Enterprise, 1990–1994

	Labour force	Labour productivity on value added, in Kč thousands	Total output, in Kč millions
1990	5,785	153	2,246
1991	4,712	137	1,975
1992	3,979	173	2,324
1993	3,743	194	2,447
1994	3,656	216	2,967

Source: Management Focus International.

Table 6.12 Breakdown of gross turnover in SSŽ, in Kč millions

	Gross turnover	Value added	Post-tax profit
1990	2,532	884	54
1991	2,611	644	48
1992	3,377	688	52
1993	3,074	726	−76
1994	3,491	789	64

Source: Management Focus International.

Table 6.12 gives a breakdown of financial results with the apparently very low level of profit, including even a small loss in 1993. This, however, was a much healthier situation than that faced by ABC. In the first place, interest payments remained very low, equivalent to less than 2 per cent of total revenues in 1991 and less than 1 per cent by 1993. The significance of wages and other labour costs was also substantially lower, amounting to only about 20 per cent of total costs, meaning that it was slightly easier to raise pay levels to recruit and retain staff.

Above all, however, the low level of profit was accompanied by an injection of Kč 243 million — equivalent to 8 per cent of annual turnover — from a new share issue in mid-1994 taken up by *Entreprise Jean Lefèbvre*. This, plus the trading profit of Kč 64 million, made it possible to finance investment totalling Kč 392 million. Part of this went into new plant and machinery while part, as outlined below, was invested in firms that came under SSŽ's control.

Privatization
The management favoured a combined method of privatization and this was accepted by the government. A 15.01 per cent share went to the foreign partner *Entreprise Jean Lefèbvre*, or EJL, which is the second largest road construction firm in France, belonging to the *Lyonnaise des Eaux* Group. A 3 per cent share went to the Restitution Investment Fund, while 82 per cent of shares were used in the first wave of voucher privatization. Roughly 95 per cent of the shares offered for vouchers were sold during 1992. The direct sale to EJL took legal effect on 2 July 1992, on which day the first general meeting of shareholders agreed to increase the capital stock allowing EJL to raise its share to 51.01 per cent. Thus, unlike the ABC case, this privatization was accompanied by an easing rather than worsening of the firm's financial position.

The management, however, still had some complaints about the privatization process. The main problem was the long-drawn-out decision-making process in the former Ministry for the Construction and Building Industry, which delayed the establishment of the company by more than a year. There was also dissatisfaction over the hiving off of two plants during 1990, before serious long-term plans could be formulated, while the negotiations with the foreign partner seemed unnecessarily slow, taking fifteen months in all.

The contrast with ABC is again very clear. The main complaint this time was that steps were not taken quickly enough. There had initially been much stronger criticisms of government policy, with a view that more should have been done to help the firm through the worst of the recession. It could, however, survive reasonably comfortably thanks to orders already on its books and to the capital strengthening with the entry of the foreign partner.

Government decisions in 1993 and 1994 on the modernization of the motorway network and railway corridors point to the prospect of expanding demand in the future, but there are still uncertainties. Thus, for example, the government has made changes to its plans for the D5 motorway connecting Prague to Munich, and a decision of August 1995 contained a commitment to slow the pace of motorway construction in favour of railways.

Problems with restructuring
External events forced some changes to the management's strategy. The main problems stemmed from the changing structure of orders, above all as a consequence of a long-term reduction in work for the Prague heavy engineering combine ČKD. Moreover, the firm failed to win an important order for a section of the D5 motorway, for which it had been preparing itself over a long time period. This caused considerable bitterness within the firm around a feeling that Czech firms should have been given preferential treatment in the selection procedure. Elsewhere, it was claimed, domestic firms are always favoured for orders subsidized or financed from the state budget.

A more immediate problem was that the decision threatened the firm with overcapitalization. A new, updated strategy was therefore formulated covering the period up to 1997, and reflecting the changes in the Czech economy in general and in the construction industry in particular. It had to react to the continuing depression in transport construction engineering and especially to the long-term stagnation of orders from the railways. The new strategy was elaborated with the help of mathematical models and so-called 'optimistic' and 'realistic' variants were chosen as the basic ones. The difference between them consisted primarily in the impact of winning or not winning the order for a section of the D5 motorway. This work was valuable in orienting management towards taking a strategic view. It was also of great practical benefit as, just as it was being completed in 1993, the foreign majority owner asked for an elaboration of the firm's prospects and plans.

An important element in the strategic reorientation was a decision to invest a part of the firm's free capital in 12 companies established either by it alone or together with other firms. Examples include three joint plants for the precoating of bituminous mixtures, the firm

Beton Lafarge for the production and transport of concrete mixtures, jointly with the Čížkovice cement works, the joint venture Preftor in Poland for modernization of tramway lines by means of large-area tramway panels using a licence from SSŽ, and the acquisition of the majority share in the joint-stock transport construction and quarrying company Silnice Nepomuk. It has also invested in a training institute jointly with a German company, and in a pension fund. It is undertaking further diversification into the mining and treatment of its own aggregates. This, it is hoped, will ensure a better quality of inputs and a greater security of supplies. This, then, is a conscious process of diversification in response to pressures from the market, unlike the purely organizational grouping of enterprises into combines and incorporation of a range of subsidiary activities that often dominated under central planning in the past.

The new owners
By 1994, the firm had undergone substantial changes, with an ownership structure as shown in Table 6.13. The foreign capital participation was crucial for the firm's success. It was used especially to aid modernization of the firm's equipment and for the introduction of new technologies. This source, together with depreciation of fixed assets of SSŽ and reinvestment of the retained profit, enabled SSŽ to spend in total about Kč 880 million for its own investment between mid-1992 and the end of 1994. It could acquire directly from the foreign partner 20 new technologies, especially in the sphere of bituminous top courses, shallow-layer surfaces, hydroisolations and the production and use of asphaltic emulsions.

Table 6.13 Ownership of shares in SSŽ in 1994, in percentages

Entreprise Jean Lefèbvre	59
Investment and Industrial Fund	33
Individual shareholders	5
National Property Fund and Restitution Investment Fund	3

Source: Management Focus International.

The precise involvement of the foreign partner within the company also brought changes to its internal structure. The membership of the Board of Directors was expanded to seven, of which four seats were occupied by representatives of EJL. Bořivoj Kačena, the Chairman of the Board of Directors, was also appointed managing director. The Supervisory Board consisted of six members, of which two were from EJL, two were nominated by SSŽ, and two were elected by SSŽ employees.

The French partner has generally kept out of day-to-day management, restricting its role to the major decisions at Board of Directors level, including the formulation of annual plans and investment programmes. However, two representatives of EJL have been working in SSŽ over a longer time period, one in the position of assistant to the managing director, in effect as the main liaison worker, and the other in the position of accountant of record-keeping, with a remit to bring the Czech firm into line with French practices.

In fact, the main impact of the French majority shareholder has been in speeding up the adoption of modern management practices. This has been done by the direct transfer of knowledge and experience and by the training of employees from all levels, involving study visits to France and seminars conducted by French specialists for SSŽ employees in the Czech Republic. It need hardly be added that the influence of the domestic owners has so far been extremely limited, as is perhaps demonstrated by the decision to pay no dividend in 1994. They have one representative who sits on the Board of Directors and one on the Supervisory Board.

The future

There are clear signs of an upturn in demand both in the Czech economy and in neighbouring countries. This is felt in the transport construction sector in the increasing pressure for construction of motorway and railway networks. The implication for SSŽ is that the time may be right to adapt the corporate strategy adopted in 1993. It is hoping for a substantial share in new orders for the modernization of the railway system and for new bridge construction. It has already won an order for the reconstruction of the railway station in Poříčany on the route of the first railway corridor which will run from the German border to a crossing close to Vienna.

It will finish its contract for a 14 kilometre section of the D5 motorway and a 10 kilometre section of the D8 motorway, which will eventually connect Prague to Dresden. It also expects a revival of investment from large industrial enterprises, such as Škoda–Plzeň and the Mělník power station, for reconstruction and modernization of their railway systems.

The prospects, then, look good, with the firm hoping to be fully recognized as one of the best Czech construction firms with a particular strength in bituminous technologies. The main remaining problem is to ensure a stable core of qualified manpower and, under the current conditions of labour shortage for many occupations, that depends on offering high enough pay and attractive enough conditions and prospects for employees. Generally, however, the process of transformation, retaining much of the enterprise's past orientation, seems to have been successful, thanks to the help of a foreign partner in overcoming financial difficulties and in filling a range of gaps in managerial and technological expertise.

7. The Restructuring of Industry

This chapter aims to introduce an assessment of the transformations of the Czech, Slovak, Hungarian and Polish economies in terms of the branch structures within industry. It builds from the well-established argument that central planning led to a bias towards extractive and basic industries. The data used here, derived from the UNIDO Industrial Statistics database and OECD STAN database, makes possible a more precise analysis. In particular, the branch structure is followed at the level of detail of the three-digit code of ISIC classification, covering 28 branches of manufacturing industry. The comparison is also broad, including the four central European countries and eight European market economies. These include the six smaller economies of Belgium, Denmark, Finland, the Netherlands, Sweden and Austria, alongside the larger economic unit of the Federal Republic of Germany.

For the purposes of this study, industries are classified into broader categories along three basic dividing lines. The first separation is into the three categories of 'early', 'middle' and 'late', corresponding to an industry's role in different stages of the industrialization process. The second division is into 'light' and 'heavy' industries. The third, referred to here as classification by use, is based on a division into four categories of food and related products, manufactured consumer goods, semi-manufactures or intermediate products, and investment goods. The three modes of classification have considerable overlap, but there are differences. The relationship between these terms and the ISIC classification of branches is shown in Table 7.1 below.

It is postulated that there should be a relationship between the level of economic development, as measured by per capita GDP, and the branch structure of manufacturing industry in terms of value added and employment. It is also assumed that this may vary with the size of the economic unit. This argument has been elaborated in

Table 7.1 Branches of manufacturing by three methods of classification

ISIC	Branch	Classification by place in development	Classification by utilization
Light industry			
311	Food	Early	Food
313	Beverages	Early	Food
314	Tobacco	Early	Food
321	Textiles	Early	Consumption
322	Wearing apparel	Late	Consumption
323	Leather and leather products	Late	Consumption
324	Footwear	Early	Consumption
331	Woodworking	Middle	Consumption
332	Furniture and fixtures	Middle	Consumption
341	Paper	Late	Consumption
342	Printing and publishing	Late	Consumption
390	Other industries		Consumption
Heavy industry			
351	Industrial chemicals	Late	Semi-manufactures
352	Other chemicals	Middle	Semi-manufactures
353	Petroleum refining	Middle	Semi-manufactures
354	Petroleum and coal products	Middle	Semi-manufactures
355	Rubber products	Middle	Semi-manufactures
356	Plastic products	Late	Semi-manufactures

ISIC	Branch	Classification by place in develop-ment	Classification by utilization
361	Pottery and china	Middle	Semi-manufactures
362	Glass	Middle	Semi-manufactures
369	Other non-metal products	Middle	Semi-manufactures
371	Iron and steel	Late	Semi-manufactures
372	Non-ferrous metals	Late	Semi-manufactures
381	Metal products	Late	Investment goods
382	Other machinery	Late	Investment goods
383	Electrical mach-inery	Late	Investment goods
384	Transport equip-ment	Late	Investment goods
385	Professional goods	Late	Investment goods

studies in United Nations publications (1963 and 1977) and in a UNIDO study (1980). It has also been used in analyses of past trends and for forecasts of structural changes in the West German economy (Fels et al.; 1971, Fels and Schmidt, 1980; and Donges et al., 1986) and for the purpose of analyzing the economic and industrial structure in former Czechoslovakia (Zeman, 1989, 1990). The assumption follows from a conception of economic growth involving structural change and the redeployment of production factors away from shrinking activities into expanding sectors. Thus, to some extent, the sectoral structure of manufacturing could be regarded as an endogenous variable, largely explained by the level of per capita GDP.

The relationship is not exact. Indeed, statistical analysis across the selected small market economies has not revealed a very precise relationship for individual branches of industry. Some countries have specialized towards different sectors. Nevertheless, three points do stand out. The first is the generally low representation of what are defined as early branches of manufacturing in countries with higher levels of per capita GDP. The second is the high weighting towards heavy rather than light manufacturing industry in east–central Europe, despite those countries' relatively low GDP levels. The third is the breadth of the spread of activities in east–central Europe, and especially the Czech Republic. This includes an emphasis on investment goods, a sector which, as frequently argued, could not avoid serious difficulties after the collapse of the CMEA.

GROWTH AND STRUCTURAL CHANGE

The theoretical framework used here can be summarized around three points, each related to a mode of classification of branches of manufacturing. Thus, the first relates to the differing behaviour during economic growth of the broad categories of light and heavy industries. Various authors (Hoffmann, 1968; Chenery and Taylor, 1968; UNIDO, 1980) have developed the argument that these two broad categories are characterized by differing long-term growth patterns. Light industries are generally assumed to require less capital per unit of production and per unit of labour employed than heavy industry. In terms of demand characteristics, light industry is mainly a supplier of basic consumer goods, while the bulk of heavy industry is made up of industrial supplies, capital goods and relatively sophisticated consumer goods. Economic development and a broadening industrial base are therefore normally associated with a growing share of heavy industry in manufacturing.

The second, closely-connected point relates to the differences in behaviour that appear when industrial branches are classified as consumer non-durables, capital goods and industrial supplies or intermediates. The definition of consumer goods overlaps with that of light industry. Industrial intermediates and capital goods, on the other hand, are supplied mainly by heavy industry. Originally, the share of investment in GDP was believed to grow rapidly in countries at early stages of development. Thus, as income increased, the growth of domestic demand would favour industries that produced capital goods and consumer durables. This pattern of structural change was expected to prevail in developed as well as in developing countries, both because specific industrial branches, such as machinery and transport equipment, would continue to absorb a growing share of investment and because the proportion of capital goods in total exports would rise as a country became more industrialized.

The third point relates to the classification of branches by their significance at different levels of economic development. Thus, following the approach developed by Chenery and Taylor (1968), each branch can be related to a stage in development, or level of per capita GDP, at which it makes its main contribution to industrial growth. Industries classified as 'early' were those which supplied essential needs at low levels of income. The share of these industries in total manufacturing value added did not rise with the growth in income. 'Middle' industries were those whose share in manufacturing value added expanded rapidly at intermediate levels of per capita income, but made only modest gains once per capita income reached a comparatively high level. 'Late' industries represented the most rapidly expanding field of manufacturing once the country had reached an advanced stage of development, as indicated by a high level of GDP per capita.

This rather simple presentation of the argument obviously ignores a whole range of further determinants of structural change, such as the extent of state involvement, the production technologies employed and the degree to which they can be transferred internationally, and the structure of firms. All or any of these can affect the development of an industry or a group of firms within that industry.

Economists originally attributed the contraction of early industries to the income elasticities of domestic demand for the products of those industries and to their reliance on relatively simple technologies. Governments, however, seldom permit the domestic production of basic necessities to decline indefinitely. They are amenable to the arguments of interest groups and may indirectly support such industrial branches as food, beverages, tobacco and textiles. The protection of agricultural production in many advanced countries is a clear illustration of this. Moreover, there is potential for massive technological change even in those activities that grew very early in the industrialization process and, in view of the ever greater scope for international trade, their potential for growth need no longer be restricted by domestic demand elasticities.

Changes in the form of ownership are another factor influencing preconceived notions of structural change, since they affect industries' access to finance and to various forms of government assistance. The number of state-owned or otherwise publicly controlled firms did rise in many countries in particular historical periods. The governments of central and eastern Europe countries, in their desire to foster industrialization, initiated projects in the steel, petroleum and other heavy industries, while governments in the developed market economies have resorted to various forms of market intervention to limit contraction in some industries, or to encourage expansion in others. One effect of this public ownership or control may be to neutralize the growth constraints imposed by the income elasticity of domestic demand. It can be added that the transformation policies in four east–central European countries, from 1990 to 1994, themselves influenced the restructuring of the manufacturing sector in this period through the undervalued exchange rates and the extremely low unit labour costs. The importance of all these factors becomes apparent when attention is focused on specific industrial branches rather than on the manufacturing sector as a whole.

BEFORE THE TRANSFORMATION

As Table 7.2 indicates, the structural pattern of manufacturing industries in the east–central European countries at the beginning of the transformation process was oriented towards industries which are the main contributors to the growth in manufacturing at an advanced stage of economic development. This might appear surprising in view of the lower level of GDP per capita in these countries, as indicated in Table 7.3. It was, however, the result of the 'socialist' industrial policies which pushed the branch structures, in terms both of value added and of employment, towards an emphasis on heavy manufacturing industry. This brought the east–central European structures close to those of the developed market economies with a higher level of economic development, a considerably larger economic size and more substantial technical and technological potential.

Table 7.2 Manufacturing value added in 1990 by broad sector

		Early industries	Middle industries	Late industries
Czechoslovakia	1989	18.1	15.4	65.2
	1992	18.3	16.3	63.8
Poland	1989	26.4	16.6	55.5
	1992	27.7	17.5	53.7
Hungary	1989	12.7	18.2	67.1
	1992	15.3	19.8	63.1
Austria	1989	19.3	19.1	60.7
	1992	20.0	19.1	60.0
Germany	1989	11.9	16.3	71.3
	1992	12.5	18.1	68.7

Note: Figures are percentages of total value added in constant 1990 US dollars.

Source: UNIDO.

Table 7.4 shows the position across east–central Europe, indicating that the bias towards heavy manufacturing was the strongest in Czechoslovakia in terms of employment but the strongest in Hungary in terms of value added. The difference between these two countries cannot be considered large. Poland's structure, however, does point to a greater share for light manufacturing. Table 7.5 shows how this differs from the position across the comparators chosen from European market economies, suggesting again that Poland's structure could be considered the least distorted.

Table 7.3 GDP per capita of selected countries in US dollars by purchasing power parity

	In US dollars			As percentage of German level		
	1990	1992	1994	1990	1992	1994
Czech Republic	8,844	7,623	8,000	56	41	42
Slovakia	7,834	6,645	6,936	50	37	37
Poland	4,636	4,693	5,541	29	25	29
Hungary	6,766	6,120	6,744	43	33	36
Austria	16,623	18,744	19,664	105	101	104
Germany	15,779	18,649	18,936	100	100	100

Source: Havlík, 1995.

The striking point is the still stronger bias towards heavy manufacturing in the German case, a large and powerful economic unit, as against the smaller weight for those sectors in smaller economies with which in other respects Czechoslovakia might be expected to have a great deal in common. Tables 7.6 and 7.7 show this in more detail, pointing towards significant differences in the precise breakdown within these broad categories between Czechoslovakia and Germany.

Table 7.8 further reinforces the point with figures comparing manufacturing branch structures from the point of view of the role of production in consumption, in other words by dividing into use for current production, for investment, and for two forms of private consumption. Again, the high share for investment goods sets Czechoslovakia somewhat apart from the others in east–central Europe, although Hungary also had a bias in that direction.

It also sets Czechoslovakia apart from the smaller market economies and somewhat closer to the German branch structure, despite the lower level of economic development as indicated by the comparisons of per capita GDP.

Table 7.4 Percentage share of light and heavy manufacturing in total manufacturing value added and employment in east–central Europe

	Czechoslovakia	Poland	Hungary
Value added			
Light manufacturing			
1989	28.5	39.2	26.9
1992	28.7	36.0	26.4
Heavy manufacturing			
1989	71.5	60.8	73.1
1992	71.3	64.0	73.6
Employment			
Light manufacturing			
1989	33.6	42.2	43.3
1992	31.8	42.7	45.5
Heavy manufacturing			
1989	66.4	57.8	56.7
1992	68.2	57.3	54.5

Source: UNIDO.

This manufacturing structural 'deformation' in the former Czechoslovakia, in Hungary and in its slightly different form in Poland, is only partially explicable in terms of specific natural resource endowments or specific historical conditions. The basic differences in the branch structure of manufacturing in these countries in comparison with the structural pattern of manufacturing in comparable developed market economies, or with the 'normal' structural pattern corresponding to the level of economic development, are the result of the 'socialist' industrial policies implemented during the period 1948–1989.

Table 7.5 Share of light and heavy manufacturing in Czechoslovakia compared with selected market economies

		Czechoslovakia	Belgium	Finland	Holland	Austria	Sweden	Germany
Value added								
Light manufacturing	1989	28.5	35.9	47.7	35.0	36.1	34.1	20.4
	1992	28.7	39.1	47.1	36.1	37.3	35.0	21.7
Heavy manufacturing	1989	71.5	64.1	52.3	65.0	63.9	65.9	79.6
	1992	71.3	60.9	52.9	63.8	62.7	65.0	78.3
Employment								
Light manufacturing	1989	33.6	39.0	49.4	38.8	37.7	33.4	21.9
	1992	31.8	38.9	48.4	39.4	37.9	33.8	22.2
Heavy manufacturing	1989	66.4	61.0	50.6	61.2	62.3	66.6	78.1
	1992	68.2	61.1	51.6	60.6	62.1	66.2	77.8

Note: Figures are calculated from data in 1990 US dollars.

Source: UNIDO.

This set the role of their manufacturing production within the context both of a relatively high degree of domestic autarky and of the division of labour in the former CMEA, with the former USSR as an exporter of raw materials and energy and an importer of manufactured goods from these countries. The more extreme nature of the deformation in the Czechoslovak case reflects the closer dependence of that country on trade with the CMEA partner countries and its status as the provider of a disproportionate share of heavy capital equipment. It can be added that the survival of this sector has already proved highly problematic. The point is that heavy investment goods are typically sold with the help of long-term credits, and the small Czech economy lacks the financial strength to compete with exporters in other countries now that the special arrangements within the CMEA have disappeared.

The high representation of heavy manufacturing industry in the east–central European countries at the start of the transformation process depended on slightly different shares for its individual components across the region. Thus, as Table 7.8 shows, it was influenced by the relatively high share of semi-manufactures — including chemical products, non-metallic mineral products and basic metal industries — which accounted for 32.1 per cent of value added in Czechoslovakia, 27.4 per cent in Poland and 35.5 per cent in Hungary. In the Czechoslovak and Hungarian cases it was also strongly influenced by the high share of investment goods, or engineering, making up 39.4 per cent and 37.6 per cent, respectively, of total value added in manufacturing.

The Polish manufacturing structure was characterized by a bias towards light manufacturing. The share of consumption goods and food production, at 23.3 per cent and 15.9 per cent, respectively, was significantly higher than in Czechoslovakia, with 19.2 per cent and 9.3 per cent, respectively, or Hungary, with 17.2 per cent and 7.0 per cent, respectively. This reflected the somewhat different position of the Polish economy. Food and consumer goods were important export sectors, the CMEA was less dominant in the country's export structure and, as befits an altogether larger economic unit, there was a greater emphasis on production for the domestic market.

Thus, although the high share of engineering industries in the former Czechoslovakia's manufacturing value added was partly a result of the country's long industrial tradition, it must be seen

Table 7.6 Percentage shares in manufacturing value added

	Czechoslovakia		Poland		Hungary		Austria		Germany	
	1989	1992	1989	1992	1989	1992	1989	1992	1989	1992
311	7.3	7.2	6.2	11.3	4.7	7.6	7.1	8.0	5.0	5.7
313	1.8	2.6	8.7	8.6	1.8	1.7	2.6	2.6	2.2	2.3
314	0.2	0.2	1.0	2.0	0.5	0.5	4.7	4.7	2.2	2.3
321	6.8	6.3	9.5	4.7	4.6	4.5	4.2	4.0	2.3	2.0
322	1.8	1.8	3.3	1.9	2.6	2.9	1.8	1.5	1.1	0.9
323	0.6	0.5	0.9	0.5	0.6	0.5	0.3	0.2	0.2	0.2
324	2.0	2.0	2.0	1.1	1.1	1.0	0.7	0.7	0.2	0.2
331	2.1	2.3	2.0	1.3	1.0	1.0	2.3	2.5	1.1	1.0
332	1.2	1.2	2.0	1.3	1.6	1.5	3.3	3.8	1.4	1.7
341	2.5	2.0	1.4	1.5	1.7	1.5	4.4	4.1	2.3	2.7
342	0.9	1.0	0.7	0.7	2.0	1.9	3.8	4.3	1.9	2.0
351	5.7	5.5	3.7	4.6	7.3	7.0	4.3	4.0	7.4	6.7
352	1.1	1.5	2.7	2.7	5.6	6.3	3.5	2.9	5.4	5.0
353	2.8	2.6	4.7	6.1	3.8	4.5	1.9	1.6	3.4	4.2

	Czechoslovakia		Poland		Hungary		Austria		Germany	
	1989	1992	1989	1992	1989	1992	1989	1992	1989	1992
354	0.6	1.7	0.3	1.1	0.1	0.1	0.2	0.2	0.2	0.3
355	1.3	1.0	1.0	0.8	1.4	1.7	1.1	1.5	1.3	1.3
356	0.2	0.4	1.1	1.2	1.9	2.0	1.6	1.8	3.0	3.1
361	0.3	0.4	0.6	0.5	0.9	0.8	0.4	0.3	0.3	0.3
362	2.3	2.4	1.1	1.0	1.1	1.2	1.6	1.8	0.9	0.9
369	3.7	3.2	2.2	2.7	2.8	2.7	4.8	4.5	2.3	2.4
371	12.4	10.1	6.6	8.3	6.4	6.1	7.6	5.9	4.0	3.1
372	1.7	1.9	3.4	4.1	4.3	6.2	1.8	1.3	1.6	1.4
381	4.6	4.8	5.1	4.8	3.9	3.8	7.9	8.3	6.9	7.6
382	18.4	20.8	11.5	11.4	10.7	10.0	9.8	9.7	15.1	14.0
383	6.6	7.2	7.3	6.1	11.4	10.5	11.7	12.8	13.7	13.2
384	9.2	7.1	8.6	7.8	6.5	5.8	5.0	5.3	12.6	13.3
385	0.6	0.7	0.9	0.8	5.1	4.9	0.7	0.8	1.5	1.7
39	1.3	1.6	1.5	1.1	2.0	1.8	0.9	0.9	0.5	0.7

Source: UNIDO.

Table 7.7 Percentage shares in manufacturing employment

	Czechoslovakia		Poland		Hungary		Austria		Germany	
	1989	1992	1989	1992	1989	1992	1989	1992	1989	1992
311	6.8	7.4	11.3	13.8	14.8	16.8	8.1	8.6	5.1	5.7
313	1.3	1.8	0.9	1.2	2.1	2.3	2.0	2.0	1.2	1.3
314	0.2	0.2	0.3	0.4	0.4	0.5	0.2	0.2	0.2	0.2
321	8.2	8.3	9.7	8.2	7.5	5.9	5.9	5.5	3.4	3.0
322	3.8	2.4	5.6	6.2	5.3	5.6	3.9	3.3	2.1	1.8
323	1.0	0.9	1.2	0.7	0.8	1.3	0.5	0.4	0.3	0.3
324	2.7	2.4	2.8	2.6	2.6	2.6	1.3	1.1	0.5	0.4
331	2.4	2.2	2.2	2.2	1.1	1.9	2.6	2.9	1.5	1.6
332	2.4	1.7	2.8	3.1	2.3	2.3	4.8	5.6	2.0	2.1
341	1.9	2.0	1.4	1.4	1.2	1.2	3.2	3.0	2.3	2.4
342	1.1	1.2	1.3	1.2	1.6	2.2	3.9	4.1	2.6	2.7
351	3.6	4.0	3.2	3.3	3.3	3.2	3.3	3.2	4.4	4.2
352	1.0	1.0	2.1	2.2	2.1	2.5	3.0	2.8	4.0	4.1
353	1.0	1.2	0.5	0.7	0.4	0.5	0.6	0.6	0.3	0.3

	Czechoslovakia		Poland		Hungary		Austria		Germany	
	1989	1992	1989	1992	1989	1992	1989	1992	1989	1992
354	0.4	0.9	0.4	0.4	0.1	0.1	0.2	0.2	0.0	0.0
355	1.0	1.2	1.1	1.0	0.8	0.8	1.2	1.5	1.4	1.3
356	0.3	0.3	1.3	1.6	1.4	1.9	2.0	1.9	3.8	4.3
361	0.3	0.4	0.7	0.8	1.0	1.2	0.5	0.5	0.5	0.5
362	2.9	3.2	1.4	1.5	1.3	1.4	1.4	1.5	1.0	1.0
369	3.2	3.3	3.3	3.4	2.6	2.3	4.0	4.0	2.0	2.0
371	6.4	7.6	4.3	4.4	4.5	3.5	6.0	5.1	3.8	3.4
372	0.9	1.1	0.9	1.2	1.7	1.7	1.6	1.2	1.5	1.5
381	6.8	5.3	6.7	6.7	4.4	4.3	9.2	9.1	9.1	9.6
382	21.0	21.4	13.9	12.8	11.2	12.5	10.7	11.7	16.2	16.0
383	6.9	7.6	7.7	7.3	11.5	9.2	12.8	12.9	14.6	14.3
384	10.0	8.8	9.1	8.9	6.3	6.0	4.8	5.0	13.4	13.3
385	0.7	0.9	1.2	1.1	4.1	3.4	1.0	1.1	2.1	2.0
39	1.8	1.3	2.7	1.7	3.6	2.9	1.3	1.2	0.7	0.7

Source: UNIDO.

Table 7.8 Branch structure of manufacturing by role in consumption in constant 1990 US dollars by percentage of total

		Semi-manufactures	Investment goods	Consumption goods	Food and drink
Value added					
Czechoslovakia	1989	32.1	39.4	19.2	9.3
	1992	30.7	40.6	18.7	10.0
Poland	1989	27.4	33.4	23.3	15.9
	1992	33.1	30.9	14.1	21.9
Hungary	1989	35.5	37.6	17.2	7.0
	1992	38.6	35.0	16.6	9.8
Austria	1989	28.8	35.1	21.7	14.4
	1992	25.8	36.9	22.0	15.3
Germany	1989	29.8	49.8	11.0	9.4
	1992	28.7	49.8	11.4	10.3

		Semi-manufactures	Investment goods	Consumption goods	Food and drink
Employment					
Czechoslovakia	1989	21.0	45.4	25.3	8.3
	1992	24.2	44.0	22.4	9.4
Poland	1989	19.2	38.6	29.7	12.5
	1992	20.5	36.8	27.3	15.4
Hungary	1989	19.2	37.5	26.0	17.3
	1992	19.1	35.4	25.9	19.6
Austria	1989	23.8	38.5	27.4	10.3
	1992	22.3	39.8	27.1	10.8
Germany	1989	22.7	55.4	15.4	6.5
	1992	22.6	55.2	15.0	7.2

Source: UNIDO.

primarily as a feature of the country's position within the division of labour in the CMEA. This point can be supported from evidence in Table 7.6 of an exceptionally strong bias towards the non-electrical engineering category, which includes the kind of heavy capital equipment exported to the Soviet Union and other CMEA countries. Its representation in Czechoslovakia's manufacturing structure was even above the German level, while the Czechoslovak representation for both electrical machinery and transport equipment, less important components of exports to the East, was relatively modest. The high share for the iron and steel industries also ties in with the trade pattern both in terms of raw material-intensive heavy equipment exports and of the relatively cheap raw material imports from the former USSR.

A LASTING DISTORTION?

There have been differences in the specific policies pursued in the Czech Republic, the Slovak Republic, Poland and Hungary during the transformation period. Nevertheless the strategy of reform in all these countries is guided by the well-known common objectives associated with the creation of an open, market economy. In no case was there an explicit concept of active means to change branch structures within manufacturing. The course of restructuring was influenced rather by the broad conditions set by macroeconomic policy. This had two important consequences. The first, and most dramatic, impact of macroeconomic stabilization policies, coinciding with the collapse of the former CMEA division of labour, was the sharp decline in industrial production across east–central Europe, the extent of which was accentuated by recession in the developed market economies. The second consequence, stemming from the undervalued exchange rates of national currencies and by the extremely low labour costs, was a slowing down of the pace of structural change. Thus, substantial elements of the old pattern were reproduced.

The course and extent of the decline in industrial production in the period 1990–1993 is shown in Table 7.9 which, by indicating substantial differences across sectors, points clearly to some form of

Table 7.9 Percentage annual growth rates in industrial output in constant prices in selected east–central European countries

	Czech Republic	Slovakia	Hungary	Poland
All industry				
1990	–3.5	–4.0	–10.2	–24.2
1991	–21.8	–25.4	–16.6	–11.9
1992	–7.9	–13.8	–9.8	3.5
1993	–5.3	–10.6	4.0	5.6
1994	2.3	6.4	9.2	13.1
Mining and quarrying				
1992	–12.8	–11.7	–17.6	–8.5
1993	–7.1	–11.4	–0.1	–11.1
1994	0.9	–0.3	–14.8	6.1
Manufacturing				
1992	–14.6	–15.6	–16.9	4.8
1993	–7.7	–18.6	3.3	12.2
1994	0.2	1.4	8.6	14.9
Electricity and gas				
1992	–3.0	–5.1	–7.3	–6.0
1993	–4.6	–7.7	–2.2	–18.8
1994	–2.6	15.3	0.5	5.0

Source: Vienna Institute for Comparative Economic Studies, 1995.

structural change. The first sign of recovery leading to a restoration of industrial output growth was registered in 1992 in Poland, followed in 1993 in Hungary. The revival of industrial production in the Czech and Slovak Republics, as indicated in 1994 by growth rates that for the region as a whole were relatively modest, was delayed by the effects of the breakup of the Czechoslovak federation in January 1993. Nevertheless, in all cases the net effect even over the whole period 1990–1994 was a substantial decline in industrial output. As Table 7.9 indicates, the level in 1994 was only 65.9 per cent of the 1989 level in the Czech Republic. The decline was even greater in Slovakia while Poland, and to a lesser extent Hungary, recorded a smaller net decline, largely because growth had been resumed more rapidly.

The experience of developed market economies suggests that the restructuring of manufacturing during a period of recession or slow growth is likely to be a difficult and painful process. To some extent, the figures for east–central Europe point to a similar conclusion for the period 1989–1992. This, of course, was the time when the greatest impact of the macroeconomic stabilization policies was felt. The relevant statistical data are the value-added figures in US dollars using the three-digit level of the ISIC classification as summarized in Table 7.2. During the period 1989–1992, the structure of manufacturing industry in terms of value added was characterized by a small growth in the shares of early and middle industries alongside a decline in the shares of late industries. Nevertheless, as Table 7.4 indicates, the share of heavy manufacturing continued at an extremely high level, especially in Hungary, where it stood at 73.6 per cent in 1992, and in Czechoslovakia, where it accounted for 71.3 per cent of manufacturing value added in the same year.

Table 7.8 can be used to break this down somewhat further. 1992 figures suggest that the firmly dominant position of heavy manufacturing was maintained thanks largely to the stable and high share of semi-manufactures, at its highest in Hungary, and of investment goods production, particularly in Czechoslovakia. The semi-manufactures category continued to account for a larger share in total manufacturing value added in all three east–central European countries than in Austria and Germany. In the cases of Czechoslovakia and Poland, this was strongly influenced by the continuation of the higher share of iron and steel, as shown in Table 7.6. In Hungary the semi-manufactures category's share increased, thanks especially to the growing weight of the chemical and non-ferrous metals industries.

The figures also indicate that the high share for heavy manufacturing in the four east–central European countries is influenced by the position of engineering industries, especially in Czechoslovakia and Hungary. This can be partly explained in terms of technological weaknesses. The past orientation of both these countries towards the CMEA market ruled out access to the most modern technology and ensured that there was no strong competitive pressure forcing quality improvements. This was not entirely a voluntary choice. The scope for the Czechoslovak and other east European economies to break out from the confines of the CMEA system was also severely restricted from the western side by restrictions on the transfer of new and advanced technology and equipment, particularly in engineering, chemicals and some light industries. The result, then, was the high share of non-electrical machinery in the Czechoslovak case, in line with its role as the basic machinery producer for the eastern bloc, and the relatively low share of electrical machinery.

A decline in light manufacturing in the structure of manufacturing value added is typical for all east–central European countries. It was largely caused by the declining share of the consumer goods industry. The textile and clothing industries and the leather and shoe industries suffered a major setback because of declining domestic and export demand. In the case of the Czech and Slovak shoe industries, which were oriented primarily towards the Soviet market, the major influence was the collapse in trade with the East, alongside growing imports of shoes from developed market economies and Asian countries. By way of contrast, the share of food and beverages grew in all four cases, and especially markedly in Poland.

The share of the wood-processing industries in all these countries declined during the first period of the transformation process. At least the comparison with Austria could suggest potential for this sector. Indeed, in the former Czechoslovakia and in the Czech Republic, the industry had a long historical tradition and had achieved a substantial level of exports before 1989 to CMEA countries, especially the USSR. The relatively low shares for the paper, printing and publishing industries were typical across east–central Europe during the trans-formation process, with only Slovakia showing a share in manufactur-ing value added higher than Austria and Germany.

The conclusions from the comparative analysis of the value-added structure of manufacturing over the period 1989–1992 in Tables 7.6 and 7.7 are based on constant 1990 US dollar prices. Comparable figures are not yet available for later years. Moreover, the breakup of

*Table 7.10 Branch structure of value added in manufacturing in the
Czech and Slovak Republics compared with developed
market economies*

ISIC	Czech Republic		Slovakia	Average, market economies	Austria	Germany
	1992	1994	1994		1992	1991
31	13.3	13.8	15.6	14.6	13.4	10.6
321, 322	9.3	7.4	7.0	3.7	4.8	3.2
323, 324	3.3	1.8	2.0	0.4	0.8	0.4
33	7.1	5.8	4.4	5.3	7.1	3.3
341	2.4	2.5	4.5	4.8	3.3	2.7
342	2.9	2.3	2.5	6.1	3.7	2.0
351, 352	4.4	6.5	9.7	10.3	9.6	10.0
353, 354	1.6	3.8	5.7	2.6	2.2	3.5
355, 356	2.6	2.9	4.1	2.9	3.4	3.9
36	7.2	7.3	6.4	4.2	5.9	3.9
37	10.7	9.5	11.1	5.4	5.1	7.0
381	7.5	6.7	5.4	8.3	9.8	9.9
382	13.6	13.0	10.3	11.1	10.3	12.1
383	6.9	5.5	4.3	8.7	13.0	12.1
384	5.7	9.0	4.7	8.1	6.6	12.5
385	0.9	1.5	1.8	1.6	1.0	2.2
39	0.6	0.7	0.5	1.9	0.0	0.7

Sources: OECD, and *SR*, 1995.

the Czechoslovak federation in January 1993 adds a further complica-
tion. Figures for the period up to 1992 refer to Czechoslovakia as a
whole, while for later years a comparison is possible using separate
Czech and Slovak figures. Thus, Tables 7.10 and 7.11 give slightly
different results derived from estimates for Czech and Slovak

manufacturing value added in current prices, which are then compared with the average structure of manufacturing value added in the seven developed market economies, plus individual figures for Austria and Germany. All figures are in current prices in national currencies.

Table 7.11 Branch structure of value added in manufacturing by role in consumption in Czech and Slovak Republics, as percentage of total

		Semi-manufactures	Investment goods	Consumption goods	Food and drink
Czech Republic	1992	26.5	34.5	25.6	13.3
	1994	30.0	35.7	20.5	13.8
Slovakia	1994	37.0	26.5	20.9	15.6
Seven market economies		25.4	37.8	22.2	14.6
Austria	1992	26.2	40.7	19.7	13.4
Germany	1991	28.3	48.8	12.3	10.6

Sources: OECD, and Czech Statistical Office.

Although showing slightly different proportions from those revealed in the figures in US dollars, the results broadly confirm the previous conclusions, especially with the higher share in semi-manufactures in the Czech and Slovak Republics when compared with the developed market economies. This is a result in both countries of the higher share of basic metal industries and non-metallic mineral products and in Slovakia also of the high share of chemicals.

The share of investment goods, or engineering, is slightly lower in Slovakia than in the Czech Republic. In that latter case, as Table 7.11 shows, its share is near to the level of the average for the seven developed market economies. The main sign of a structural distortion in the engineering industry in both countries is, again, the low share for electrical machinery and the relatively higher share of non-electrical machinery.

Although the share of consumption goods in manufacturing value added in both countries in 1994 is relatively close to that in the seven developed market economies, there are signs of some specificity in the higher share of the textile, garment and leather industries in the Czech and Slovak Republics. The share for the wood-processing industries, despite a decline during the transformation period in both countries, appears from the figures in Table 7.10 to be comparable to its shares in developed market economies. The relatively higher share of paper industry in Slovakia is influenced by substantial investment undertaken in the past. These figures, based on current prices and in national currencies, do nevertheless confirm the lower share of printing and publishing in total manufacturing value added in both countries.

The position of the food-processing industries in manufacturing value added in both countries was strongly influenced by the policy of import substitution aimed at self-sufficiency pursued within the Czechoslovak federation before 1989. The sector was therefore oriented towards local markets and, with the exception of sugar and beer from the Czech Republic, very little was exported. The collapse of the CMEA market and the opening of the domestic market to outside competition therefore had only a minor impact on this branch, although there has been a growing threat from western imports. Its share in both countries is comparable to that in developed market economies, albeit a little higher in Slovakia.

Tables 7.12 and 7.13 show the changes in exports and imports of manufactured goods by SITC group, and reveal the expected close relationship to the branch structures of the individual countries. The highest share of manufactured goods, defined as SITC 6, in total exports is achieved by Slovakia, followed by the Czech Republic and Poland. The highest share for machinery is achieved by the Czech Republic followed by Hungary. The Czech Republic and Poland have lower shares for chemical and related products and Hungary has a very low share for manufactured goods. Both Poland and Slovakia have relatively lower shares of machinery in total goods export. Both the Czech Republic and Slovakia have relatively higher shares of manufacturing production as a whole in total goods exports. In all four countries the share of machinery in total goods imports is higher than its share in exports.

Table 7.12 Structure of exports by selected commodity groups, percentage of total

	Czech Republic	Slovakia	Hungary	Poland
Chemical and related products (SITC 5)				
1992	9.2	11.2	10.8	8.6
1993	9.5	12.0	12.1	6.8
1994	9.9	12.8	11.2	6.8
Manufactured goods (SITC 6)				
1992	32.3	41.9	16.0	27.1
1993	29.9	38.8	16.1	26.4
1994	30.5	39.2	16.6	27.5
Machinery (SITC 7)				
1992	25.4	17.4	20.8	19.2
1993	27.6	19.4	24.1	20.9
1994	26.1	19.4	25.6	19.6
Miscellaneous manufactured goods (SITC 8)				
1992	12.0	15.2	20.4	11.7
1993	12.7	13.4	17.8	19.4
1994	14.1	13.3	17.9	20.5
Total for these groups				
1992	78.9	85.7	68.0	66.6
1993	79.7	83.6	70.1	73.5
1994	80.6	84.7	71.3	74.4

Source: Bulletin of Central European Cooperation in Statistics, various issues.

Some analytical studies have pointed in the past to a strong similarity between the structure of exports of Hungary, Poland and former Czechoslovakia to the European Union and those of the Asian newly-industrialized countries. For both groups there was a strong bias towards such light industry branches as footwear, textiles and garments,

Table 7.13 Structure of imports by selected commodity groups,
percentages

	Czech Republic	Slovakia	Hungary	Poland
Chemical and related products (SITC 5)				
1992	9.8	9.8	12.9	13.5
1993	12.1	11.3	11.9	13.3
1994	13.1	13.3	12.7	14.7
Manufactured goods (SITC 6)				
1992	10.3	8.6	20.4	11.8
1993	15.9	15.1	18.2	18.5
1994	16.4	16.9	19.8	20.3
Machinery (SITC 7)				
1992	41.5	33.0	29.9	29.9
1993	36.1	29.3	36.6	29.4
1994	34.9	27.7	34.1	28.7
Miscellaneous manufactured articles (SITC 8)				
1992	9.3	8.3	12.2	10.3
1993	11.7	9.0	11.1	10.2
1994	11.8	8.9	11.3	9.9
Total for these groups				
1992	70.9	59.7	75.4	65.5
1993	75.8	64.7	77.8	71.4
1994	76.2	66.8	77.9	73.6

Source: As Table 7.12

broadly reflecting the comparative advantage of low labour costs.
There were, and are, however, some clear differences. Thus, Czech
exports to the European Union have shown high shares for wood,
paper and glass and also machinery and chemicals, while Slovakia has
been biased towards raw materials, metallurgy, wood, paper and

glass, Hungary towards food, agriculture and chemicals and Poland towards raw materials and semi-manufactures.

Three broad conclusions follow from this. The first is that the branch structures of manufacturing industry in east–central Europe did exhibit specific characteristics that were derived from the technological backwardness of, and division of labour within, the CMEA. The degree to which these structures diverged from what could have been expected in view of size and level of development varied somewhat between the countries, but signs of some degree of distortion are visible in every case. The second conclusion is that some changes have already taken place, leading towards a closer approximation to the structure of a small developed market economy. The decline in importance of leather and woodworking and the growth for transport equipment and industrial and other chemicals in the Czech case are examples. The third conclusion is that any specialization at the branch level seems to depend very much on the base inherited from the past. Thus, the Czech bias towards non-electrical machinery and basic metals seems to have changed very little.

This leaves predictions about the future very open. There is no need to expect the countries of east–central Europe ever to adopt branch structures identical to those of any other particular economy. They all differ in terms of historical and natural conditions. It can also be assumed that, with increasing integration of economies within Europe, individual and especially smaller countries will become more specialized in their industrial structures.

Nevertheless, a number of elements may be expected that would amount to a move closer to the branch structures of small market economies at the same level of development. In particular, the share of light manufacturing may be expected to increase, thanks especially to an acceleration in the growth of the food, paper and printing branches. These are cases in which the export potential was not realized within the framework of the CMEA. The share of heavy manufacturing may be expected to decline because of the fall in shares of semi-manufactured goods, such as chemicals and basic metals. These were well developed within the CMEA conditions, but their potential for further growth is already proving to be severely limited.

It would also be reasonable to expect a restructuring of the engineering industry with a decline in the share of non-electrical machinery and a possible expansion in the share of electrical machinery. In the meantime, the persistence of much of the branch structure inherited from the past can be taken as a further indication of the relatively early stage of structural change in the economies of east–central Europe. A great deal has changed, but a great deal more change can be expected.

Part III

Conclusion

8. Towards Sustainable Growth?

ARE THE TRANSFORMATIONS SIMILAR?

Assessments of the degree of 'success' of economic transformations, or of the policies pursued by governments, in east–central Europe typically end with a mixture of positive and negative points. Although there are differences across the region and to some extent every case is specific, it remains impossible in any case to produce a simple verdict. Nevertheless, a number of broad generalizations are possible.

The first is that in no case has there been a catastrophic failure. There were predictions from various critics in the years immediately after 1989 that attempts at a very rapid transition to a market economy would lead only to lasting economic depression, with the threat of political catastrophe. The failure of reform measures to prevent a massive fall in living standards and employment levels could, it was warned, lead to political opposition to further reform, or to a rise of the authoritarian right.

This was a major part of the opposition parties' platforms in the Czech Republic in the lead-up to the 1992 general elections. It is a continuing fear across the whole region, taken up, for example, by János Kornai (1995, p.200) in recent years, although he previously appeared as an advocate of generally radical reform measures without paying much attention to their political consequences. Above all, of course, plausible fears of catastrophe were fuelled by the sheer scale of the drop in national income from 1990 onwards, as shown in Table 4.4. Critics were quick to point out that this surpassed the impact of the depression of the early 1930s and appeared to be quite unprecedented in peacetime Europe.

It is possible to point to a number of political phenomena that may be related to problems with economic reform. Thus 'post-communist' parties have come to power in Poland and Hungary and the Party of

Democratic Socialism, an organization that grew out of the old East German ruling party, has significant support in parts of east Germany. These, however, reflect protests about more than just economic policy and do not point in any case to a strong desire for a reversal of changes that have already taken place. Moreover, no such political phenomena can be seen in the case of the Czech Republic. Economic reform has been accompanied by political stability and consolidation. Various economic indicators, such as the low level of unemployment, point to prosperity rather than permanent depression.

The course of political developments could even be used to reinforce a number of arguments that have been put forward for believing that official estimates of GDP may be misleading or inaccurate. Thus, it has been argued, the fall at the start of the 1990s may reflect a drop in output for goods that nobody really wanted and that it anyway should be set against the benefits of overcoming the economy of shortage and restoring equilibrium on consumer- and producer-goods markets. Past figures were exaggerated, as they were reported by enterprises wishing to claim higher output so as to secure bonuses for plan fulfilment. In a market economy, the pressure could be to under-report so as to evade taxes. It has also been suggested that a rapid growth in private enterprise, and possibly of an 'unofficial' economy, might not have been recorded fully.

The typical protagonists of these arguments have been staunch supporters of the reform measures that have become associated with the massive fall in recorded national incomes and living standards. This, of course, does not disprove any of the arguments, but they should not be allowed to hide the evidence of a clear drop in the production and consumption of a number of goods that people did want to buy. There therefore is good reason for believing that the macroeconomic policies at the start of the decade 'overshot' the target of achieving market equilibrium and caused an unnecessarily severe depression.

It is impossible to produce a reliable method of recalculating GDP changes in the early 1990s. According to one serious recent estimate, the fall in Czech GDP was overstated by about a third, thanks primarily to a failure to record a growth in the unofficial economy (Vintrová, 1994). There is, however, an even more important point here. The transformation, with the opening up of the economy to modern imports, widened and changed the range of choice for consumers. Money could be spent on foreign travel, or on modern consumer goods that had previously been unavailable. There was a definite shift away from food consumption, which had previously been high by international standards, and towards more sophisticated products.

It can be added that this was not purely a Czech phenomenon. In fact, one of the clearest indicators of a change in consumption patterns is the acceleration in the increase in private car ownership over the period 1989–1993, compared with the previous four years. This appears in Polish, Hungarian and Slovak statistics. It does not appear in the Czech Republic, which had already reached a higher level by 1989, and in which the population was more concerned to improve quality rather than quantity. Other indicators, however, such as modern electronic consumer goods, confirm areas of improvement in average Czech living standards.

This change in the structure of consumption is difficult to capture in a single quantity such as real wages or GDP. Aggregate national income figures therefore could have been calculated very accurately and still give a deceptive picture of how the population perceived the changes that had occurred.

This leads on to the second of the broad generalizations, which is that there clearly have been massive changes in the economic structures of the countries of east–central Europe. Any fears that they would remain stuck with the system of central planning now appear misplaced. It is even surprising that at one point policy debates were conducted in terms that implied a fear that nothing much might change. Thus, the advocates of the most radical reform measures accused their opponents of not really wanting to abandon central planning at all. Critics of the most radical steps frequently argued that pressing too hard with potentially unpopular measures could jeopardize the prospects for success and lead to a backlash, again with the end result of only limited changes from the old system.

The evidence in the earlier chapters of this book gives a clear picture of a massive transformation. It can be seen in the form and number of economic units, in the sectoral structures, and in the methods whereby the whole system functions. Open questions still remain as to what more is needed to achieve a 'complete' transformation into a modern market economy. It is also not absolutely clear precisely which policy measures have been the most important in opening the door to the changes that have occurred. Nevertheless, there is a great deal of similarity across the region, albeit with east Germany a somewhat special case, for reasons that follow directly from its incorporation into the large and powerful all-German economy.

The third broad generalization is that the results are not as good as the leading policy makers had hoped. Again, the early naivety can easily be forgotten, partly because results have been good enough not to confirm the fears of the most vociferous critics. All the governments seemed to be promising success in a relatively short period of time on the basis of relatively simple policy prescriptions. Again, the policy approach was somewhat different in the east German case, while there was more in common across Poland, Czechoslovakia and Hungary. None, however, predicted the extent of the drop in GDP in the early 1990s and nor did they predict how long it would take for growth to be resumed. That point remains valid even after any plausible re-estimation of GDP changes.

Indeed, in so far as serious attempts were made to forecast the future, the expectation was of a pretty small drop in output under the impact of liberalization and stabilization measures. This would soon be restored as enterprises quickly adapted to the new market conditions. The Czechoslovak government in late 1990 even saw the main danger in a possible sharp cut in oil and other raw material deliveries from the Soviet Union which might, under the worst conceivable circumstances, result in a 10 per cent drop in national income and a burst of inflation increasing prices by 35–45 per cent. The expectation was of a restoration of the 1989 level by mid-decade. The government tried to keep this report quiet because of a fear that it could cause 'panic' (Myant, 1993, p.188).

In fact, GDP fell by substantially more than this, assuming that the official statistics should be considered accurate, while inflation was higher and more persistent than forecast. Moreover, the fundamental cause of the GDP decline was a drop in demand — both domestic and for export — rather than any shortages of raw material inputs. The Czechoslovak government had failed to understand the nature of the economic processes that were coming into play.

This is not surprising. The transformation from a centrally-planned economy was itself unprecedented before the 1990s. It might have been possible to spot some of the problems ahead by extrapolating from Poland's experience in 1990 of a GDP fall currently recorded and shown in Table 4.4 as 10.2 per cent, following the introduction of the 'Balcerowicz Programme' in January 1990. This was very similar to the macroeconomic package applied in Czechoslovakia in January 1991 which, along with the drop in demand for exports following the collapse of relations within the CMEA, must be seen as the principal cause of the fall in national income. Generally, however, there was hardly time for busy policy makers to appreciate fully the significance of developments in another country.

The real point here is to emphasize the unexpected complexity of the transformation process. The notions of 'success' and 'failure' in the early years were themselves largely a reflection of this naivety. As is now clear, the alternatives were not simply a 'modern' market economy, as existed in the advanced countries of western Europe, or some form of chaos or even a return to central planning. The changes that have taken place, and the stage now reached, point to the need for a consideration of a more subtle range of possible alternatives.

HAS ECONOMIC THEORY FAILED?

If governments, and leading economists, were naive in their predictions and expectations, then that can justify posing again the question raised in Chapter 1 as to whether economic theory itself could not be judged to have 'failed'. The answer is twofold. In the first place, there is no single body of economic theory that could give a universally acceptable guidance on how a centrally-planned economy should be transformed. In the second place, no purely economic theory could ever provide an adequate framework for interpreting the complex changes that have taken place across east–central Europe.

The evidence in earlier chapters points to the diversity within economic theory, demonstrating very clearly that different philosophies were applied in east Germany and in the Czech Republic. It could be argued that there was no specific transformation strategy in east Germany. Policy was dominated by the speediest possible adoption of practices and institutions that had been tested and proved in the Federal Republic. Alongside this, however, was at least an implicit notion of what was needed. The actions of the *Treuhand-*

anstalt suggest that the weaknesses in the centrally-planned economy were to be overcome by bringing expertise, skills and contacts from west Germany. Private ownership alone was very clearly not considered the key issue. It was considered crucially important that real power in the economy went to the most appropriate people.

Viewed from the outside, that sounds both very pragmatic and very sensible. The strategy was followed with some interest across east–central Europe as an alternative to the methods of privatization actually adopted. A large, specialist institution, able to examine and assess business plans and impose conditions on new owners, could have great advantages over the very small Czech Ministry for Privatization, which was committed to leaving as far as possible all the difficult business decisions and judgements to new owners. East Germany, however, has clearly not provided a foolproof model. The extent of the negative consequences of the THA's privatization strategies have been covered in Chapters 1, 2 and 3 and are referred to again below.

In the Czech Republic, the approach to policy making was based on a very different theoretical perspective. Indeed, it could appear to have been far more ideologically based than the German approach, although, perhaps paradoxically, the effect in practice was to impose less rigid rules on some of the actors in the economic system.

Thus Czechoslovak, and subsequently Czech, policy making was strongly influenced by what Václav Klaus likes to refer to as 'standard' economic theory. By this he means neoclassical, or sometimes neoliberal theory, as presented in many 'standard' textbooks. The key element is the notion of a market economy functioning, in line with elementary textbook theory, through instantaneous adjustments in response to price signals. From this followed the insistence on macroeconomic stabilization measures, in line with the orthodox IMF thinking and also a precondition in theory for the normal functioning of a price mechanism, plus the approach to privatization. Once firms were in private hands, so it was believed, there would be pressure on managements to improve efficiency.

There are obvious differences here from the east German approach. In that case, privatization was linked with bringing in expertise, experience and better management practices. In the Czechoslovak, and subsequently the Czech, case, the issue was one of creating a structure of controls and incentives. This has continued to be a starting point for a great deal of subsequent research — including some referred to in Chapter 5 — on changes at the enterprise level, with a strong focus on the issue of 'corporate governance'. The initial questions have related to the impact of the new ownership structures created by privatization on managements and hence on changes within enterprises. A common conclusion has been that ownership explains less than might be expected in terms of simple economic theory.

More generally, it can be argued that this kind of economic theory is bound to 'fail' when confronted with the realities of economic transformation in east–central Europe. It leads to too abstract and too oversimplified a view of the world. Moreover, the nature of the abstraction makes it impossible to encompass a number of other factors, and even theoretical perspectives, that are essential to an understanding of the transformation processes at work. Indeed, no purely economic theory can be a fully adequate starting point because the changes under way go beyond the narrow confines of economic questions. Four key areas can be identified in which what Klaus refers to as 'standard' economic theory is inadequate.

The Role of Politics

The first is the area of interrelationships between economic and political or social factors. The comparison between east Germany and the Czech Republic demonstrates the immense importance of politics in setting the direction of economic changes. Czech advocates of rapid reform measures argued that economic theory pointed to no alternative to the policies they were pursuing. In east Germany there seemed to be 'no alternative' to a completely different set of policy measures. In both cases the choices made are explicable in terms of the political backgrounds.

In east Germany a ready-made model seemed to exist, available for importing from the West. With this went a willingness to wipe out the heritage of the GDR to a far greater extent than was possible in any other part of the former Soviet bloc. Thus, the combines that had dominated the centrally-planned economy could be swept aside as an unfortunate aberration that had no lasting place within German society. Privatization could amount almost to a completely fresh start for what had become a regional economy.

In the Czech case, there was no practical model available but rather a set of guidelines, or even an ideological position, that could be derived from what is currently mainstream economic thinking. There were strong political reasons for the success of thinking associated with prestigious international bodies, such as the IMF, and with the 'radical right' that had inspired Margaret Thatcher and Ronald Reagan in Britain and the United States, respectively. This seemed to be the clearest, most decisive and safest guarantee of a complete break from the communist past. With it came the priority to macroeconomic stabilization and hence a whole number of policies that have affected changes within enterprises. An example is the cautious handling of debts inherited from the past which, unlike the east German case and partly as a result of fears and pressures from the IMF, were carried forward into the new market system, causing severe problems to many enterprises.

In some respects, however, the comparison with east Germany can illustrate how far the past was not rejected. Thus, there were free market economists who looked with contempt at the giant companies that had dominated the Czechoslovak economy under central planning, but their thinking could not determine policy making. The government ministers in charge of economic policy — especially Vladimír Dlouhý, who took charge of the State Planning Commission in December 1989 and went on to become Czech Minister for Industry and Trade after June 1992 — made it absolutely clear from the start that they would not allow the destruction of the 'core' of the economy. Above all, they stepped in to defend large engineering combines when faced with financial catastrophe. This partly reflected fears of social consequences. It also reflected a sense of national pride in the industries and firms, such as Škoda, ČKD and others referred to in earlier chapters, which had grown up with the modern Czech nation.

Ideology was also tempered by a further important form of Czech pragmatism. The aim was almost universally accepted as the creation of a modern market economy similar to the advanced countries of western Europe. This is not the same as the picture of an economic system built up from the abstractions of economic theory. Indeed, neoliberal thinking typically leads to strong criticisms of the degree of state involvement that is found in western Europe's market economies. State intervention is frequently dismissed as a factor distorting the otherwise perfect functioning of a market mechanism and reflecting a willingness to yield to political lobbying.

There have, therefore, been inevitable conflicts between the policy recommendations that can be derived from two different possible starting points. Neither has dominated in total. Elements of a western European interventionist approach have been adopted, such as some forms of advice and support to new small businesses. Others have been resisted. Thus, internal demands for a consistent policy of support to exporters which, as indicated in Chapter 7, would help above all the large engineering firms that can only sell their heavy equipment on the basis of extended credits, have met with only partial success and only after very substantial delays. The key obstacle has been the opposition of Prime Minister Klaus to what he sees as the effort of a powerful lobby to gain softer conditions for itself.

Thus, a purely economic theory cannot explain the course even of the purely economic aspects of the transformations. As a result, it cannot on its own be an adequate guide to policy making. Ignoring constraints from the political and social spheres can only lead to inconsistent policy making. A clear example is precisely the Czech approach towards the large firms inherited from the past. On the one hand, there was no consistent policy for handling the problem of old debts and creating conditions for future success, for example with the creation of a framework for encouraging R&D and for guaranteed export credits. On the other hand, however, the same enterprises were not left to die, in the hope that their place could be taken by newly-emerging firms. The result, as critics have frequently pointed out (for example, J. Klacek, *Hospodářské noviny*, 20 April 1995), was a series of *ad hoc* measures that lacked consistency.

The Firm in Transition

The second area in which economic theory appears inadequate relates to the theory of the firm. 'Standard' theory starts with the assumption that all firms are the same and, in the simplest and most abstract version, are concerned only with adjusting price and output of a single product so as to maximize profit. The firm has no internal life or structure. Nor does it have a history with a body of experience built up over years. It is in effect an entity that does no more than undertake an arithmetical calculation.

This abstract theory cannot explain the growth and existence of large, multiproduct firms, bringing together R&D, marketing and other specialist activities. There clearly is something missing in the theory, not least because differences in performance between economies are often related to differences between their firms, including issues such as how they are financed, how managements interact with owners and how firms relate to state bodies.

In fact, one of the problems for purely economic theory has been to explain exactly why large firms exist at all when, in theory, all relationships could be successfully mediated through the market. Thus, for example, a firm need not set up its own R&D department but could buy in services as required. It appears, however, that success in some sectors depends precisely on the close integration within one organizational structure of research, production and selling.

Large parts of modern market economies are therefore dominated by sizeable companies that emerged and grew, often towards the end of the nineteenth century. There clearly are advantages in complex organizational structures which bring together 'complementary assets', and build up experience, their own culture and networks of relatively stable relationships with other firms (Dosi, Teece and Winter, 1992). Success, then, is not just instantaneous adjustment to market signals. Moreover, the permanence and organizational complexity of the modern firm mean that changes do not occur suddenly and completely. They have to be built on the past, whether classified as 'adaptive', meaning responses to the changed environment, or 'initiative', meaning the development of completely new activities.

The point could be related to a somewhat different approach to the theory of the firm, combining elements from economics and the study of organizations. A possible starting point is Alfred Marshall, a father figure to an earlier generation of British economists. Although often 'blamed' for the theory of the firm that spread through textbooks from the 1930s onwards, he consistently tried to base his theories on empirical generalization rather than on pure abstraction. One such case was the notion of the 'life cycle' of the firm.

In this view, a new firm is born out of the enthusiasm of an entrepreneur, goes through a period of growth, but eventually dies when another generation is expected to take over management but lacks the will and determination (Marshall, 1920, Chapter 13). This is a typical story of a family firm. Schumpeter (1943, Chapter 13), albeit less dramatically, also put forward a kind of life-cycle view, in which the firm would be established by an enthusiastic entrepreneur but eventually stagnate into a lifeless and boring bureaucracy.

The history of large companies does not fit with either of these views. Both Marshall and Schumpeter were guilty of linking the fate of the firm to the individual entrepreneur who founded it. They probably exaggerated the significance of a founding individual even at the very start. Leaving that aside, the successful company must over a period of time create structures that can enable it to keep adapting to new circumstances. It is, then, possible to develop a life-cycle theory that does not assume death. Indeed, a firm that is chronologically old may be able to behave in a youthfully innovative manner.

On this basis, it is possible to distinguish a number of phases in a firm's life. The most difficult and problematic is likely to be the initial formation of the firm. This requires some kind of original idea, which is unlikely to be developed by one person alone without a circle of business contacts. It also needs finance, and this is frequently cited as the major barrier. Anything beyond the most rudimentary form of business organization also requires managerial expertise, and that often does not come with entrepreneurship in the purest form. Already, the complexity of the task of forming a new business points to the need to consider a comprehensive institutional and policy framework based on an understanding of how the process works.

Once a firm has been established in a line of business activity, it can hope to grow and develop relatively stable internal structures and relationships with other businesses. It will, however, almost certainly be faced by the need at some point to react to changes in the external environment. The ability to adapt is therefore crucial to business success. It is, to repeat, not a question of reacting to immediate market signals in the form of a change in prices. The real problems relate to the need for more substantial forms of adaptation, for example when the product range is judged to have become obsolete. Needless to say, this is a stage at which many firms do fail.

How, then, does adaptation take place? The central message from studies of past experience is that it is not a question of dramatic changes. Nor, however, is it a matter of 'muddling through' with no clear longer-term strategic vision. Writers in the field, such as John Kay (1993, p.4) and Mintzberg and Quinn (1991, pp.97–8), refer rather to 'adaptive and opportunistic' strategies which emerge by linking together 'strategic subsystems' by a process of 'logical incrementalism'. Adaptation, then, builds on ideas and experiences from within the existing organization. It therefore cannot be based on a complete rupturing from the past.

These general points are to a great extent reflected in the visible structures of large companies today. They typically have undertaken some degree of diversification, but into fields that clearly are related to their primary activities. That has led to very different structures from those of the giant firms or combines under central planning, as outlined in Chapter 2. It is consistent with past behaviour based on a gradual process of learning from acquired experience. A firm's history both creates possibilities for future development and creates constraints, ruling out changes that would be too dramatic.

This account points to possible criticisms of policies in both east Germany and the Czech Republic. In the German case, where the desire to sweep away the past was at its strongest, little attention was paid to possibilities of an 'adaptive' process, building on the past. As is pointed out in Chapters 2 and 3, it is unclear what the results would have been from different privatization strategies. The currency unification plus the collapse of trade with the traditional partners in the East presented immense problems for east German enterprises. It is therefore impossible to say with confidence what different outcome might have been achieved. Nevertheless, there may well have been a price for an oversimplified view of how the adaptation process could take place.

The relationship between theory and Czech practice is more complex, largely because the results of policy decisions were even further removed from the expectations that could be derived from pure theory. The point can be illustrated in two parts. The first relates to the expected impact on firms of the twin reform measures of macroeconomic stabilization, meaning the drastic reduction in the level of demand, and privatization.

The aim, of course, was to impose the discipline of hard budget constraints on enterprises that had lived under the 'soft' conditions of central planning. The argument above rather suggests that this misses the point. Far from requiring strict financial discipline at all times, success depends on a *soft* budget constraint *in the short run*, albeit with the threat of competition and bankruptcy essential in a longer-term context. This is in line with Schumpeter's observation that entrepreneurship, in the sense of inventive business ideas, needs to be combined with relatively easy access to various forms of credit.

A related implication is that firms do not need continual rigorous control from owners. The separation between ownership and control in capitalist economies in the inter-war period was documented by Berle and Means (1968). Subsequent studies suggest that, particularly in 'management-intensive' activities which require substantial expertise and knowledge of the specific business area, there are clear advantages for management-controlled firms (Chandler, 1990). The whole argument above suggests that controlling managers, and hence much of the emphasis on research into the area of corporate governance, is only one, and probably not the most important, issue. More important issues relate to how firms can find finance on terms that are not too strict and how far they can formulate and implement strategic decisions. It is a matter of enabling as much as of controlling managements.

Set in this context, Czech privatization strategy presents rather a mixed picture. In theory the aim, particularly behind the voucher method, was to find new, private owners as quickly as possible. They were then to exert the required pressure on previously indolent managers. In practice, however, as outlined in Chapter 5, voucher privatization left considerable power in the hands of existing enterprise managements.

Although this was one of the grounds on which voucher privatization has been criticized, it could be seen as a strength. In Chapter 6 it is even suggested that one of the great advantages for Czech enterprises is the lack of rigid control over their managements, who have scope to develop new strategic thinking. They have not in all cases taken advantage of this freedom, and different methods of privatization might have put them under greater pressure to do so.

One alternative would have been to create an agency able to give advice and lay down conditions. It would not, of course, have been possible to reproduce in total an analogy to the THA. No Czech agency could have ignored to so great an extent the interests of the area in which it operated. Nor, however, could it have claimed the same access to expertise on the operation of a market economy.

The remarkable point about the arguments in Chapter 6 is the extent to which policy choices look different when viewed from the enterprise. Thus, for example, one important part of the thinking behind arguments for subjecting enterprises to a sudden 'shock' appears to have been misplaced. The view was that a hard blow, with the very rapid conversion of a sellers' into a buyers' market, would force them to recognize that the good times from the past were over.

In fact, as Chapter 6 indicates, managements were aware of the need to seek alternatives as soon as the political system changed. They were almost immediately looking to the establishment of new international contacts. The speed with which foreign trade was reorientated confirms that they were not all sitting in idle paralysis. Thus, the policy package implemented in January 1991, involving liberalization and the depression of domestic demand, was just one episode that impinged on an ongoing adaptation process.

Very much the same can be said of privatization. It did represent a very important change, but it has to be set in the context of a more prolonged process of change within enterprises. It could be a sudden break, when a completely new management took over. That, however, was far less typical in the Czech Republic than in east Germany. Its importance in other cases has been greatest when linked to finding means to overcome financial difficulties or weaknesses in managerial expertise.

This, it can be emphasized, was not recognized by the key decision makers in the Czech government. Indeed, leading officials privately admitted during the early 1990s to having very little information on what was really going on at the enterprise level. Their policy making was guided by generalizations derived from a theoretical framework which suggested that macroeconomic policies and privatization should have been the key factors.

Market Economies are Different

The third area in which economic theory appears inadequate follows on from the recognition of differences between firms and between political environments. Thus, there are differences among market economies. This argument was treated with understandable suspicion by policy makers in the early stages of the Czech transformation, partly because it was used as a foundation for criticisms of the key government policies in both the macro- and the microeconomic fields. If accepted, so it was argued, it could have led to dithering, indecision and a failure to take any radical steps at all. In fact, the observation that the state may play a larger role in some developed market economies than others was used as an argument against speedy privatization (for example, M. Matějka, *Hospodářské noviny*, 1990, No. 7).

The point here is slightly different and can be divided into two themes. The first is that market economies are themselves subject to rapid change. This is not just a matter of economic growth in the sense of an increase in a single quantity. It is also a matter of structural change, involving a development of the institutional and infrastructural framework. This affects the criterion of 'success' set out at the start of the book. The aim is not just the creation of a market economy in the simplest sense of a price mechanism and private ownership. The aim is a 'modern' market economy, and that has only grown up over a long period time during which it was helped by a complex policy framework.

The second theme is that different countries have different possibilities that relate to features independent of the economic system. Thus, each one of the former centrally-planned economies has a different endowment in terms of infrastructure, skill levels, inherited sectoral structures, geographical position and political background. Comparisons between the Czech Republic and Slovakia in Chapters 4 and 5 point to some clear differences in the extent of 'new' growth, particularly around the export of products from the engineering industry, and in the nature of regional problems. There are also differences in the potential for tourism to the two countries. A very careful assessment of the prospects for the Czech economy from the research team working for the main trade union centre even suggested that the country was living off 'investment by our ancestors' in the form of the historical monuments built in former centuries (Útvar makroekonomick ých analýz a prognóz, 1993, p.8).

This comparison could be taken further. Countries further to the East have far less chance of achieving the kind of structural changes outlined for the Czech Republic in Chapter 5. The implication must be that there need be no universal 'theory' of, and no 'standard' recipe for, a successful transformation. Different policies may be appropriate to different countries. Indeed, different targets may be appropriate, with the Czech Republic enjoying a heritage from the past and a geographical location that must raise hopes of an early, full integration into western Europe.

Static Equilibrium Is Not Enough

The fourth area in which economic theory appears inadequate relates to the workings of the market mechanism itself. Static equilibrium analysis implicitly assumes instantaneous adjustments to price signals, or at least it assumes that the time taken for adjustment to occur is irrelevant to the outcome. The reality is that different processes occur over different time periods and incidentally also depend to differing extents on a favourable policy framework. Thus, as emphasized in Chapter 1 and reaffirmed across east–central Europe in Chapter 4, the reduction in output in response to a fall in demand can come very quickly. Growth in new output takes varying periods of time, depending most obviously on the amount of investment needed.

This point has been used by Kornai (1995) to explain the 'transformation recession' and subsequent recovery. A fall in GDP was, he suggests, an inevitable result of no more than this chronological mismatch. 'Recovery' takes the form of structural change, with growth appearing in different kinds of activities after varying time lags. As Kornai points out, however, some elements of 'new' growth may be heavily dependent on the creation of a more sophisticated institutional framework. Referring particularly to Hungary, he pinpoints problems with the weak development of the financial sector and some areas typically subject to substantial state involvement in advanced market economies. His conclusion is that there needs to be some degree of policy reorientation towards the active creation of the preconditions for further, secure growth.

A THREE-STAGE TRANSFORMATION

This can be developed further into a comparative account of transformations that makes an attempt to divide the process into stages. At least three can be identified in a comparison of east German and Czech experience, although there are substantial differences between the two countries.

The first stage was one in which three important developments broadly coincided. The first was the fall in output from the large enterprises oriented both to export and to the domestic market. The second was the rapid growth in new small businesses, especially in the service sector. They, initially at least, were based on very low levels of capital investment, were not part of complex networks and for the most part lacked the preconditions for growth into larger firms. Thus a substantial very-small-business sector came into being, bringing with it a lot of benefits, but its prospects for further growth are severely limited. The third early new development was a reorientation of exports to western markets, affecting initially those sectors that required no significant adaptation of the product. That largely meant raw materials and basic products such as steel.

In east Germany the first, and to a lesser extent the second, elements mentioned above are clearly present. The difficulties in the large enterprises were, however, substantially more severe, leading to disintegration rather than just crisis. The position now is that reports from DIW and other research institutes have pinpointed the absence of large firms as one of the identifiable weaknesses of the east German economy, also hampering the development of smaller firms. Moreover, the growth in raw material exports appears to have been less important than in east–central Europe, and this could help explain the sharper drop in overall industrial output.

The differences between countries in this first export success can be related to some extent to the inheritance from the past. Poland had greater potential for a rapid growth in food exports while its metallurgy exports grew more slowly after 1989, having risen rapidly in the 1980s at a time of severe domestic difficulties.

Generally, however, the differences between countries owe a great deal to their different exchange-rate policies. East Germany obviously suffered from the currency reunification. Comparisons across east–central Europe in Chapter 4 also rather suggest that the greater the undervaluation of the currency the greater the potential for raw material exports. That is hardly a surprising conclusion. The dangers of setting the exchange rate too high too soon are also clear from the pressure for devaluation across the whole region. Nevertheless, this does not appear to provide a basis for sustained growth. All the signs are that this was largely a one-off event with export levels tending towards a plateau.

In the second stage, the Czech transformation continued with a sharp increase in exports to western Europe of manufactured goods, including products of the engineering industry. These were cases either where new selling arrangements had to be established or where some adaptation of the product was necessary. Privatization may have helped, especially where it involved closer links with a foreign partner or some degree of subdivision of existing large enterprises. The low exchange rate and low wage levels were clearly important in attracting orders from nearby western firms for particular components or production processes. There is little evidence of major changes in technology, apart from some case of direct foreign investment.

There were analogous tendencies in Poland, particularly with the growth from light industry, which jumped from 7.0 per cent of total exports in 1991 to 15.9 per cent in 1993, or 20 per cent of exports to the EU. This required some adaptation of the product but was possible on the basis of existing technology. A growth in Czech consumer goods exports into the EU, including a strong representation for textiles, occurred at roughly the same time. Analogies in Slovakia, where the key exports continued to be basic products and raw materials, are harder to find. That may reflect a permanent weakness in the Slovak economy or it may be no more than a matter of timing with this stage somewhat delayed. Figures for 1995 still show the intermediate products category accounting for 41.2 per cent of exports, compared with 38.8 per cent in 1993. The smaller shares for engineering and consumer goods had declined further over the same period.

There is an east German equivalent to this new kind of export activity in the 'extended work-bench' with western firms covering for capacity shortages, often only short term, by using newly-acquired east German facilities. That, however, was more likely to be associated with full ownership by the western firm and appears not to have been anything like as substantial a phenomenon. As suggested in Chapter 1, west German firms may have found it more advantageous to seek partners in the lower-wage economies of east–central Europe.

The key question, however, is the potential for future development. An 'extended work-bench' can be abandoned in times of lower demand. Alternatively, it may become the basis for further investment and development. There are examples in the Czech Republic of links starting with orders for a specific component and developing into full integration into a major production programme, including substantial outside investment. Such cases are, however, not as yet typical.

Two comments can be made on this 'stage' in the transformation process. The first is that its importance varies across east–central Europe. It is much more visible in the Czech Republic than in Slovakia, a country with fairly similar macroeconomic preconditions. The Czech success depends, it can be suggested, on geographical proximity to western Europe, the good transport and communications network that came with the high level of development achieved in the past, a reliable workforce available at very low rates of pay and, finally, the heritage of an industrial structure that could adapt fairly quickly in this way.

The second comment is that this may not be a 'necessary' stage. Only some of these preconditions exist in east Germany but, thanks to the closer integration into the all-German economy, there are probably greater possibilities for jumping over this stage altogether, with the development of new production processes using completely new technology. That, however, is still a relatively small phenomenon. Nevertheless, the relative weakness of this stage in east Germany could already be partly compensated by a different transformation route. There has been far more new investment in the infrastructure, itself encouraging a boom in the construction sector and in construction-related manufacturing. Higher incomes have also contributed to growth in those sectors of manufacturing that stay close to their markets, including much of the food industry. Again, then, the structural changes in east Germany have been following a different pattern with 'new' growth taking a somewhat different form.

This brief account points to two conclusions. The first is that transformations in different countries are following somewhat different paths, although this may not be obvious from macro-economic indicators alone. The second is that many of the individual processes that make up the full transformation seem to have only a limited potential. It is not clear that a basis has yet been created for sustainable and rapid growth. That rather depends on entering a new, third stage in which new technologies are used to make new, internationally-competitive products.

The discussion of the experience of east Germany and of the Czech Republic leaves open the precise prerequisites for this. In the analysis of east German experience, especially in Chapters 1 and 3, there has been a strong emphasis on the importance of interrelation-ships between different kinds of firms and on the need for a structure that includes both large and smaller enterprises. The policies adopted, however, have led to the effective disappearance of the larger firms. It is unclear whether this can be overcome, and if so by what means. The framework within which policy for east Germany is being decided rather suggests that it will develop as a peripheral region within the all-German economy, without a secure economic base of its own.

A major emphasis has been placed on developing the basic infrastructure of a modern economy, and this could be expected to make the region more attractive to inward investment. So far, however, the results are not particularly impressive. Indeed, it is not clear that the Czech Republic, in which infrastructural investment has not been a priority, has suffered for tending to ignore this area. This could, however, prove a far more substantial barrier to a future transition into that elusive third stage of the transformation process.

It is not even clear what the key firms would be in the full development of a modern market economy. There could, however, be a major role for large enterprises inherited from the previous economic system, many of which have established close partnerships with western firms. They have not been given all the help they could ask for but, in contrast to the German case, they have been allowed to survive.

Although solid arguments have been given above as to why policies could not be based on a purely economic logic alone, an ideal transformation strategy might have involved different elements from the two cases considered. There were clear advantages in adopting a German, or west European, policy and institutional framework rather than allowing policy to be influenced in many cases by an excessively abstract theory. This, however, needed to be combined with a conscious strategy for developing from the heritage of the past, and in particular for ensuring that big firms not only survived but were also given an environment in which they could adapt and formulate long-term strategies. That was bound to take time, reinforcing arguments for protecting the early stages of the transformation with an ample exchange-rate cushion.

Unfortunately, there were very good reasons why such a hybrid model was not applied in practice in either of the two cases under consideration. The important question today is whether further policy measures will be required to ensure self-sustaining growth across the region. At the time of writing it is very much an open question as to whether this is imminent.

Results for 1995 across east–central Europe have pointed to very encouraging GDP growth, reaching 7.0 per cent in Poland, 7.4 per cent in Slovakia, 4.8 per cent in the Czech Republic and a less impressive 1.1 per cent in Hungary. In each case, industrial output growth has been particularly strong. In Hungary and Slovakia, this has been associated with signs of a reorientation towards exports. In Poland and the Czech Republic it has been associated with increasing trade deficits. It remains to be seen whether common forces are at work in the different countries. It may all prove to be part of another sub-stage with limited potential — perhaps with domestic industry adapting to cover some of the increase in domestic demand — or it may be the start of consistent and self-sustaining growth based on the creation of a new technological base.

References

Auer, J. and W. Müller (1993), 'ECP: Bilaterale Wirtschaftsvergleiche mit Polen, Ungarn, ČSFR, Jugoslawien, Rumänien und Sowjetunion', *Statistische Nachrichten*, No. 8.

Berle, A., and G.C. Means (1968), *The Modern Corporation and Private Property*, New York: Harcourt, Brace & World Inc.

BfW (1995a), *Entwicklung des Mittelstandes in den neuen Bundesländern zum 31.12.1994*, Berlin.

BfW (1995b), *Wirtschaftsdaten Neue Länder*, Berlin.

Burrows, R. (ed.) (1991), *Deciphering the Enterprise Culture: Entrepreneurship, Petty Capitalism and the Restructuring of Britain*, London: Routledge.

BVS (1995), *Abschlußstatistik der Treuhandanstalt per 31.12.1994*, Berlin.

Carlin, W., J. van Reenen and T. Wolfe (1994), *Enterprise Restructuring in the Transition: An analytical survey of the case study evidence from central and eastern Europe*, Working Paper No. 14, London: European Bank for Reconstruction and Development.

Chandler, A. Jr. (1990), *Scale and Scope: The Dynamics of Industrial Capitalism*, Cambridge, Mass.: Belknap Press.

Chenery, H. and L. Taylor (1968), 'Development patterns among countries and over time, *Review of Economics and Statistics* **50** (4), pp.391–416.

DIW (1993), *Stand und Entwicklungsperspektiven des Forschungspotentials der chemischen Industrie im Raum Halle, Merseburg, Bitterfeld*, Report to BfW, Berlin.

DIW (1994), *Aufbau des industriellen Mittelstands in den neuen Bundesländern*, Berlin.

Donges, J.B., H. Klodt, and K.D. Schmidt (1986), *The West German Economy Toward the Year 2000: An Analysis of Structural Change*, Working Paper No. 268, Kiel: Institute of World Economics.

Dosi, G., D.J. Teece, and S. Winter (1992), 'Towards a theory of corporate coherence: preliminary remarks', in G. Dosi, R. Giannetti, and P.A. Toninelli (eds), *Technology and Enterprise in a Historical Perspective*, Oxford: Oxford University Press.

Fels, G., K.W. Schatz, and F. Wolter (1971), 'Der Zusammenhang zwischen Productionsstruktur und Entwicklungsniveau. Versuch einer Strukturprognose für die westdeutsche Wirtschaft', *Weltwirtschaftliches Archiv*, No. 106.

Fels, G. and K.D. Schmidt (1980), *Die deutsche Wirtschaft im Strukturwandel*, Tübingen: Kiel Institute of World Economics.

Gemeinnützige Gesellschaft für Wissenschaftsstatistik (1993), *Forschung und Entwicklung in der Wirtschaftsstatistik. Ergebnisse und Schätzungen 1991 bis 1992*, Essen.

Hálek, I. (1993) 'Vyzrávání středního stavu', *Národní hospodářství*, No. 12.

Havlík, P. (1995), *CEEC–EU Trade: Recent Trends and Some Hypotheses of the Future Integration and Competitiveness*, Vienna: Vienna Institute for Comparative Economic Studies.

Hejkal, J. (1994), 'Manažeři a vlastníci', *Ekonom*, No. 30.

Hoffman, W.G. (1968), *The Growth of Industrial Economies*, Manchester: Manchester University Press.

Hornich, S., et al. (1993), *Kombinate: Was aus ihnen geworden ist*, Berlin/Munich: Verlag Die Wirtschaft GmbH.

IWH (1991), *Schlussbilanz der DDR*, Halle.

Karasz, P. (1995), *Foreign Trade Development in East and Central Europe*, Bratislava: Institute for Forecasting, Slovak Academy of Sciences.

Kay, J. (1993), *Foundations of Corporate Success: How Business Strategies Add Value*, Oxford: Oxford University Press.

Klvačová, E. (1994), 'V těžké roli vlastníka', *Ekonom*, No. 49.

Klvačová, E. (1995), 'Vláda v rukou managementu', *Ekonom*, No. 48.

Kornai, J. (1995), *Highway and Byways*, Cambridge Mass.: MIT Press.

Lemoine, F. (1994), *CEEC Exports to the EC (1988–1993): Country Differentiation and Commodity Diversification*, Document de Travail No. 94, Paris: CEPII.

Marshall, A. (1920), *Principles of Economics*, 8th edn, London: Macmillan.

Mintzberg, H. and J. Quinn (1991), *The Strategy Process: Concepts, Contexts, Cases*, 2nd edn, Englewood Cliffs, NJ: Prentice-Hall.

Myant, M. (1993), *Transforming Socialist Economies: The Case of Poland and Czechoslovakia*, Aldershot: Edward Elgar.

Myant, M. (1994), *New Firms in East Central Europe: The Case of the Czech Republic*, European Studies Working Paper No. 3, Paisley: University of Paisley.

Myant, M. (1995), 'Transforming the Czech and Slovak economies: evidence at the district level', *Regional Studies*, **29** (8) pp.753–760.

OECD (1994), *Economic Survey: Czech Republic, Slovak Republic*, Paris: OECD.

Oswald, E. (1994), 'Po první vlně: vyřešila kuponová privatizace vlastnické vztahy?', *Ekonom*, No. 21.

Pöschl, J. (1995), 'WIIW Forecast for 1995-1997', *Monthly Report of Vienna Institute for Comparative Economics*, No. 11.

Rittenau, R. (1995), 'Wirtschaftsvergleiche mit Östereichs Nachbarländern', *Statistische Nachrichten*, No. 9-10.

Schäfer, R. and J. Wahse (1990), 'Prognostische Einschätzung des Einflusses moderner Technologien auf das gesellschaftliche Arbeitsvermögen in der DDR', *Mitteilungen aus der Arbeitsmarkt- und Berufsforschung*, No. 1.

Schumpeter, J. (1943), *Capitalism, Socialism, and Democracy*, London: George Allen & Unwin, Ltd.

Štatistický úrad Slovenskej republiky (1994), *Údaje o prímoch domácností za SR*, Bratislava.

Statistisches Bundesamt (1994), *Sonderreihe mit Beitragen für das Gebiet der ehemaligan DDR*, Vol. 19.

THA (1994), 'Bericht des Vorstands der THA über den Abschluss der Arbeiten zum 31.12.1994', *Informationsblatt der THA, letzte Ausgabe*, December.

UN (1963), *A Study of Industrial Growth*, New York: United Nations.

UN (1977), *Structural Change in European Industry*, New York: United Nations.

260 References

UNIDO (1980), *World Industry since 1960: Progress and Prospects*, Vienna: United Nations Industrial Development Organization.

Útvar makroekonomických analýz a prognóz (1993), 'Základní vývojové tendence české ekonomiky', *Pohledy*, No. 1.

Vintrová, R. (1994), 'Co nezachycuje statistika v ekonomickém růstu', *Statistika*, **31** (12).

Wetzker, K. (ed.) (1990), *Wirtschaftsreport — Daten und Fakten zur Wirtschaftlichen Lage Ostdeutschlands*, Halle: IWH.

Zeman, K. (1989), 'Structural Change in Czechoslovak Economy to the Year 2000', in W. Krelle (ed.), *The Future of the World Economy. Economic Growth and Structural Change*, Springer-Verlag.

Zeman, K. (1990), *Model for Testing Development Trends in the Structure of the Czechoslovak Industry*, Prague: Ústřední ústav národohospodářského výzkumu.

Zemplínerová, A. and R. Laštovička, (1994), 'Pomohla privatizace podnikům?', *Ekonom*, No. 52.

STATISTICAL PUBLICATIONS

Annual Abstract of Statistics, produced annually by UK Central Statistical Office.

Bulletin of Central European Cooperation in Statistics, joint publication with statistics from Czech and Slovak Republics, Poland and Hungary.

Bulletin ČSÚ, monthly bulletin of Czech Statistical Office.

Czech and Slovak Labour Force Surveys, published quarterly by Czech and Slovak Statistical Offices.

HSR (Historická statistická ročenka ČSSR), Historical Statistical Yearbook, Prague: Federal Statistical Office, 1985.

SR (Statistická ročenka), Statistical Yearbook, produced annually by Czechoslovak and then Czech Statistical Office.

Statistisches Jahrbuch der DDR, Statistical Yearbook of GDR.

FURTHER STATISTICAL SOURCES

Czech Statistical Office.
Czech National Bank.
Eurostat, *Analytical Tables of Foreign Trade.*
Eurostat, *Labour Force Survey.*
Management Focus International
OECD, STAN database.
UNIDO, Industrial statistics.
United Nations.
Vienna Institute for Comparative Economic Studies.
World Bank.

PERIODICALS

DIW Wochenbericht, DIW weekly report.
Ekonom, Czech economic weekly.
Hospodářské noviny, Czech economic daily.
Lidové noviny, Czech daily paper.
Práce, Czech daily paper.
Tagesspiegel, German daily paper.
Wirtschaftswoche, German economic weekly.

Index